Private Lives, Proper Relations

Private Lives, Proper Relations
regulating black intimacy

CANDICE M. JENKINS

University of Minnesota Press
Minneapolis
London

Chapter 3 was originally published as "Queering Black Patriarchy," *Modern Fiction Studies* 48, no. 4 (2002): 969–1000; copyright Purdue Research Foundation; reprinted with permission of The Johns Hopkins University Press. A version of chapter 4 was published as "Pure Black: Class, Color, and Intraracial Politics in Toni Morrison's *Paradise*," *Modern Fiction Studies* 52, no. 2 (2006): 270–96; copyright Purdue Research Foundation; reprinted with permission of The Johns Hopkins University Press.

Published by the University of Minnesota Press
111 Third Avenue South, Suite 290
Minneapolis, MN 55401-2520
http://www.upress.umn.edu

Library of Congress Cataloging-in-Publication Data

Jenkins, Candice Marie, 1974–
    Private lives, proper relations : regulating black intimacy / Candice M. Jenkins.
        p.   cm.
    Includes bibliographical references (p.) and index.
    ISBN 978-0-8166-4787-3 (hc : alk. paper) — ISBN 978-0-8166-4788-0 (pb : alk. paper)
    1. American literature—African American authors—History and criticism.   2. African Americans—Intellectual life—20th century. 3. Literature and history—United States—History—20th century. 4. African Americans in literature.   5. Identity (Philosophical concept) in literature.   6. Sex in literature.   7. Race in literature. I. Title.
    PS153.N5J46 2007
    810.9'896073—dc22
                                                                    2007004540

Printed in the United States of America on acid-free paper

The University of Minnesota is an equal-opportunity educator and employer.

12 11 10 09 08 07   10 9 8 7 6 5 4 3 2 1

Contents

Introduction
Vulnerable Subjects

The dedication of Miss Packard and Miss Giles was total.
—"Spelman College History" circa 1992

According to Lillian Faderman's book *To Believe in Women,* Sofia Packard and Harriet Giles, the two white missionaries who founded my undergraduate alma mater, Spelman College, were a lesbian couple. Spelman was established in 1881 as a seminary to educate formerly enslaved women, and more than 125 years later it remains dedicated to the education of black women from all over the world. Faderman quotes a passage from an early history of the college, which describes its founders' relationship thusly: "It would have been impossible for a school girl of those days to speak or think of one without the other. They dressed alike and in leisure hours were nearly always together."[1] Not only this, but the two women were buried together, under a single tombstone which "bears their names on one side, and on the other [bears] the inscription 'Founders of Spelman Seminary.'"[2]

I was only recently made aware of this aspect of Spelman's history, although like every other first-year student, or "freshwoman," I had been required by campus tradition to learn the aforementioned names of our school's founders, along with other salient aspects of the college's history and legacy. In fact, I still have a dog-eared photocopy of the

"Spelman College History" (from which this introduction's double-entendre epigraph is drawn) that was handed to all first-year students sometime during orientation week along with the instruction that we were to memorize that history, then approach upperclasswomen and ask to be quizzed on aspects of it. If we passed their various examination questions, we could amass their signatures, which were eventually collected as a part of our "initiation" into Spelman's sisterhood.

Still, all of this attention paid to learning how Spelman came to be never included mention of even the *possibility* that Packard and Giles were romantically involved—the notion was so suppressed that I don't even recall speculation about it on campus.[3] In a recent essay addressing this phenomenon, alumna Sheila Alexander-Reid wonders, "why isn't the story of Packard and Giles taught as part of the Spelman curriculum?" and bemoans the fact that although the campus houses buildings named after both Packard and Giles, "no one bothered to say they were a loving couple in a long-term relationship."[4] At other (predominantly white) women's colleges, many of which Faderman suggests were also founded by lesbians, this history is common knowledge, and is celebrated by students and alumnae—or so Alexander-Reid insists. She goes on to explain the suppression of Packard and Giles' relationship, and black homophobia more generally, with the statement "The African American community is light years behind the rest of the civilized world."[5]

As intrigued as I was to see an alumna "outing" the lesbian history of my alma mater in print, as Alexander-Reid has attempted to do, I must admit that I bristled when I read this last statement of hers, as I always do when someone suggests that African American communities are reticent about matters of sexuality, and particularly about what some might call "transgressive" sexual practices like lesbianism, simply because they are less civilized than other groups. If for no other reason, such rhetoric is unsettling because the dominant notion of "civilization" is such a loaded one, heavy with the burden of white supremacy, Western imperialism, and the so-called "savagery" of nonwhite people across the globe. As one historian of the nineteenth century writes, "Civilization denote[s] a precise stage in human racial evolution—the one following the more primitive stages of 'savagery' and 'barbarism.'"[6] Indeed, the concept of African peoples as *un*civilized has been used, historically, to justify a whole host of violations against and assaults upon black bodies.[7] As such, for an African American uncritically to take up this discourse of imperialist exploitation and racial exclusion by suggesting that what ails African Americans is our inability to keep up with "the civilized world" seems mildly negligent at best and seriously irresponsible at worst.

In addition, however, Alexander-Reid's statement erases a whole history of black American efforts to keep pace with "the civilized world" on matters of sexuality, though in a different manner than she might prefer. These efforts—their origins, their complexities, and their appearance in African American literature of the twentieth century— are the subject of this book, and are the reason I begin my introduction with the silenced lesbian history of Spelman College. While this silence about lesbianism and other so-called "deviant" intimate behaviors among both Spelmanites and African Americans in general does constitute what Alexander-Reid calls "[k]eeping [our] collective head in the sand," in this book I argue that the communal burial of heads in sand is neither coincidental nor the result of an African American lack of refinement or sophistication. Instead, it might be read as a deliberate attempt, however misguided, to gain access to the respectability of "civilized" status by ignoring or suppressing any so-called sexual deviance—including a lesbian history like Spelman's—precisely because blacks' alleged sexual and familial pathology has historically been one major justification for our exclusion from the privileges of "civilization" by whites.[8]

Along with other marginalized groups, African Americans "have long experienced simultaneously the wish to be full citizens and the violence of their partial citizenship."[9] If it is fair to assume that one of the ways full citizenship operates in the United States is through membership in America's "civilized" sociopolitical world, with all the respectability and assumed normalcy such membership would entail, then this statement gets to the heart of the problem that my work hopes to address. It points to the ways in which an assumed and enforced partial citizenship, particularly in the realm of the intimate, collides in African American culture with the wish not only to *be* full citizens, but to be *understood* as such. I am deeply interested in the silences and suppressions that such a collision engenders, the vulnerabilities that it exposes, and the way that these silences and vulnerabilities are addressed in twentieth-century African American literature.

The collection of historical tensions and suppressions surrounding black erotic and domestic behavior suggests to me that intimacy in general has political significance for black people, and is related to who African Americans are as civic subjects, to the very shape of the black "body politic." This book argues that African American subjects have a particularly complex relationship to the exposure of intimacy, and to its peculiar vulnerabilities, because of the vulnerability that many blacks already experience through racial identity and its associated dangers. Indeed, part of this racial vulnerability has to do with the manner in which African American sexual and familial character has traditionally been stigmatized as *un*civilized in the United States, from the days of slavery onward—and I would suggest that this stigma attached to race, as well as repressive intraracial responses to it, are under continuous interrogation in African American literature, particularly that written by women.

In her brutally honest memoir *The Black Notebooks*, Toi Derricotte uses precisely the language of vulnerability to explain the obsessive attention to appearances she observed as a child among other middle-class blacks:

> I don't know why it is that we fear others' thoughts so. It seemed especially true of the black middle-class people in my childhood. It seemed that it was so important to keep up appearances, to not let people know there were problems, as if problems meant we were failures. I am sure that years of conditioning in a society that blamed us for our own destruction—they're animals, they don't deserve any better—being aware of what power white people's thoughts had over our lives, made us feel especially vulnerable.[10]

For Derricotte, the always-present, judgmental gaze of whites who expected the worst from black people created a kind of constant assault on the African American community. As Derricotte is quick to point out, this assault has never been merely psychological or symbolic: "This is not just a hangover from slavery, it is an accurate assessment of the danger in the world we live in today. Just about every black person I ever met has some tale of arbitrary cruelty."[11] In other words, black subjects in a racist society are at literal risk on a daily basis, and are constantly susceptible to the consequences of the culture's barely concealed racial hostility. As Elizabeth Alexander notes in another context, African Americans "have been taught a sorry lesson of their continual, physical vulnerability in the United States."[12] In this book, I suggest that this vulnerability, the vulnerability of blackness, might make the vulnerability of sexual and familial intimacy somewhat more burdensome for the African American subject, creating literally a "double jeopardy" around these issues that is repeatedly reflected and interrogated in the literature.[13]

The Black Body Politic: Contexts

I will return to this issue of doubled vulnerability, so crucial to the overall project, later in this introduction. At this point, however, it may be worthwhile to examine a bit of the historical background of these concepts, "citizenship" and "civilization"—at least as they have taken shape in the realm of the intimate, my focus throughout this project. At the same time, I want to elaborate some of the ways that black people's alleged sexual and domestic character, our intimate lives, so to speak, have been stigmatized in American cultural parlance, usually in connection with these discourses of civic membership. The two go hand in hand because early white middle-class norms of family structure and sexual behavior have had a great deal to do with the ways that African Americans have been scripted out of narratives of American national belonging.

A number of related concepts, whose roots lie in nineteenth-century Victorian culture, bear examination here. The first of these is "the republican family ideal," which in the early 1800s accompanied the gradual division of work and home into radically separate spheres (defined, respectively, as public and private, masculine and feminine) and which centralized the nuclear, father-headed family as normative.[14] It is worth noting, here, that several more contemporary analyses of nineteenth-century culture have questioned the ultimate accuracy and usefulness of the "separate spheres" model in addressing the complexities of the period; nonetheless, I believe it is possible to take this politicized concept of family seriously without wholeheartedly embracing the "separate spheres" metaphor that it references.[15] According to the republican family ideal, the nuclear family was imagined to be a microcosm of the unified republic, and thereby acquired civil as well as social importance as a marker of cultural stability and "national well-being."[16] And at the center of this new understanding of family was the heterosexual marriage coupling, a contractual bond sanctioned both figuratively and literally by the state.

This conception of family, as the small-scale mirror of the nation and the hallmark of political and personal wholeness, was distinctly bourgeois in its origins. It grew in time, however, to infiltrate Euro-American culture as a whole: "A middle-class creation, the republican family dominated household ideology and practice in an increasingly bourgeois nation[. . . .] the reorganized family affected every class, region, and institution."[17] At least one group of people, however, was visibly and purposely excluded from legitimate participation in this national family. Enslaved blacks not only retained some aspects of West African kinship patterns in their lives on white farms and plantations, patterns that frequently diverged from European family norms, but they were also prohibited from marrying legally because of their status as chattel.[18] Even slaves' nonlegal "marriages" and extended families were in constant danger of being disrupted through sale or other owner-directed separation. Rather than the hierarchical nuclear enclave privileged in the bourgeois American understanding of "family," enslaved blacks "were *forced* into patterns of *dispersal* . . . by the legal arrangements of enslavement"—forging lateral bonds that were dependent on choice, not state sanction.[19]

Contemporaneous to the developing republican family ideal was the similarly pervasive "cult of True Womanhood," an ideology about appropriate feminine demeanor that outlined specific principles for (white) women's behavior within and outside of the home. The cult of true womanhood and the republican family ideal were actually two sides of the same coin, for an appropriately behaved woman was seen during this period as the cornerstone of a stable home, and by extension a stable nation. The four primary criteria for judging a woman's suitability for her influential role as wife and mother were her "piety, purity, submissiveness and domesticity."[20] Special attention was given to the ideal of purity, for perceived sexual immodesty—and any expression of overt sexuality might qualify as such—could banish one from the realm of womanhood entirely. In true womanhood ideology, "[p]urity was as essential as piety to a young woman, its absence [. . .] unnatural and unfeminine. Without it she was, in fact, no woman at all, but a member of some lower order."[21] Such a prescription makes clear that the cult of true womanhood was never assumed to include all women. Instead purity and sexual innocence, or the appearance of such, gained its bearers entry into a separate and privileged class.

This select group of women retained their privilege, however, in contrast to and at the expense of that aforementioned "lower order," a group made up primarily of enslaved black women. Because of the conditions of their enslavement—for example, their subjection to field labor or strenuous domestic chores and their vulnerability to the exploitative sexual interest of their owners—black women rarely exemplified the fragility, gentility, or chastity required of "true women." Indeed, the cult of true womanhood relied upon this backdrop of black female "nonwomen" in order to more clearly define true womanhood as white, frail, and virtuous—everything that black women supposedly were not. My use of the word "supposedly" is deliberate; enslaved women in this period were neither ignorant of nor uniformly acquiescent to their disadvantaged positioning within this ideology, as the calculated resistance of a figure like Harriet Jacobs makes clear.[22] Still, black women were typically understood by whites to "[e]xist outside the definition of true womanhood"—a peculiar irony, since black female sexuality was nevertheless used to demarcate those boundaries.[23]

Of course, men were hardly exempt from Victorian behavioral

strictures; instead, "[t]rue manhood was equally crucial to antebellum middle-class identity" among whites.[24] Dominant conceptions of "civilization" were linked to race and gender ideology more broadly in the mid-nineteenth century, which meant that Victorian concepts of "manliness," defined by "honesty, piety, self-control, and a commitment to [. . .] industry, thrift, punctuality, and sobriety" also circulated widely in the discourse of the period.[25] Enslaved men were similarly excluded from this dominant understanding of "manliness," although peculiarly enough, contemporaneous racist narratives of black male "savagery" frequently returned to the sexualized body of the black woman, represented in nineteenth century iconography as the ultimate "source of corruption and disease."[26]

The figure of the "oversexed-black-Jezebel," for instance, exemplifies a particularly virulent assertion about African American racial "pathology" with roots in the antebellum era.[27] Enslaved women of this period were assumed to be black Jezebels, their supposed sexual licentiousness not only situating them outside of antebellum prescriptions for feminine behavior, but also dooming the larger black population to depravity and disease, given the common association between black women's assumed sexual excesses and the sexual and domestic failures of the race as a whole: "The black female [. . .] comes to serve as an icon for black sexuality in general."[28] Indeed, black men "were thought capable of [. . .] sexual crimes because of the lascivious character of the women of the race in a time when women were considered the foundation of a group's morality."[29] It is also no coincidence that this fantasy of the black Jezebel helps to justify white male sexual exploitation of enslaved women; part of the means by which whites in the antebellum United States excused the existence of slavery more generally was through the creation of mythologies that dehumanized enslaved Africans. Again, a discourse of "civilization," or the lack thereof, is invoked around communities of black people in order to exclude them from protected status.

Such discriminatory practices continued well after slavery ended, even as Victorian ideologies of gender began to fall from favor at the turn of the century. During this period, the United States "underwent a transformation from a producer-oriented to a consumer-oriented society"—as a result, "[a] modern ethos of masculinity supplanted earlier nineteenth-century notions of [Victorian] manliness."[30] Contemporaneous with this shift, however, was a peak in the American eugenics movement, "the science of breeding better human beings," most often associated with the writings of Francis Galton and Charles Darwin.[31] Indeed, the related notion, that Darwin's theory of biological evolution via natural selection could also be applied to humanity's social systems and institutions, has frequently been given the shorthand term "social Darwinism."[32]

Eugenic theory "was rife with raced, classed, and gendered conceptions of fitness," nearly all of which privileged white, Anglo-Saxon racial "stock" as superior.[33] As such, it should hardly be surprising that just as in the antebellum period, in the early twentieth century black people were understood in dominant cultural parlance to be a physically and morally inferior "race." Such assumptions about black inferiority, in the early decades of the twentieth century, were accompanied by a preoccupation with black sexuality and reproduction and fear that the rapidly expanding "lower races"—including not just blacks, but white ethnic groups such as the Irish—would eclipse Anglo-Saxon supremacy.[34] Yet while eugenics eventually met an ignominious end in the United States, as the horrors of the Holocaust brought the "ugliness and immorality" of so-called biological selection home to white Americans, racist cultural narratives of black deviance never suffered quite the same fate.[35]

Indeed, by the second half of the twentieth century, black people would have another allegation of intimate "pathology" to combat. This one, even more than the image of the lascivious black Jezebel, was specifically aimed at the black woman's role within the household. In his widely debated and refuted 1965 study of the black family, sociologist Daniel Patrick Moynihan suggested that because slave men had been unable to support their wives and children due to their forced submission to white owners, black families from antebellum America to the present "reversed [the] roles of husband and wife"—which for Moynihan was a pathological situation, dooming blacks to inferiority because it deviated from dominant American patterns of male-female interaction.[36] E. Franklin Frazier, a black sociologist whose work actually preceded and inspired Moynihan's, made similar assertions, commenting on the black woman's allegedly excessive power within the black domestic sphere, power which she used to dominate her husband and children.[37]

In the decades since Frazier and Moynihan voiced these pronouncements, the myth of the "Negro matriarchate,"[38] as Frazier called it, has taken on unusual power in dominant twentieth-century-U.S. ideology, merging with the still-lingering stereotype of the oversexed-black-Jezebel to create a hegemonic narrative of black sexual and familial pathology that shows no sign of dissipating in the twenty-first century. As Rhonda Williams suggests:

> Black families have long functioned as markers in the public imagination: they generally signify and manifest a morally problematic sexually [sic] agency, a cultural degeneracy. The conventional social scientific wisdom is clear: "the problem" is that so much black sexuality and kinship formation transgresses the boundaries of married (and therefore healthy) heterosexuality.[39]

In other words, the perceived inability of African Americans to conform to middle-class understandings of family and appropriate sexual behavior has hardly diminished since its origins during the antebellum period. Long after explicit invocations of the "cult of true womanhood" or the "republican family ideal" have disappeared from dominant U.S. cultural parlance, blacks' alleged deviance from Victorian norms of respectability, propriety, and morality remain central to an American national narrative. Contrary to whites, African Americans continue to "live without the benefit of an assumed familial and sexual wellness[.]"[40] Indeed, as Nell Painter suggests, "[t]he depiction of the oversexed-black-Jezebel [. . .] in American culture [. . .] has sufficient visibility to haunt black women to this day."[41]

The notion that these carryovers from slavery "haunt" the present moment is a telling one, reiterated in more recent arguments that slavery "haunts the peripheries of the national imaginary" or constitutes a ghostly presence in American culture, an "ending [which is] not over."[42] Like other specters created during slavery, Jezebel reappears in contemporary American culture through such figures as the "welfare queen," the image of an unwed and unfit black mother feeding voraciously on white tax dollars and producing hordes of literally and figuratively "dangerous" black children. I say figuratively dangerous because while some of the fear of such children grows from the sense that they will become, as adults, the urban criminals who allegedly threaten the safety of American streets, another part of the "danger" of these children is found in their (assumed) numbers—and the accompanying sense that they have the power to engulf whites with a peculiarly destructive blackness. In other words, the mythological black welfare mother, because of her reproductive capacity, is painted as the very "agent of destruction, the creator of the pathological, black, urban, poor family from which all ills flow[.]"[43] The hysteria that has surrounded this figure in recent years is remarkably similar to the eugenic furor surrounding fears of white "race suicide" nearly a century ago, suggesting that racist preoccupation with black reproduction and the black domestic sphere has continued to exist in American culture long after the public admission of such fears and assumptions has fallen out of favor.[44]

At the center of these phantasmagoric associations is the black woman's alleged sexual degeneracy, her inability to fit within the boundaries of "acceptable" (married) sexuality. The "welfare queen" is who she is because she is *sexually* irresponsible, unable to refuse the carnal pleasure that leads to pregnancy, and, perhaps because of this alleged immorality, unable to legitimate herself or limit her offspring through marriage and the nuclear family structure. Actual legislation reveals how literally this logic, which privileges marriage over all other family forms, operates in U.S. national policy. The Personal Responsibility and Work Opportunity Reconciliation Act (PRWORA)—otherwise known as the Welfare Reform Act—signed into law in August 1996, opens with a section entitled "Findings," which details the presumed connection between marriage and family legitimacy:

The Congress makes the following findings:

(1) Marriage is the foundation of a successful society.

(2) Marriage is an essential institution of a successful society which
promotes the interests of children.

(3) Promotion of responsible fatherhood and motherhood is integral
to successful child rearing and the well-being of children. [. . .]

(8) The negative consequences of an out-of-wedlock birth on the
mother, the child, the family, and society are well documented. [. . .]

(10) Therefore, in light of this demonstration of the crisis in our
Nation, it is the sense of the Congress that prevention of out-of-
wedlock pregnancy and reduction of out-of-wedlock birth are very
important Government interests[.][45]

The language of "crisis" used in reference to out-of-wedlock births is
telling. Although no reference to race is made in the text of the law,
popular (and inaccurate) assumption that the majority of welfare recipients are African American means that "irresponsible" black parents,
particularly mothers, are the source of this so-called crisis.

Responding to Calumny: The Salvific Wish

One not-so-surprising reaction to such narratives of black sexual and
domestic deviance is the attempt by blacks, particularly black women,
to regulate black behavior in the service of creating an inviolable respectability. This response from African American women, particularly middle-class women, to narratives of black pathology began as an
earnest attempt at racial uplift, entailing to some extent the embrace
of the very same Victorian values that had been used to exclude black
people from ideals of kinship and sexuality. One example of this was
the black women's club movement, which began in 1895 with the first
national conference of the "Colored Women of America." The public
defamation of black female sexuality through repeated characterizations of black women as sexually promiscuous and immoral "provided
both the occasion for and the substance of the conference."[46] Similar
movements existed within the black church, with an only slightly more
spiritually driven focus on the same issues.[47] In both cases, the activist

women involved worked to recuperate black women's sexuality from infamy by exemplifying propriety and family stability and encouraging other black women to do the same. The club movement's recuperative mission was explicitly tied to the emulation and promotion of bourgeois values, the same values that white women of the middle class had long held dear.[48]

Importantly, however, black women's embrace of bourgeois Victorian convention was not merely mimetic, a misguided attempt to emulate their white counterparts. Instead, it constituted a "race-conscious mission" with a political emphasis, for the stakes involved included not simply black women's moral reputation, but that reputation's consequences for their physical safety. During the period, dominant American attitudes about black sexual depravity "were getting black men lynched and black women raped and exploited."[49] Indeed, in the post-Reconstruction South in particular, "[s]exual exploitation was so pervasive that it drove black women north in search of safer climes."[50] In the face of such concrete vulnerability to whites, it is hardly surprising that middle-class black women in the late nineteenth century saw the need to insist upon their own "inclusion in the category of protected womanhood," even if that meant the strategic acceptance of values that historically had been designed to disallow them.[51]

These nineteenth-century gestures toward communal uplift through the adoption of bourgeois values are the beginnings of the pattern of black female and middle-class desire that I call the *salvific wish*.[52] As may be evident, the term "salvific" is related to the word "salvation," which, due to its religious connotations has significant linguistic resonance in African American communities. In the Christian religious tradition, spiritual salvation for all human beings is won through the sacrifice of the "lamb" of God, Christ—a voluntary scapegoat for the sins of the world. The salvation alluded to in the term "salvific wish" also depends upon voluntary sacrifice, but in this case that sacrifice is political and social, and the scapegoat black women themselves. According to the salvific wish, black women (and, to a much lesser extent, black men) could pay with their bodies, or rather with the concealment and restraint of those bodies, for the ultimate "safety" of the black community as a whole.

In other words, the content of the salvific wish—a black, largely female, and generally middle-class desire—is a longing to protect or save black women, and black communities more generally, from narratives of sexual and familial pathology, through the embrace of conventional bourgeois propriety in the arenas of sexuality and domesticity. I say "largely" female and "generally" middle class because the salvific wish, essentially shorthand for a preoccupation with propriety in the realm of intimacy, actually need not be limited by either gender or class. In that the salvific wish is focused on the well-being of the group and resistant, in obvious ways, to the insidious nature of racist ideology, it is certainly a desire that black men are capable of expressing—though as I explore at length later, masculine articulations of and demands for domestic and sexual propriety often have a slightly different resonance, given that black women have historically been painted as "the primary carriers of black familial pathology."[53] Precisely because women are more typically present in the intimate arenas with which the salvific wish takes issue, they have far more responsibility than men for maintaining the wish's hoped-for decorum, which means that a female version of the salvific wish is generally bound up with a call for self-control or self-denial, while male expressions of the salvific wish tend toward the disciplinary and externally corrective.

In addition, while the struggle for respectability among African Americans may have originated among bourgeois blacks, in many ways it is a phenomenon that crosses boundaries of class, particularly in its relationship to uplift ideology. Economic status has not historically been the sole determinant of blacks' participation in uplift ideology, of which the salvific wish is one small part.[54] Instead, actual economic position was less of a marker of class standing than the *aspiration* to respectability. Michele Mitchell uses the phrase "aspiring class" to denote blacks who, while not members of the black economic elite, nonetheless sought class mobility through hard work and sacrifice. She notes that "[t]he characteristic common to the overwhelming majority of the black aspiring class during the late nineteenth and early twentieth centuries was an abiding concern with propriety[.]"[55] In other words, in the late nineteenth and early twentieth centuries, the embrace of uplift ideology was one means by which blacks lacking the material comforts of the middle class could still gain some access to bourgeois status.

Although the salvific wish originates in the Victorian era, and is a kind of subcategory to ideologies of black uplift popular during that period, it certainly has remained a part of the African American cultural imaginary throughout the twentieth century and arguably into the twenty-first, and has continued to be linked to the sphere of black intimacy and black sexual practice. For instance, what historian Darlene Clark Hine identifies as a black and female "culture of dissemblance" around sexuality is one way that such a desire continues to show itself in African American culture.[56] Similarly, Evelynn Hammonds notes that what began with the recuperative project of black club women at the turn of the century has developed into a "public silence about sexuality which . . . continues to the present."[57] These recurrent silences on issues of black female sexuality—which would include the silence around homosexuality that Sheila Alexander-Reid identifies—suggest that the salvific wish remains culturally relevant in the present moment.

In this book, I read the salvific wish as the "public" face of black middle-class desire. I am concerned with the larger cultural context and content of the salvific wish, a kind of social narrative that is informed by American and African American history. This narrative, existing not merely in individuals' behavior but in collective idioms such as "don't air (our) dirty laundry in public," or "don't put family business in the streets," might be considered a form of the "everyday ideology" named by Wahneema Lubiano in reference to black nationalism.[58] The salvific wish functions similarly, and constitutes a particularly public kind of black desire because it surfaces in response to a common negative characterization of African American sexual and familial patterns that has taken as its project the public (mis)marking of these patterns as deviant. Furthermore, the salvific wish as ideological response to such characterizations highly values the public reputation of African Americans, among both blacks themselves and among whites. In other words, although one might identify the salvific wish as an intraracial gesture toward communal protection, it represents equally a concern with how the black community is seen *inter*racially, observed and evaluated across racial lines. The wish may be community-minded, but it is interested in both the actual and the *perceived* safety of blacks as a group.

Doubled Vulnerability and the Black Intimate Subject

I use the word "safety" advisedly, for it recalls, again, the notion that black subjects are vulnerable in particular ways. This racialized vulnerability becomes a double burden when coupled with the possibility of intimate vulnerability. Indeed, it seems to me that the ultimate motivation for African Americans' continued preoccupation with propriety around all forms of intimacy is the potential danger of publicly signifying such intimacy in a racialized context—particularly to a larger "public" already likely to misinterpret black signification. I would suggest, in fact, that in the realm of the intimate, black subjects experience a doubled sense of endangerment to the self that is akin to DuBois's now familiar notion of "double consciousness," in which one always "look[s] at one's self through the eyes of others, [and . . .] measur[es] one's soul by the tape of a world that looks on in amused contempt and pity."[59] We might recall, again, Toi Derricotte's words, which highlight this sense of a (white) world looking on, judging the failures of black communities—and as I have already noted, the racial threat that Derricotte's comments imply is not limited to panoptical observation.

Here one might ask, however, why intimacy's "zones of familiarity and comfort" constitute a parallel threat, rather than simply a source of enjoyment, even a possible corrective to the violence of racial stigma.[60] If sexual desire, in particular, is accurately described as "an experience which overwhelms," I would argue that its overwhelming character stems in part from desire's ability to break through indifference, to encourage corporal and emotional vulnerability. Who could be more vulnerable than a desiring subject, a human being in the throes of an "intimate, deeply compelling and profoundly *private* experience"?[61] This is particularly true given the ways that "attachments make people public, producing transpersonal identities and subjectivities," such that one's "private" experience can always already be perceived as a public endeavor.[62] Certainly, if desire is understood as both attraction and appetite, its expression in the sex act is also a site of human vulnerability; after all, "sexual excitement . . . shatters the will and disintegrates the constructed self."[63] The extreme vulnerability—to pain, to weakness, to exposure, as well as to pleasure and joy—that both experiencing and expressing desire thus engenders is always a complicated status to endure, but could become much more burdensome to those whose bodies and psyches are already vulnerable in other ways.

In addition, while we might be tempted to focus solely on the potential vulnerabilities of *sexual* excitement and connection, I would also argue that the vulnerabilities that can exist between close family members in the home are related to these sexual vulnerabilities. Nonsexual relationships that exist within the domestic sphere still must confront the "aggression, incoherence, vulnerability, and ambivalence" typically associated with desire, albeit with less sociocultural support, given the ways that the domestic sphere is usually (mis)read as "safe."[64] The sheer proximity of the sibling, the parent, the child—and indeed, the other iterations of family that might inhabit the home space—means the body of the family member is *knowable,* and accessible, in a way that is rarely possible in other social interactions. Yet at the same time, the family "as a whole" remains particularly tenuous, constantly in danger of breaking or being broken apart; indeed, "the family unit is never *solely* the family unit; people and propositions articulated and unarticulated lurk at its borders."[65] In other words, the peculiar depth of human exposure that is possible within the household makes that space at least as potentially threatening as the individual sexual coupling, particularly given that the seemingly sacred space of the "home" is subject to the same transformations, violations, and assaults as the separate individuals who constitute it. Therefore the notion that "homespace today is [. . .] a source of confusion as much as, if not more than, renewal," should not be surprising.[66]

This problem of sexual and domestic vulnerability, of intimate exposure, has special resonance for black people. This is particularly true since African peoples in the United States have not, historically, had consistent access to the so-called private space that can exist between lovers or family members, a space that would presumably provide a "safe" place for the exposure of human connection—either because enslaved relatives and spouses were always in danger of being separated by the social and financial interests of slave owners, or because one of the two "lovers" was participating under duress.[67] The problem of black sociosexual vulnerability has certainly continued to exist after slavery's demise, in part a function of the "painful representations" of black sexuality that are still "haunting the present," in the words of bell hooks (and hooks's language recalls, again, what I have already noted here—slavery's spectral relationship to the present-day American imaginary).[68]

In 1994, Elizabeth Alexander argued that "[b]lack bodies in pain for public consumption have been an American spectacle for centuries[,]" adding, "this history moves from public rapes, beatings, and lynchings to the gladiatorial arenas of basketball and boxing [. . .] African American bodies on videotape have been the site on which national trauma—sexual harassment, 'date rape,' drug abuse, racial and economic urban conflict, AIDS—has been dramatized."[69] Though Alexander refers specifically to the televised infamy of Clarence Thomas, Mike Tyson, Marion Barry, Rodney King, and Magic Johnson, to this list we might certainly add O. J. Simpson, whose face was famously darkened on the cover of *Time* magazine, in order to "expel O. J. from the lighter, celebrity realm of affluent Brentwood, returning him to the darker, underworld of black crime and the L.A. County Jail."[70] The vast majority of these figures share a particularly sexualized cast to their social scandals, which easily recalls a much earlier narrative of black degeneracy—one tied to the "public rapes, beatings, and lynchings" Alexander first invokes. Just as systematic rape of black women both during and after slavery was justified through reference to their "promiscuity," lynching has historically been justified by making reference to the out-of-control sexuality of black men.[71] This is precisely the history that Clarence Thomas hoped to invoke when he referred to his Senate hearings as a "high-tech lynching."[72]

In fact, the spectacle of "black bodies in pain"—of black bodies, period—has always had at least some relationship to the spectacle of an assumed black sexual degeneracy—even as we add more recent figures to the above list, such as popular singer R. Kelly, indicted in Chicago in 2002 on twenty-one counts of child pornography because of a videotape that allegedly showed him having sex with an underage girl, or NBA basketball star Allan Iverson, charged with criminal trespass, assault, and a number of gun-related offenses after barging into a cousin's apartment looking for his estranged wife, whom he had reportedly ejected naked from their home following a domestic dispute. It may not be coincidental that each of the names on our list of modern-day racial spectacles is a black man—as Alexander reminds us, "American narratives of violence against blacks in the popular imagination are usually figured as male[,]" perhaps because "black men present a particular kind of physical threat in the white imagination, [which. . .] must be contained."[73] Nonetheless, the spectacle of degenerative blackness that such figures create by no means excludes black women, particularly in the cases of Kelly and Iverson—in which the sexualized (and in one case, explicitly "naked") bodies of black females are the subtext of the scandal.

Each of these contemporary representations, and the assumptions about black intimate pathology that they reinforce, has repeatedly exposed black families and black sexual relationships to public scrutiny, creating what can appear to be a ceaseless and indiscriminate vulnerability for blacks as a collective to whites' judgments or to actions based on those judgments. Indeed, the vulnerability that African Americans have been subject to at the hands of white racism often *is* the vulnerability of intimacy, not simply because black people have been the objects of white desire, but because black bodies have been assumed always to be excessively proximate and desirous bodies, bodies too readily revealed or exposed, too willing to reveal and expose others. In such an over-determined cultural framework, in which one's black body is always already assumed to be signifying desire, the added vulnerability that comes with expressing something as personal and deeply felt as sexual attraction, filial affection, human tenderness, or need, takes exposure to a painful extreme.

In this context, the repressive efforts of the salvific wish can be understood as attempts both to limit such exposure *and* to create a kind of hyperprivate black space within which the vulnerability of intimacy is once again possible. This protected, hyperprivate space is the space of conventional domesticity, the heterosexual marriage coupling and traditional nuclear family so valued by the salvific wish. Indeed, the domestic space of the marriage is understood within the confines of traditional bourgeois propriety to be the only legitimately "private" and protected sexual arena, such that "[b]edroom privacy is secured [solely] for marital genital intercourse."[74] Thus the expression of black intimacy outside of that arena is suppressed by the salvific wish in order to allow for the "safe" expression of that intimacy within its confines.

The paradox of cloaking aspects of intimacy in a suppressive silence, or of masking other aspects of it in a veil of protective propriety, is that the very nature of human connection is to explode such masks: we might recall the assertion that excitement "disintegrates the constructed self." Human beings take risks—emotional, physical—when we connect with one another. These risks, of loss, of violation, of betrayal, not to mention, in the case of the sexual encounter, of illness and even premature death, in many ways cannot be mitigated, may even grow deeper over time as intimate connection itself becomes deeper and more profound. Certainly intimacy can also bring rewards, and the imagined promise of such rewards usually motivates our movement toward one another. Yet to disavow the dangers of intimacy—the "unbreakable links between intimacy, vulnerability, and risk"—and to imagine rewards with no cost is at best naïve, and at worst, a denial of the very truth of human existence.[75] In other words, no matter how hard one tries, intimacy simply cannot be made "safe." The impossibility of such efforts may explain why the texts I address interrogate and critique the salvific wish on multiple levels.

Narrating the Black Intimate Subject

Of course, black literature has always had an interest in addressing issues of family and sexuality, particularly as these issues emerge from and influence the black "community-at-large"; early nineteenth century black writers, for instance, by "producing a familial narrative of the national union, a domestic fiction," essentially brought the black literary and social body into being.[76] Indeed, in the nineteenth century, writing in general "was a site where race got manufactured, deployed, disseminated, contested, and claimed."[77] Such constitutive fictions are at least as important in the twentieth century, precisely because of the increasing ubiquity of challenges to the very *possibility* of black domestic and sexual integrity. Yet while nineteenth and even early twentieth century texts may have had a somewhat uncritical investment in the salvific wish, and the notion of "uplift" out of which it grows, texts in the latter twentieth century, which are my focus in the body of this project, have a much more complicated relationship to the phenomenon. Indeed, part of what I argue here is that twentieth century texts bear reexamination around the issue of intimacy precisely because they address the politics surrounding this issue, born in the nineteenth century, in new and consequential ways.

Critic Claudia Tate has already demonstrated how a version of the salvific wish, expressed in nineteenth-century black women's domestic fiction, actually evidenced a political desire for black progress, one which was highly appropriate to the time period in which these novels were written. Tate suggests that early fictional visions of idealized domesticity constituted "a fundamental cultural symbol of the Victorian era for representing civil ambition and prosperity[. . . .] a symbol that black women writers in particular used to promote the social advancement of African Americans."[78] Tate is not the only scholar to consider how issues of domesticity and/or sexuality operate in specifically political ways in early African American literature, but I focus on her work here because it is in some ways emblematic of the serious attention that has been paid to how these issues surface in work by black writers throughout the nineteenth century—and into the first two or three decades of the twentieth century.[79] Literature of the twentieth century, however, does not explicitly follow the pattern Tate identifies in earlier works: "By the 1920s the allegorical link between idealized domestic tropes, on the one hand, and liberational racial and sexual desire, on the other, had become disengaged," replaced by "explicit depictions of racial protest."[80] Indeed, twentieth century narratives are more likely to portray a black domestic and sexual life that is fraught with confusion and chaos, the antithesis of the "idealized" black domesticity that Tate examines.

Still, in *Private Lives, Proper Relations: Regulating Black Intimacy,* I disagree with Tate's suggestion that in the twentieth century's post-Victorian society, domesticity and the home suffered "diminished political significance." Instead, I would argue that only the perceived *function* of the home as political signifier was modified in the twentieth century, and that domesticity remained conceptually vital in the civic arena. In other words, while blacks in the nineteenth century had believed it was possible for the political problems that plagued African Americans—problems assumed to be caused by racism and centuries of disadvantage—to be transformed by the embrace of conventional domestic patterns, the twentieth century eventually ushered in a conception among both whites and blacks that African Americans' political problems in fact *originated* with their group's inability to recreate such domestic patterns. The Moynihan report and resultant controversy are perhaps the best example of this shift in focus from externalized racial oppression to a supposed internal pathology reflected by the "troubled" black family structure.

Thus I argue, counter to Tate and a number of other scholars who have undertaken similar work, that the political significance of black intimacy remained high in the twentieth century, well after the widespread influence of Victorian moral codes had waned. What has changed is blacks' perceived control over black intimacy's associative potential. For African Americans, popular invocations of black familial/ sexual practice now operate less as group-initiated instruments of social transformation, and more as tools that can be used against the group by outsiders, cited as evidence in an all-too-familiar narrative of black pathology.

It should therefore not be surprising that the salvific wish, an earnest longing to rescue the black community from such narratives of pathology, remains a central part of the black cultural imaginary, even as the actual prospects for its success, particularly as attempted through the embrace of conventional sexual and familial behaviors, are much less widely accepted than in the Victorian era. Neither should it be surprising that this wish continues to resurface in African American literature as a subject of increasing contention and interrogation; unlike black women's writing in the nineteenth century, twentieth-century African American literature comments upon and finally critiques the tenets of the salvific wish, pointing out the internal sacrifices and suppressions it makes necessary, and highlighting the structures of vulnerability that it hopes to conceal. Indeed, as I suggest in the early chapters of this volume, the wish seems to operate in these texts as a narrative trope—a way to foreground representations of intraracial class, gender, and color conflict as these pertain to intimacy.

I read narrative invocations of the salvific wish as useful points of access to the larger issue of intimacy in African American cultural production, because they signal a self-conscious attention to the black doubled vulnerability that underlies the wish. Certainly, one aspect of such a reading is a kind of implicit commentary on the desires and experiences of real people—given that my analysis alludes in very specific ways to social forces surrounding African American cultural production, it would indeed be impossible not to speak, in some sense, for the lived reality of the individual African American subject, and about the intimate involvements of individual black bodies. Throughout this book, I take the rather traditionalist position that works of fiction are both products of and responses to a given sociohistorical and political moment, and that it is possible to learn something useful about our "reality" through rigorous examination of the stories that are told about it. I take this position not because I buy into "the assumption that [black] literary texts transparently reflect preexistent social realities," but because I believe African American fiction participates in and speaks back to larger cultural narratives that are *constitutive* of black subjectivity in the United States.[81] If, in fact, "[n]arrative is one of the ways in which identity, the ideological subject, is manufactured," then it stands to reason that close reading of African American narrative in particular might offer us insight into the ideological complexities of black subjectivity.[82]

This position obviously betrays my belief that African American literature "continues [. . .] to be grounded in a lived experience of blackness."[83] It also, however, reveals my indebtedness to the writings of Michel Foucault, particularly on the notion of "discourse" and the concept of power. Foucauldian "discourse," summarized by one scholar as "a set of ideas and practices which, taken together, organize both the way a society defines certain truths about itself and the way it deploys social power," is useful to my project in *Private Lives, Proper Relations* because it highlights the interrelated nature of ideologies that circulate within the social real and the cultural products that invoke, challenge, or reinforce those ideologies.[84] This interrelation speaks to what Foucault sees as the promiscuous operation of power:

> What makes power hold good, what makes it accepted, is simply the fact that it doesn't only weigh on us as a force that says no, but that it traverses and produces things, it induces pleasure, forms knowledge, produces discourse. It needs to be considered as a productive network which runs through the whole social body, much more than as a negative instance whose function is repression.[85]

In *Private Lives, Proper Relations* I argue that the power of the dominant culture operates "productively" at precisely those moments when African Americans participate in their own victimization through the project of self-imposed sexual and familial propriety—in these moments, power "traverses" or inhabits blackness, and contributes in complex ways to its larger social meaning.

Foucault even speaks directly to the role of "fiction" in the operation of discourse, noting in an interview, "It seems to me that the possibility exists for fiction to function in truth, for a fictional discourse to induce effects of truth, and for bringing it about that a true discourse engenders or 'manufactures' something that does not yet exist, that is, 'fictions' it."[86] Part of what I claim in this book is that the writing of twentieth-century African American authors itself "fictions" intraracial resistance to the persistent ideology of the salvific wish—in the process engendering new ways of thinking about black intimate vulnerability. Invocations of the salvific wish in the literature under study here offer an insistent challenge to the value of intraracial discipline as a means of achieving community sanctity. Ultimately, the texts that I examine in this project reveal the essential *violence* of the salvific wish, the manner in which its restrictive, disciplinary assault upon black bodies constitutes a fearful denial of not simply black intimate expression, but of the chaos and vulnerability of human encounter more broadly conceived.

A Paradigmatic Text: Nella Larsen's *Passing*

A brief look at Nella Larsen's 1929 novella, *Passing,* might be useful here as illustration of this phenomenon. *Passing* is an ideal text to inaugurate the critical discussion at the center of *Private Lives, Proper Relations* because these issues—decorum and respectability, as well as the racialized vulnerability of intimacy—are at the very surface of Larsen's narrative, and are addressed therein quite directly. This should perhaps not be surprising, since Nella Larsen's work was clearly subject to the salvific wish's contemporaneous external influence. This is so, in spite of the fact that in the years following World War I, "[t]he day for supporting [. . .] uplift and civilization for the masses was rapidly passing."[87] In part, uplift's demise had to do with the country's movement away from Victorian ideology, which as I have already noted accompanied the shift, in the early years of the twentieth century, from a producer- to a consumer-oriented economy.[88]

The shift away from uplift ideology was also due to a shift in the location of the black poor and working class; once large numbers of African Americans migrated from the rural South to the urban North, where many of the original middle-class proponents of uplift resided, it became increasingly difficult for black elites to generalize about the "ignorance" or "backwardness" of the far-removed black masses. Hazel Carby has noted that while black intellectuals at the turn of the century "did not doubt or question their position of leadership as members of the 'Talented Tenth' speaking from the North to the majority of blacks who lived outside it[,]" following World War I, "[n]o longer was it possible to mobilize an undifferentiated address to 'the black people[.]'"[89] Carby's use of the phrase "Talented Tenth" here likely references W. E. B. DuBois's 1903 essay of the same title, which discusses the need to educate a small group of capable blacks who could then work to educate and uplift the masses of African Americans.[90] Joy James argues, however, that this term was actually coined nearly a decade prior to the appearance of DuBois's essay, by "Northern white liberals of the American Baptist Home Missionary Society (ABHMS), which established Southern black colleges to train Negro elites"—a reminder of the complex and sometimes troubling racial politics behind the term and behind the notion of racial uplift more generally.[91]

Perhaps not surprisingly, given these politics, the belief among both whites and elite blacks in black rural "incompetence," to use the language of Fannie Barrier Williams, began to be replaced in Larsen's era with an equally sinister (mis)understanding of black urban culture. In the years following World War I, whites (and some blacks as well—Claude McKay and Wallace Thurman are two examples) began to espouse a romanticized and stereotypical view of the black urban proletariat as primitive and "closer to nature," a refreshing counter to the allegedly sterile character of the Western world. This newfound admiration for the black working class "tended to follow in the traditional patterns of anti-black prejudice," celebrating blacks' alleged "sensual and passionate, high-spirited and exotic" natures.[92] As such, the sense that black women were lascivious was still common in the period during which Larsen wrote. Indeed, this primitivist mythology is one way that Larsen and her contemporaries were subject to a peculiarly racialized vulnerability around sexual expression. Here as elsewhere in the twentieth century, this vulnerability served as a primary impetus for the misguided discipline of the salvific wish.

Understandably, then, the demand from some blacks for properly "behaved" African American literary works was as explicit during the New Negro Renaissance as it had ever been previously. As an example one only need turn to the oft-cited comment from W. E. B. DuBois that in reading Claude McKay's freewheeling novel *Home to Harlem* he was made to feel "'distinctly like taking a bath.'"[93] *Home to Harlem* depicts a "hard-drinking, fast-living, sexually emancipated army deserter" named Jake, whom McKay fashions into a kind of larger-than-life, urban and working class black hero.[94] DuBois, like other bourgeois blacks of this period, was highly critical of texts such as McKay's, which seemed to reinforce popular stereotypes of black sexual and social immorality. Indeed, Martin Summers points out the homosocial and in some cases homoerotic overtones of McKay's portrayal of black working-class men, which may have had a great deal to do with conservative DuBois's aversion to the novel.[95]

DuBois's use of bathing, with its connotative connections to physical cleanliness and spiritual purification, as a metaphor to register his *political* distaste for McKay's work is certainly instructive; the idea of the bath serves as a reminder that perceived breaches of morality could figuratively "dirty" other blacks in multiple ways. We might consider, as well, how the desire to bathe can be understood as capitulation to social judgment—the recipient bathes not just to improve his own physical comfort, but so that he will not be *perceived* as unclean by the larger community. Interestingly enough, DuBois's review of *Home to Harlem* in the *Crisis* was paired with a review of Larsen's *Quicksand*, which appeared at the same time; DuBois praised the latter book as "'on the whole, the best piece of fiction that Negro America has produced since the heyday of Chesnutt'" while simultaneously condemning the hypersexuality and violence of McKay's narrative.[96] For DuBois, presumably, Larsen's novel avoids the sexual excesses of McKay's work, crafting a less offensive tale of racial disquietude and individual tragedy.

As Deborah McDowell has rightly noted, however, Larsen's work was hardly asexual in its content; in fact, Nella Larsen's "peculiar problems" as an author were shaped by her desire to write fiction about female sexual identity while remaining mindful of conventional patterns of decorum in her community:

> The questions confronting [Larsen] might well be formulated: How to write about black female sexuality in a literary era that often sensationalized it and pandered to the stereotype of the primitive exotic? How to give a black female character the right to healthy sexual expression and pleasure without offending the proprieties established by the spokespersons of the black middle class?[97]

McDowell argues that Larsen succeeds by "attempting to hold these two virtually contradictory impulses in the same novel."[98] Yet I would suggest that Larsen maintains control of her precarious position only by displacing sexual freedom *and* sexual exoticism onto the body of the mixed-race figure, the mulatta. In both *Quicksand* and *Passing,* but particularly in the latter, mulatta figures are sexualized even as fellow characters are denied sexual expression; their erotically "liberated" behavior counters patterns of proper bourgeois behavior exemplified by other black female characters in the texts they inhabit.[99] This sexual character forms the basis of a racial threat; the mulatta's refusal to be contained by the bourgeois mores of the salvific wish marks her as culturally disloyal in Larsen's texts because she is disruptive to the behavioral strictures required by bourgeois racial community.

Indeed, Larsen's mixed-race figure frequently behaves in a manner by which other bourgeois blacks in Larsen's fiction cannot abide—disrupting codes of morality which, I argue, are in many ways constitutive of "blackness." When J. M. Favor suggests that "discourses of black identity have as some of their basic premises rules for the expression of sexuality that determine one's standing as a racial being,"[100] he anticipates Gayle Wald's claim that cultural pressures exist "to maintain and/or secure sexual and gender 'respectability' as a means of *racial* self-assertion."[101] Both statements remind us that the central aim of the salvific wish, "respectability," might itself be understood as a marker of black racial identity. To demonstrate a deliberate resistance to codes of respectability is thus to disregard racial community, at least in the bourgeois context about which Larsen writes. The mixed-race woman in *Quicksand* and *Passing* betrays bourgeois black culture by challenging racialized attempts to confine black women's sexual expression to the sphere of the black bourgeois family structure. In doing so, she presents an appearance of *sexual* impropriety that decorum-obsessed characters like Irene Redfield and Anne Grey cannot tolerate.

Of course, the irony of reading respectability, defined by conformity to patriarchal family structures, as a mark of "blackness," even bourgeois blackness, is that the conventional domestic structures that are the criterion of that respectability actually issue from white, Western ideology—in particular, Victorian gender ideals.[102] Hence I find myself in the paradoxical position of arguing that an aspect of white cultural ideology serves to define blackness. Yet I make this claim not to suggest that black identity is generally dependent on hegemonic structures of dominance for its own coherence, but to call attention to, and problematize, the ways in which intimate behavior has always been a part of how black people choose to situate themselves as *political* subjects.

The policing of black female sexuality in the dubious service of racial protection is the hallmark of the salvific wish; thus it should be no surprise that in the novel *Passing,* sultry character Clare Kendry is a source of both fascination and aversion for Irene, the textual representative of black bourgeois "uplift."[103] I should make explicit, here, my interpretation of Irene as a "black" rather than "mulatta" character. Not only does Irene see herself as a black woman, but the text gives readers no serious evidence that Irene's biological ancestry is mixed. Unlike Clare, Irene comes from a black bourgeois home, with two putatively "full-blooded" black parents. Larsen makes a point of narratively identifying Clare's white American ancestry, courtesy of the interracial indiscretions of her father's father, while seeming to suggest (by omission) that Irene's equally light skin is merely a kind of inexplicable accident of her birth into a wealthy black family.[104]

Clare's seductive behavior disrupts, in multiple ways, the racialized respectability that Irene so reveres. In part, this disruption arises from

Clare's sexual availability to white men: not only is she married to the racist Bellew, but she dallies with still other white men on the side, if her indiscretions at the Drayton Hotel are any indication. Clare may perform this sexual liberation while living as a white woman, but it is precisely her affiliation with "blackness" that makes her behavior threatening—witness, for example, Irene's mental note, once she has recognized Clare as black, that the latter woman's flirtatious behavior toward a male server is inappropriate: "Again that odd upward smile. Now, Irene was sure that it was too provocative for a waiter" (152). The emphasis created by the comma after "now" makes it clear that Irene's suddenly confident disapproval is based in Clare's black ancestry, which only takes shape in the temporal space following their introductory conversation, the period of Irene's racial recognition of Clare.

Further, Clare's sexually daring interactions with whites seem to parallel her perceived availability to married black men, a group just as socially forbidden by the black bourgeois community. The sexual and domestic propriety embraced by uplift-driven, race-conscious figures such as Irene Redfield absolutely prohibits those behaviors that would threaten the safe function of the black nuclear family and its attendant patriarchal stability, the "security" that Irene clings to throughout the novel. This social prohibition suggests that Irene's suspicion of Brian and Clare's sexual involvement is based at least in part on an assumption about Clare's *political* disloyalty. Of course, no concrete evidence is given in *Passing* for the adulterous indiscretion, and beginning with Deborah McDowell's groundbreaking analysis of the novel as a covertly lesbian text, numerous critics have suggested that Irene's suspicions only expose her sublimated desire for Clare.[105] Whether or not Irene's suspicions are founded in truth, however, or merely based in her own desires and jealousies, there remains a sense in the text that Clare would be *capable* of such betrayal, empowered as she is with the "ability to secure the thing that she wanted in the face of any opposition, and in utter disregard of the convenience and desire of others" (201). Clare's potential for an adulterous involvement with Brian is emblematic of the potential for racial "infidelity" that resides in the mulatta figure more generally in Larsen's work. The sense throughout Larsen's novels that these figures are capable of "taking quietly and without fuss the things which [they] wanted" (*Quicksand*, 129) is a reference to selfishness, yes, but a selfishness that translates into disregard for black codes of social convention more generally.

It is no wonder, then, that the novel concludes in Clare's death, ostensibly at Irene's hand. Because of her obsessive need for bourgeois propriety, Irene must destroy the mixed-race character, as that character's misconduct proves too much for her to tolerate. This misconduct betrays a "respectable" reconceptualization of blackness—and insofar as the mulatta's sexual transgressiveness recalls common primitivist stereotypes about black erotic excess, it also reifies a stigmatized version of blackness that bourgeois blacks of the period longed to escape. If, as already noted, this primitivist stigma highlights the peculiar vulnerability of the black community around sexuality, then restricting the sexual indiscretions of a figure such as Clare Kendry might be understood by Irene as a way to suppress that vulnerability—to save herself, and her community, from the social stigma that Clare's behavior invites or, perhaps, confirms.

Passing may thus be the ideal test case for an analysis of how the salvific wish, and the peculiar vulnerability that underlies it, surface in black women's literature of the twentieth century. Larsen's novel nonetheless has a somewhat less multifaceted approach to these issues than do some of the other works I consider in this volume. In addition, perhaps because of the lingering relevance of uplift ideology in the period, the sexual politics of the Harlem Renaissance have been addressed in some detail by previous scholars of black intimacy, making Larsen's work an inevitable but hardly inventive inclusion in *Private Lives, Proper Relations*.[106] Few scholars have considered, however, how writing from the latter years of the twentieth century takes up and treats similar issues in innovative ways—this explains my focus on post–World War II narratives in the body of this book. Both the narrative content and the surrounding conditions of African American writing develop and intensify at later points in the twentieth century;

as such, close attention to black writing from the years after the Second World War offers the possibility of truly new insight into the question of black intimate subjectivity.

In *Private Lives, Proper Relations,* I analyze individual narratives both thematically and historically. Each primary text, centerpiece of a given chapter, has its own way of troubling black intimacy and invoking or questioning the ideology of the salvific wish, and each novel also grows out of a specific historical context that includes particular social discourses around black intimate character. It is worth noting, however, that although these contexts sometimes overlap and are frequently interrelated, they do not constitute a clear-cut, sequential narrative spanning from one end of the century to the other. Indeed, although the book proceeds in what might be understood as a loosely chronological order, this order is not at all seamless. In general, *Private Lives, Proper Relations* is less interested in constructing a linear account of intimacy in "the" African American literary tradition than it is in identifying and examining how and why the issue of intimacy arises as a source of tension in particular texts from notable moments during the twentieth century. At the conclusion of her related monograph *The Coupling Convention,* Ann DuCille suggests that "[t]raditions and the canons which confirm them are made not born, constructed not spawned."[107] If I am constructing a tradition of sorts with the group of texts I have selected for inclusion in the body of *Private Lives, Proper Relations*—Ann Petry's *The Street,* Toni Morrison's *Sula* and *Paradise,* Alice Walker's *The Color Purple,* and Gayl Jones's *Eva's Man*—this is in the service of accumulating literary examples that best elucidate the recurrent sociopolitical and cultural power of racialized intimacy in a variety of circumstances throughout the century.

I should note here, as well, that although part of my argument in this book is that the black subject's doubled vulnerability in the realm of the intimate has implications for all African Americans, my work focuses on texts by black women only, for two related reasons. First, as I have already noted, women have historically been understood as the gender most responsible for maintaining domestic and sexual decorum—a Victorian convention that in the case of black women has also served as a marker of racial inadequacy, given persistent assumptions in American culture that black women are incapable of appropriate domestic and sexual comportment. In addition, and perhaps as a result of this history, intimacy in general has continually been understood within black culture itself to be a women's issue. Questions of filial and sexual connection have appeared in some form in the work of most black female authors of the twentieth century, and have been rejected by most of their black male contemporaries in favor of "weightier" topics such as racial identity and political empowerment—this is precisely what Claudia Tate suggests when she writes that early black fiction's idealized domestic tropes are replaced, in the twentieth century, with "explicit depictions of racial protest."[108]

There is an unspoken and false opposition in Tate's words here, an opposition between politics and the racial intimate. Indeed, *Private Lives, Proper Relations* resists precisely this sense that domestic fictions lose their political valence once they shift away from the idealized narratives of the late nineteenth and early twentieth centuries. Instead, I argue that the gendered opposition of racial politics and intimacy constitutes a major oversight in contemporary understandings of African American sociopolitical subjectivity, that in fact the "political" and the "intimate" may be mutually constitutive signs for the black subject, given the fraught history of African American intimacy in the United States. In other words, it may not be possible, or sensible, to think about racial identity without thinking, simultaneously, of intimate subjectivity—for African Americans, the "public" and "private" faces of blackness cannot, and perhaps should not, be distinguished with any great ease, a point that has been made in other contexts by recent scholars of black queer studies.[109]

Private Lives, Proper Relations is divided into five chapters, each of which considers a different primary text and a different constellation of sociocultural narratives about black identity and black intimacy—narratives that influence the reading of a given text both within and beyond its moment. The first two chapters, concerned, respectively, with Ann Petry's *The Street* (1947) and Toni Morrison's *Sula* (1973), consider in particular how self-protective responses to racist narratives of black pathology both rely upon and reinforce class-based hierarchical distinctions between African American women. While my analysis of Petry's text leaves me with more questions than answers regarding the possibility of escaping a peculiar critical angle of vision that defensively naturalizes such hierarchies, my reading of *Sula* suggests that that novel's continual subversion of seemingly naturalized social oppositions offers one way of challenging—and even exploding—the divisive but persistently recurring rhetoric of the salvific wish.

In the third and fourth chapters, I shift to an analysis of the masculinist investments of the salvific wish and the relationship between black intimacy and patriarchal narratives of black nationalism. In my analysis of Alice Walker's *The Color Purple* (1982) in chapter 3, I pinpoint how, and why, Walker's reenvisioned gender dynamics threatened the coherence of a rigidly patriarchal and heteronormative black masculinity, and identify the salvific wish as one of the motivations behind critical hostilities toward Walker's work. In chapter 4, I suggest that Morrison's recent novel *Paradise* (1997) defines the black "national" subject through complex representations of intraracial intimacy—ultimately arguing that the disciplinary labor of the salvific wish is an effort to control not merely black intimate behavior but the literal appearance of a fearfully unknowable black body.

The fifth chapter of the book is perhaps the most significant, in that it most fully examines the notion of "doubled vulnerability"—the black subject made susceptible to exposure and violation by the simultaneous operation of racial scrutiny and human intimacy. This chapter not only points out how depictions of violent desire in Gayl Jones's 1976 novel *Eva's Man* mirror the repressive safety-seeking of the salvific wish, but also attends to reasons why the vulgar language and shocking imagery of the novel themselves seem deliberately to challenge conventional notions of propriety and decorum. Ultimately, using Jones's text as a starting point, I address the indelible risk, the inevitable chaos, of human desire—a chaos that in the end renders the most tenuous efforts of the salvific wish ineffective and even dehumanizing. Finally, in the epilogue of *Private Lives, Proper Relations*, I return to the seemingly irresolvable tension between the particular vulnerability of black intimacy and repressive efforts to remedy this vulnerability, considering whether a communal rejection of heteronormative sexual culture might offer a more productive way of performing, and reading, black intimate subjectivity.

In the end, this project is about what African Americans hope to protect, and what they inadvertently but inevitably lose, in the desperate search for entry into the "civilized world." When Sheila Alexander-Reid suggests that black people are "light years behind" that world, she unwittingly echoes a discourse of pathology that has always worked to exclude black people from so-called normalcy, particularly in the realm of the intimate—a discourse of pathology that constitutes part of the danger in which black subjects repeatedly find themselves. African Americans' reaction to this discourse, in the form of the salvific wish, has facilitated the "problem of denial" that Alexander-Reid so abhors.[110] And I contend that reading twentieth-century African American women's narratives through the prism of these issues is absolutely critical because these stories recall the potentially disastrous consequences of countering one kind of dehumanizing repression with another, more rigid one, this version self-imposed. As Hortense Spillers has written on the subject of black women's sexuality, "the unsexed black female and the supersexed black female embody the very same vice, cast the very same shadow, inasmuch as both are an exaggeration—at either pole—of the uses to which sex might be put."[111] Hiding the doubled vulnerability of black intimacy behind such an exaggerated façade of propriety and "normalcy" does little to alleviate the real pressures of that vulnerability, or to create new social and personal spaces for intimacy, spaces complex enough to move us beyond fantasies of an intimate life made "safe."

Chapter 1

Domestic Oversights

The Negro intellectual is still largely in psychological bondage [. . .] to the fear of breaking the tabus [sic] of Puritanism, Philistinism and falsely conceived notions of "race respectability" [. . . .] The releasing formula is to realize that in all human things we are basically and inevitably human, and that even the special racial complexities and overtones are only interesting variants. Why, then, this protective silence about the ambivalences of the Negro upper classes, about the dilemmas of intra-group prejudice and rivalry, about the dramatic inner paradoxes of mixed heritage, both biological and cultural, or the tragic breach between the Negro elite and the Negro masses[?]
— ALAIN LOCKE, "SELF-CRITICISM"

In the special "Symposium: Survey and Forecast" section of the December 1950 issue of *Phylon*, a group of black male intellectuals ruminated upon the condition of black literature in the post–World War II period.[1] The *Phylon* Symposium was likely modeled on a similar series that had appeared in *The Crisis* nearly a quarter of a century earlier. Entitled "The Negro in Art: How Shall He Be Portrayed," *The Crisis*, led by W. E. B. DuBois, posed seven leading questions about black literature to the journal's readership and published the responses from March to November of the same year.[2] One significant difference between the two symposia, apart from the earlier journal's serial release of the discussion, was that nearly two-thirds of those whose responses were printed in *The Crisis* were white writers and intellectuals, including Carl Van Vechten, H. L. Mencken, Joel Spingarn, Alfred Knopf, and Sinclair Lewis. Indeed, a surprising number of these cautioned black readers against being "too sensitive" and displaying a "lack of humor" about racist portrayals of blacks by white writers such as Octavius Ray Cohen.[3]

By contrast, *Phylon*'s version—led by Alain Locke, the "grand old man of black American letters"[4]—outlined a new, *intraracial* vision for African American writing, largely optimistic but filled with clear criticism for the work of years past. Nearly all of the contributors to the volume touched in some way upon how and why it remained appropriate for black writers to discuss race in their work, most concluding that while dwelling gratuitously upon racial struggle was limiting, "race-experience" nonetheless had an important place in a newly mature black literary oeuvre. Essays such as Nick Aaron Ford's "A Blueprint for Negro Authors," for instance, advised black writers favorably on the "continued use of racial themes," and articles contributed by two of the great names in black literary scholarship—Hugh M. Gloster and J. Saunders Redding—both argued that racial material was "full of lessons and of truth for the world."[5]

Locke himself, in an essay entitled "Self-Criticism: The Third Dimension in Culture," suggested that a forthcoming black artistic maturity would be marked by "an objective, thoroughly humanized treatment" of "Negro materials."[6] This treatment would shift black literary production from a narrowly parochial "chauvinism" to a vision capable of expressing the "universal" aspects of the racial subject. For Locke, such a feat would well surpass the efforts of the New Negro Renaissance, which to him was presently analogous to black literature's adolescence—"gawkly and pimply, indiscreet and overconfident, vainglorious and irresponsible[.]"[7] "Self-Criticism" goes on to suggest that Richard Wright's 1940 novel *Native Son* had been the first gesture toward a corresponding "manhood," though its extreme racial protest ideology and ultimate dehumanization of the black male subject (in the form of nuanceless protagonist Bigger Thomas) meant that it certainly fell far short of the promise of universality for which Locke and other *Phylon* contributors hoped.

Surely, however, if *Native Son* constituted black writing's first clumsy gesture toward literary adulthood, then Ralph Ellison's *Invisible Man*, published only two years after the contributors to *Phylon* outlined their vision, could be its crowning achievement, given that novel's much more subtle attention to the black experience in the United States—indeed, its portrayal of this experience as a fundamentally American conundrum with consequences for the nation as a whole. Sigmund Ro has argued that "the pivotal process of the novel *[Invisible Man]* is the metamorphosis of the black experience into a paradigm of tribulation and overcoming in a crisis-ridden and shrunken world."[8] The shrunken world that Ro speaks of was a product of the "moral vacuum" which existed in the United States following the Second World War, and the related sense among whites that Western civilization needed a "redemptive ethos purged in the crucible of history," which the American Negro was finally well-poised to provide.[9] In other words, in the postwar period, the metaphorized black experience was increasingly understood as a cultural resource both for blacks and for whites, one means of better understanding the human condition in a world no longer insular and categorically secure. Ellison himself suggests such a project when he writes, in a 1981 introduction to *Invisible Man*, that "my task was one of revealing the human universals hidden within the plight of one who was both black and American[.]"[10]

I begin the first chapter of *Private Lives, Proper Relations* with attention to this postwar conversation about a newly mature black American literature in order to highlight two phenomena. The first, which will perhaps hardly be surprising given the time period and the actors involved, is the particularly male-centered or masculinist language in which such literary conversation is couched (witness, for example, Locke's distinction between the literary "adolescence" of the New Negro Renaissance and the "manhood" for which it was frequently mistaken).[11] In Locke's metaphorical structure, African American literary development is assumed to be a matter of black *masculine* empowerment—a rhetoric remarkably similar to what Michele Wallace would later identify as "Black Macho," the notion, prevalent among leaders of the Black Power movement, that when it came to blacks' struggle for autonomy, "manhood is more valuable than anything else."[12] An enormous body of black feminist scholarship from the late twentieth century, including Wallace's own controversial efforts, has pointed out the limitations of such rhetoric—particularly as it worked in tandem with white liberal feminism to exclude black women from dialogues about both race and sex.[13] It is beyond the scope of this chapter, and indeed this volume, to rehearse such counter-arguments fully—nonetheless I invoke this history as a way of highlighting the simultaneously ubiquitous and anticipatory nature of Locke's masculinist language. Penned in 1950, Locke's recourse to a linear narrative of literary evolution ending in racial "manhood" was neither the first nor the last time such a script would be used figuratively to render African American progress.

The second phenomenon I want to remark upon here is closely related to this gendered rhetoric of racial advancement—simply, the extraordinary lapse of vision evidenced by the black male critical establishment in regard to black women's writing of the era. Again, perhaps this lapse is less than surprising, but it is nonetheless impossible simply to sidestep. The epigraph of this chapter, also drawn from "Self-Criticism," is particularly illuminating on that score. In it, Locke details a number of topics he would like to see addressed in African American literature, topics which, in his estimation, black writers had avoided because of cultural "tabus," in particular "Puritanism, Philistinism," and "race respectability."[14] These taboo topics, shrouded in an apparently unbroken "protective silence," include attention to the complexities of "mixed [biological or cultural] heritage," as well as the causes and consequences of class difference within the black community.[15] Ellison's *Invisible Man* certainly addressed a number of these issues, and undoubtedly must have pleased Locke—who, coincidentally, died only two years after that novel's publication. Still, even in the years prior to *Invisible Man*'s appearance, the "protective silence" that surrounded such subject matter was not, in fact, as thorough and impenetrable as it might have seemed to certain critics.

Black women writers had long addressed such questions; the work of Harlem Renaissance author Nella Larsen, as I noted in the introduction to this volume, was particularly driven by the "ambivalences" of the black upper classes and the dilemma of multiracial ancestry—as was the writing of her contemporary, Jessie Fauset.[16] Zora Neale Hurston, also usually understood as a Harlem Renaissance author despite the late publication date of her best-known work, the 1937 novel *Their Eyes Were Watching God*, certainly broached "the dilemmas of intra-group prejudice and rivalry" as well as "the dramatic inner paradoxes of mixed heritage" in her work—at least if *Their Eyes*' protagonist Janie, daughter of a biracial mother and the object of sometimes rancorous envy for her waist-length hair and fair skin, is any indication. All three of these authors, deeply constrained by the same taboos Locke outlines in his essay, nonetheless managed to address in significant ways the very topics he considered to be the "great themes" of black literature.

Why, then, did Locke overlook the work of Larsen, Fauset, and Hurston as he bemoaned the silences and omissions present in modern black writing? One might suppose that Locke lumped such narratives, insightful as they may have been, in with everything else produced during an earlier period in black literary history. Along with a great many men's texts, the writing produced by Renaissance authors Larsen, Fauset, and Hurston could presumably also be understood as the immature scribblings of a black literary adolescence. It remains unclear, however, why Locke's discussion failed to notice more contemporary novelists such as Ann Petry or Dorothy West—both of whom had published major works of fiction less than five years before the symposium issue of *Phylon*, both of whom also addressed a number of the taboo topics Locke himself found so crucial to a new and more mature vision of African American humanity.

I want to suggest that Locke and other critics of the postwar period refused to read or acknowledge writings by these and other black women authors not simply because of their gender difference—i.e., out of straightforward sexism—but rather because the *context* within which these female authors addressed questions of racial identity made it impossible for most male critics to see those texts as a part of the newly mature, "universalizing" efforts of the black writer. Frequently, postwar women authors such as Petry and West (as well as, writing slightly later, Paule Marshall) couched their innovative approaches to topics such as class difference, mixed heritage, intraracial rivalries, and the like, within depictions of the racial intimate—the domestic sphere and the sexual and familial relationships constituting that sphere. Given that such domesticity has historically been understood as the purview of women alone, it is no wonder that the writing of female authors would slip beneath Locke's critical radar—while in search of a racial "universal," the uncovering of black women's narratives would seem only to present an uncomfortable tangent into the particular, the narrow, the categorically "private."

Still, the rigid opposition of public and private, masculine and feminine spheres—an ideology that has been linked, in particular, to studies of nineteenth-century sentimentalism and domestic culture—is a false one, as a number of scholars have recently argued.[17] This may be particularly so for the African American subject, who historically has had an unusually complex relationship to notions of "house" and "home." Robert Reid-Pharr has written, for example, that "there can be no coherent (black) body prior to the interposition of the domestic sphere."[18] In thus linking black subjectivity and black domesticity, Reid-Pharr anticipates Maurice Wallace's recent assertions specifically about black masculine identity, that "the house [. . .] is the very image of the structure of black masculinist consciousness as well as a principal object, materially and metaphorically speaking, of African American men's literary and cultural figuration."[19] Indeed, according to Wallace, the "black masculinist fondness" for enclosed spaces, including the space of the house, actually "speaks for a *longing* to [. . .] retreat away from the public sphere where the gaze tyrannizes into the remote interiority of that other construction of space: consciousness."[20] In other words, for black men, the putatively "private" space of the household can function as escape from an oppressively scopic and panoptic public arena, the home providing not an occasion for "Oedipal dread," but a welcome "figure for black masculine self-possession[.]"[21] Black men are thus, at least metaphorically, as bound by the domestic, the intimate, as are black women—in different ways, perhaps, but with no less crucial a symbolic resonance.

If Locke's analysis seems on its surface to miss this resonance, however, his language nonetheless betrays an awareness of the numerous contexts through which African American intimacy and domesticity might be read and understood. Locke speaks with disdain of the "race respectability" preventing some authors from writing freely of the "great themes"—going so far as to outline it as a significant danger to black literary production:

> Consciously and subconsciously, these repressions [Puritanism, Philistinism, and race respectability] work great artistic harm, especially the fear of being accused of group disloyalty and "misrepresentation" in portraying the full gamut of Negro type, character, and thinking. We are still in the throes of counter-stereotypes.[22]

For Locke, then, contemporary authors were choosing not to portray the "full gamut" of the black experience because they feared the potential repercussions, particularly the accusations of race betrayal that would come with so-called "negative" images of African American character. Such authors seemed to prefer images that would argue against negativity, in the form of "counter-stereotypes." An informed reader might ask, however, what precisely these "counter-stereotypes" are designed to *counter*. From where do accusations of "group disloyalty" arise—what or whom, for that matter, does the "silence" Locke overhears attempt to protect? Perhaps most crucially, how do the black female authors to whom I have already alluded manage to speak to and through these silences and omissions in their own articulation of the very themes Locke sees lacking in other (male) artists' work?

"Race Respectability": The Salvific Wish and Narratives of Black Pathology

Here I want to turn, again, to the concept of the "salvific wish." As I outlined in this book's introduction, the salvific wish is best defined as the desire to rescue the black community from racist accusations of sexual and domestic pathology through the embrace of bourgeois propriety. Most frequently a class- and gender-inflected response—a largely though not entirely feminine and middle-class phenomenon—the wish is an outgrowth of ideologies of racial uplift that circulated in the late nineteenth century. It might be understood as a response to the peculiar vulnerability of the black subject with regard to intimate conduct, for not only must African Americans, like all individuals, wrestle with the human risks involved in familial and sexual connection, they must also contend with a fiercely invasive body of myths that designate the African American community incapable of healthy intimate bonds. Black bodies, understood as sites of sexual excess and domestic ruin in U.S. cultural parlance, are thus doubly vulnerable in the intimate arena—to intimacy itself as well as to the violence of social misperceptions surrounding black intimate character.

The salvific wish, with its attempts to repress and discipline black intimate conduct in hopes of limiting that conduct to patterns of "respectability"—thereby shattering, through force of will, the distortions and myths surrounding black eroticism and domesticity—is thus a sociopolitical response to a discursive and ideological dilemma. The salvific wish, and racial uplift ideology more generally, has its roots in the nineteenth century. Part of what I argue throughout this volume, however, is that twentieth century African American literature and culture are no less concerned with such issues, not only because of the continued vulnerability of the black subject to American cultural narratives of black sexual and domestic pathology, but also due to an increasing recognition that the propriety-minded salvific wish is ultimately a repressive, even *destructive,* response to persistent, pathologizing narratives about the black intimate in majority culture.

One example of such pathologizing narratives, mid-twentieth century, is the black degeneracy thesis advanced by a number of post–World War II historians and sociologists. Patricia Morton suggests that a great many mid-century scholars of African American culture worked diligently, often by manipulating data, to advance a thesis of black pathology rooted in a degenerate black domestic sphere:

> Given the snowball effect whereby each scholar drew from and cited
> his predecessors to build and substantiate his own analysis, history and
> sociology worked closely together to confirm that the Negro's "back-
> wardness" was due to what he did and did not learn in the Negro home

[. . . .] Central to this consensus was the notion that the decrepitude of
the black family was the cause as well as the effect of Negro pathology,
and in turn that the linchpin of this was the inadequacy of Negro
women as women.[23]

Remarkably similar to the vernacular racist discourse about black
women and black families that circulated in the late nineteenth century (the originating era of the salvific wish), such accusations were
now couched as intellectual analysis, though as Morton notes, much
of this "research" was built upon the unabashedly racist attitudes of
earlier writers.

Given the racist history behind such theories, it is also ironic that
one major mid-century contributor to black degeneracy ideology was
a well-respected black sociologist, E. Franklin Frazier. His writings,
particularly 1937's *The Negro Family in the United States,* focused on
the "dominating position" of the black mother during and after slavery, and the negative manner in which the "disorganization of Negro
family life" contributed to black "demoralization" and "delinquency."[24]
Frazier's work, along with that of other liberal scholars of the 1930s
and '40s, had far-reaching implications, later serving as the impetus for
Daniel Moynihan's controversial 1965 report, "The Negro Family: The
Case for National Action." Moynihan's report built upon and extended
Frazier's theory of a pathological black "matriarchate" responsible for
various African American social weaknesses and shortcomings.[25] Thus
in 1950, a moment when Locke argued decisively against "falsely conceived notions of 'race respectability,'" the justification for such repressive efforts was certainly still at the center of American cultural discourse around black identity—indeed, its transformation from shared
colloquial or anecdotal knowledge to scientific, "objective" scholarship
meant such theories were becoming more invidious because they were
more difficult simply to dismiss.

The increasing popularity of such theories in the period directly
following World War II was also due, in part, to reactionary gender
politics in the larger culture. White (and black) women may have en-
tered the workforce in unprecedented numbers during the war, but

once soldiers returned home, these newly minted workers were often expected to return to their "rightful places" as housewives and mothers.[26] As Susan Hartmann notes, most World War II initiatives for women "were based on a temporary wartime need: those powers which tolerated, even urged, women to step outside their customary sphere couched that invitation in terms which fortified traditional convictions about sex roles."[27] This "feminine mystique," in the later words of Betty Freidan, came to dominate postwar popular culture, demanding that women re-embrace lives as stay-at-home mothers and housewives in spite of many working women's dissatisfaction with such conventional roles.[28]

African Americans were hardly immune to such traditional ideologies of femininity, in spite of the fact—or perhaps because of the fact—that few black women, historically, were financially capable of eschewing work outside the home. Because black men were closed out of jobs due to racial discrimination, black women were more likely than majority women to work for wages, especially given the continued demand for black women as domestic servicepeople in the homes of whites.[29] As I will explore more fully later in this writing, Ann Petry's novel *The Street* actually addresses just this dilemma—readers are made to understand that work outside the home leads to the breakup of protagonist Lutie Johnson's marriage, as her chronically unemployed husband becomes increasingly unhappy once she has, in desperation, left their home to accept a position as a live-in domestic. Here the dire economic situation of most African Americans does little to displace a set of guidelines for appropriate feminine behavior that limit female productivity to the tasks of homemaker and family caretaker.

Part of what I argue in the remainder of this chapter, however, is that in the postwar moment, black women writers—particularly best-selling author Ann Petry—resist the rigidity of such guidelines in their work, using the trope of the salvific wish, and associated questions of black intimacy, as points of entry for this resistance. I focus on Petry here because her work's unusual commercial success indicates its particular usefulness as a cultural touchstone for postwar readers; nonetheless, such issues were equally at stake in other, less popular novels, such as

Dorothy West's *The Living Is Easy* (1948), Gwendolyn Brooks' *Maud Martha* (1953), and Paule Marshall's later text, *Brown Girl, Brownstones* (1959). In many of these post–World War II novels, black female characters whose behaviors are guided by the salvific wish ultimately damage, even destroy, the domestic environments under their influence. By highlighting, and interrogating, the disciplinary stance of the salvific wish toward black intimate conduct, authors of the period challenge rigidly gendered "spheres," ironically demonstrating the potential danger of the black wife and mother whose power is limited strictly to her household. New attention to such texts can help today's readers consider the consequences—for all of black humanity, not just black women—of such socially imposed limitations upon the black intimate sphere.

Ann Petry: Beyond Naturalism

To that end, I now turn to Ann Petry's popular first novel, *The Street* (1946). *The Street* was somewhat of an anomaly in its period, precisely because of the attention it received from critics, as well as its unusual financial success. The first novel by a black woman to sell more than one million copies, Petry's work received what one scholar calls "a warm and enthusiastic reception" at the time of its publication.[30] This reception was warmer financially than critically, however; although most early critics found it appropriate to acknowledge Petry's novel because of its superficial similarities to Richard Wright's hugely successful *Native Son* (1940), acknowledgment did not extend to sincere praise. The comparison of Wright and Petry is certainly plausible, as both novels are naturalist in approach, and both depict the debilitating effects of a hostile urban environment on young, black protagonists. For the novel's earliest critics, however, Petry's novel was rarely seen to measure up to Wright's volume. Scholars such as Robert Bone and Addison Gayle ultimately dismissed the novel as an inferior "carbon copy" of Wright's text.[31]

In subsequent years, feminist critics and others writing from a less myopic perspective have done much to recuperate *The Street* from this categorization.[32] Most point out that Petry's novel, far from being a copy of Wright's, actually is more complex because it points out the crippling influence of not just race and class, but sex as well—Lutie Johnson is oppressed because of her blackness and her poverty, but she is also, crucially, victimized because she is a woman. Rather than repeat such arguments, which have been made successfully elsewhere, I would instead like to look more closely at something most critics of *The Street*, whether favorable or unfavorable, seem repeatedly to overlook—that is, a specific choice that the novel's protagonist, Lutie Johnson, makes near the beginning of the text, a choice that sets the rest of the narrative's events in motion. I refer, here, to Lutie's decision to move out of her father's flat and into the unfortunate apartment on the "street" of the novel's title. In fact, I want to suggest that in depicting this choice, Petry's text makes Lutie's unwitting contribution to her own victimization quite clear, much more clear than the text's naturalist approach would initially seem to support.

M. H. Abrams tells us that naturalist fiction is based upon the philosophy that a human being "is merely a higher-order animal whose character and behavior are entirely determined by two kinds of forces, heredity and environment."[33] It is easy to understand Lutie Johnson as a naturalist character, born a poor black woman and trapped by her environment—the Harlem street where she comes to live—into an existence circumscribed by racial, sexual, and class oppression. Petry's narrative makes this explicit by the end of the text: "[A]ll those years she'd been heading straight as an arrow for that street or some other street just like it. Step by step she'd come, growing up, working, saving, and finally getting an apartment on a street nobody could have beaten."[34] And, indeed, Lutie does not beat the street—as the novel ends, she is leaving New York after having committed a gruesome murder, abandoning her young son to an uncertain fate and fleeing toward an equally bleak urban environment, Chicago.

As readers we might ask, however, how and why Lutie comes to live on this street that defeats her. I have already noted that Lutie's marriage breaks up because she is forced, by her husband's persistent unemployment, to take a job as a live-in domestic with a wealthy family, the Chandlers, in Connecticut. When Lutie comes home to New York from the country early one afternoon, she discovers that "there was another woman living there with Jim" (53). Unsympathetic to her shock and rage, her husband scoffs, "'What did you expect? Maybe you can go on day after day with nothing to do but just cook meals for yourself and a kid. [. . . .] But I can't. And I don't intend to" (54). Implicit in Jim's response is a possible comment upon the gender roles occupied by the two spouses. Maybe Lutie can go on with only cooking meals and childcare as her daily tasks, and maybe she *should*—after all, such is the expected behavior of a housewife. That Lutie is, instead, the family's breadwinner, separated from her husband in order to make money, "sending practically all her wages, month after month" (54) back to Jim and their son, Bub, is a clear reversal of Western culture's traditional sexual order.

What Jim's callous dismissal of such a reversal also suggests, however, is the generally demoralizing nature of the housewife's expected labor, particularly when cooking and childcare come "[w]ith just enough money to be able to eat and have a roof over your head" (54). In other words, since Jim's statement makes no explicit reference to Lutie's gender, it is also possible to read his comments as a reminder that a woman's traditional role can be unsatisfying not just to men, but to women as well, particularly when coupled with poverty. As Angela Davis wrote some thirty-five years after *The Street* was published, "[R]epetitive, exhausting, unproductive, uncreative—these are the adjectives which most perfectly capture the nature of housework."[35] In the same essay, Davis goes on to argue that in spite of the superficial appeal, to many women, of the "househusband" as an idea, the "desexualization of domestic labor would not really alter the oppressive nature of the work itself."[36] For either sex, then, such a life as Jim led while unemployed might be experienced as unfulfilling and monotonous, because of the actual character of domestic labor.

Nonetheless, Lutie is less than sympathetic to the means by which Jim has chosen to improve his unfulfilling life, and she packs up her son and her furniture and moves out of their rented house in Jamaica, Queens (53). Contrary to what we might expect, based upon how the novel is summarized by other critics, Lutie does not move directly from the home she shared with Jim to the street of the novel's title. Instead, she and her son move in with Lutie's father, into a "crowded, musty flat on Seventh Avenue" (55). Not one of the scholars who have written about *The Street* pays significant attention to how Petry depicts this period in Lutie's history. Such scholars summarize early pages of the text by describing Lutie as the novel's "apartment-hunting protagonist" or as a woman whose family has "run into trouble," forcing her to rent "a cubbyhole of a place in the heart of the ghetto."[37] Yet such abbreviated portrayals of Lutie's situation following her marital separation overlook a significant moment in the character's life. In fact, Lutie's unhappy perception of her father's home, as depicted in the narrative, is crucial to her decision to take the ill-fated apartment "in the heart of the ghetto," on 116th Street in Harlem.

Central to Lutie's uneasiness in her father's apartment, and her decision to move out on her own with her son, is her dislike of her father's live-in girlfriend, Lil, whose presence in the space is described this way:

> There seemed to be no part of [the flat] that wasn't full of Lil. She was always swallowing coffee in the kitchen, trailing through all seven rooms in housecoats that didn't quite meet across her lush, loose bosom; drinking beer in tall glasses and leaving the glasses in the kitchen sink so the foam dried in a crust around the rim—the dark red of her lipstick like an accent mark on the crust; lounging on the wide bed she shared with Pop and only God knows who else; drinking gin with the roomers until late at night. (10)

The preceding passage is narrated in the third person but evidently limited to Lutie's perspective. It makes clear that the younger woman's discomfort with Lil has a great deal to do with her perception of Lil as a morally lax individual, excessive in her dress, grooming, and personal habits. Lutie's obsessive belief that the spacious seven-room apartment is "spilling over with Lil" indicates her anxiety about this excess, her fear that it will engulf her and her child. This is particularly clear in the description of Lil's "lush, loose" breasts; inadequately restrained by brassiere or housecoat, they are signifiers of an equally loose sexuality, an unrestrained access to pleasure that Lutie, like Larsen's Irene Redfield, cannot tolerate. The accompanying description of "the wide bed [Lil] shared with Pop and only God knows who else" also slyly alludes to promiscuity—or at least to sexual expression unregulated by legal marriage, as the text is careful to identify Lil as a "girlfriend" rather than a wife.

Seemingly, Lutie is justified in her horror over this aspect of her living situation, particularly since Lil has apparently already begun to pass her habits on to eight-year-old Bub: "And what was far more terrifying[:] giving Bub a drink on the sly; getting Bub to light her cigarettes for her" (10). Yet the text also suggests that Lutie's discomfort with Lil leads Lutie into destructive behavior toward her son, the very person she ostensibly intends to protect: "Only last night Lutie had slapped him so hard that Lil cringed away from her dismayed [. . .] 'Jesus!' [Lil] said. 'That's enough to make him deaf. What's the matter with you?'" (10, 11). Here, Lil, ostensibly the source of moral peril, is actually the one who moves to defend Bub, and Lutie's violence seems to offer a more clear and present danger to the child's welfare. Reading such a scene, it becomes evident that Lutie's hysterical fear of Lil's influence is based in more than concern for her child's physical and moral safety—indeed, we might take her violent slap as an indication that Bub's well-being is tangential to the situation. What, then, motivates Lutie's discomfort with Lil, and her subsequent decision to leave her father's apartment?

I want to suggest that Lutie's behavior is motivated, quite simply, by the salvific wish. This is apparent in the particular objections Lutie has to Lil—her drinking and smoking, her careless housekeeping, her dark red lipstick, and her already-mentioned buxom breasts and uninhibited sensuality—all of which signal domestic disorder and sexual immodesty, the very characteristics the salvific wish is intended to police. In addition, however, Petry gives us a number of clues about Lutie's class aspirations, which also suggest that she strives for bourgeois "respectability," that quality that adherents to the salvific wish hold so dear. In just one example, when Lutie discovers that Bub has industriously put together a shoeshine box to earn extra money, her reaction is just as violent as her response to Lil's influence: "[S]he slapped him sharply across the face. His look of utter astonishment made her strike him again—this time more violently, and she hated herself for doing it, even as she lifted her hand for another blow" (66). Here, Lutie's violence seems grossly out of proportion to Bub's "crime," indicating, perhaps, that she is lashing out at something larger. And indeed, Lutie's rage-filled verbal assault, which follows the physical one, reveals precisely her reasons for disliking the shoeshine box as an idea: "'I'm working to look after you and you out here in the street shining shoes just like the rest of these little niggers" (67). The sense that Lutie and her son are, must strive to be, better than "the rest" of the blacks on the street is implicit in this statement.

As a number of other critics have noted, much of Lutie's sense of herself as better has to do with her exposure to the Chandlers, a wealthy white family whose central goal is to remain "filthy rich" (43).[38] Lutie herself acknowledges this influence: "After a year of listening to [the Chandlers'] talk, she absorbed some of the same spirit" (43). Ironically enough, however, even as Lutie models her own class aspirations after those of the wealthy whites who employ her, she is aware that these very whites perceive her as little more than a sexual object—which is precisely the cultural stereotype that the bourgeois strivings of the salvific wish are intended to counter. White women friends of Mrs. Chandler invariably make assumptions about Lutie's morality and her sexual availability to their husbands: "Sure, she's a wonderful cook. But I wouldn't have any good-looking colored wench in my house. Not with John. You know they're always making passes at men. Especially white men'" (40). Here Lutie is scripted into a narrative of black (female) sexual pathology that simultaneously affirms her alleged moral degeneracy and steadfastly denies the danger Lutie faces from white male employers who see black women as ready sexual prey. Even as the white women speaking acknowledge that Lutie's physical appearance might make her desirable to men—hence the qualifier "good-looking"—they insist that any sexual contact between their white husbands and black domestics would be initiated by the "colored wench" in question, willfully erasing or overlooking the truth of historical precedent, the "sexual harassment that many [black women] confronted in white homes."[39] In this way, the words of Lutie's white female employer and her friends enact a kind of violence against Lutie, in their erasure of and indifference to the frequent realities of her subject position.

Lutie at first denies the abusiveness of these women's assumptions, as she reminds herself of her own "respectable" status: "It didn't make her angry at first. Just contemptuous. They didn't know she had a big handsome husband of her own; that she didn't want any of their thin unhappy husbands. But she wondered why they all had the idea that colored girls were whores" (41). Of course, Lutie's mental rebuttal of her employers' prejudgments is immaterial, given that the assumption of her promiscuity has little to do with whether she has a "big handsome husband of her own." In fact, given popular beliefs about the disorganization of black family life (to borrow E. Franklin Frazier's language), most whites probably would not believe that Lutie's marital status could prevent her from making "passes" at other men. Nonetheless, the fact that Lutie is "highly respectable, married, mother of a small boy" (45) is crucially redemptive in Lutie's eyes, even though it is unlikely to salvage her in the eyes of whites whose preconceived notions of black intimate character assume an always willing and available female body.

Rather than souring her on the values of the upper classes, however, Lutie's two years with the Chandlers only serve to solidify her class aspirations, her desire for more money and, equally important, greater social status and respectability. Perhaps since she already sees herself as holding an elevated status because of her husband and her "respectable" home, Lutie seems willing to embrace the hierarchy that the Chandlers value, the very one that would exclude her on the basis of race. And indeed, if one goal of the salvific wish is protection of blacks (individually and as a group) from accusations of pathology, Lutie's embrace of bourgeois social hierarchies and the recuperative power of "domesticity" might be expected to exempt her from the Chandlers' racism, or to prove it wrong. In understanding Lutie's persistent view of herself as a certain kind of black person, then, one who is better than "the rest of these [. . .] niggers," we might also better understand her desperate desire to escape her father's apartment and the buxom, "blowsy" Lil.

For Lutie, driven by the bourgeois strivings of the salvific wish, "the thing that really mattered" was escaping Lil; anything, "[d]ark hallways, dirty stairs, even roaches on the walls" was better than another month dominated by her influence (4). Here, Lutie expresses her willingness to endure a host of humiliating and degraded living conditions rather than remain for one more moment in her current environment. One could certainly read these conditions symbolically, as merely an alternate form of the moral "darkness" and "dirt" Lutie believes Lil's presence imparts. It is just as important to note, however, that in the literal sense, this setting signifies *physical*, not moral, discomfort; darkened hallways, dirty stairs, even the ultimate evidence of ghetto crowding and filth—roach infestation—indicate a domestic space burdened only with *external* depravity, potentially unmarked by the more interior sort of contamination that Lil represents.

Lutie seems to believe that she can create a "safer" intimate space in the midst of such materially unpleasant surroundings than she can while living with Lil, a more indelible source of peril. This anxiety, this determination to escape one kind of danger for another, supposedly lesser kind, is no doubt motivated by the fact that Lutie's husband, the former marker of her carefully maintained "respectability," is no longer a part of her life. A newly single mother, Lutie is now uncomfortably close to fitting the stereotype of black female sexual availability and domestic disorder that circulated with increasing regularity in the post–World War II moment, the very stereotype assumed (and enforced) in the comments Lutie overhears from her white female employers. This is so in spite of the fact of Lutie's actual celibacy, which, as Evie Shockley points out, is a requirement of her social position and ethical strivings—her nonlegal separation from her husband prevents sanctioned physical pleasure within a new marital relationship, but her rigid sense of morality also prevents her from seeking sexual release extramaritally.[40] Indeed, one wonders whether Lutie's discomfort with Lil is motivated at least in part by *resentment* of Lil's easy access to carnal pleasure, unconstrained by the legal strictures of marriage, via Pop's "wide bed." Such pleasure is out of reach for Lutie precisely because of her strict moral code, a moral code shaped by her determination to resist racist whites' preconceptions. Thus, prior to her marriage's dissolution, Lutie takes multiple forms of comfort in Jim's body, her "big, handsome husband" serving as not only the object of Lutie's later-frustrated desires, but also as the obvious antidote to her employers' violently demeaning ideology.

Indeed, in a reminder of the traditional function of bourgeois masculinity, Jim's presence in Lutie's life creates a symbolic barrier between Lutie and the unmarried, sexually and socially "loose" Lil, clearly demarcating Lutie's position on the safe side of a sociocultural boundary between "ladies" and "women." Writing about bourgeois men's encounter with working-class women in the Victorian period, Griselda Pollock has suggested that "the apparently deregulated sexuality of working women[. . . .] was threatening to the sex-gender system by which the bourgeoisie defined its class identity at its most vulnerable and therefore most urgently defended point—defended through the codification of the feminine and the absolute regulation of female sexuality and productivity."[41] In other words, in the nineteenth century, bourgeois men's role was to delimit female sexuality—and the distinction between the idle, bourgeois "lady" and her working-class counterpart was precisely the fact that working-class women's bodies were not made safe by legally sanctioned male control. In the working class, "bourgeois men discovered another kind of female 'body' which appeared to control its own sexualities and its own productivity rather than being exchanged between fathers and husbands."[42] While Pollock refers specifically to Europe in the late nineteenth century, her analysis relates quite cogently to the distinction that Lutie sees between herself and Lil—especially since the very notion of "respectability," one goal of the salvific wish, in fact originates in white, Western bourgeois values from the Victorian era, as I have already noted in this book's introduction. The social hierarchies espoused by the Chandlers and embraced by Lutie are simply an extension of such values.

For the married, "highly respectable" Lutie, then, she and Lil literally occupy different spaces, both ideologically and physically. Once Jim departs, and Lutie reenters her father's household, Lutie and Lil not only are forced to cohabitate, but they again occupy a similar *discursive* space as black women. They may have always shared this space in the perception of whites, as race persistently nullifies any such class-based distinctions in the larger cultural imaginary, but from Lutie's point of view, the intraracial potential for differentiation was crucial. After Jim's departure, not even Lutie herself can maintain an adequate barrier between herself and Lil, except one that she must constantly reinforce through violence—hence her repeated, excessive corporal disciplining of Bub, whose youth and innocence make his body the contested site over which the two women compete for control. This literal and figurative proximity to Lil, as well as the possibility of losing a competition with such stakes, is too much for the salvific wish–driven Lutie to bear. It is no wonder, then, that after her marriage is over, Lutie is increasingly desperate to create a household that will distance herself and Bub from socially "inappropriate" black women like Lil—and the sexual frankness associated with them.

Thus readers eventually arrive at a crucial moment in the text, one that reveals Lutie's thought process as she decides, against her better judgment, to take the apartment on 116th Street. In this moment, the salvific wish provides the motivation for Lutie's deliberate endangerment of herself and her son. Lutie convinces herself that the apartment is her only option, in spite of her feelings of dread as she walks past the madam living in the first-floor apartment, Mrs. Hedges, and in spite of "the instinctive, immediate fear she had felt when she first saw the Super" (20). Ignoring her own sense of the street, the apartment, and the super as threats to her own and her son's well-being, Lutie uses her salvific wish–driven distaste for Lil's character as justification for a bad decision, soothing her fear by imagining herself to be under the protection of the local police:

You've got a choice a yard wide and ten miles long. You can sit down
and twiddle your thumbs while your kid gets a free education from
your father's blowsy girlfriend. Or you can take this apartment. The tall
gentleman who is the superintendent is supposed to rent apartments,
fire the furnace, sweep the halls, and that's as far as he's supposed to
go. If he tries to include making love to the female tenants, why, this is
New York City in the year 1944, and as yet there's no grass growing in
the streets and the police force still functions. Certainly you can holler
loud enough so that if the gentleman has some kind of dark designs on
you and tries to carry them out, a cop will eventually rescue you. That's
that. (19)

Weighing Lutie's distaste for Lil, who, no matter what her alleged
moral failings, never presents enough of a threat to require police protection, against Lutie's intuition that the super might try to cause her
actual, physical harm, makes it clear that Lutie's decision-making is
skewed in the direction of propriety, at the expense of her own safety.
Unlike the distinction between materially distasteful living conditions
and Lil's moral laxity, Lutie here decides in favor of serious physical
danger over the potential moral threat. The foolishness of this decision
is borne out by the text. Not only does the super in fact attempt to rape
Lutie (and she is rescued not by a kindly Harlem police officer, but by
the "snake-eyed" Mrs. Hedges, who herself hopes to hire Lutie out as a
prostitute), but the super is also responsible for getting Bub into trouble,
and the lawyers' fees Lutie naïvely believes she needs to get Bub out of
juvenile detention are what lead to the tragic denouement of the novel.

In other words, Lutie's decision to take the apartment sets the rest
of the narrative's events in motion, and proves to be a destructive and
foolhardy choice with painful consequences for both Bub and Lutie
herself. Obsessed with creating a "respectable" home for herself, away
from Lil's generally harmless, if "improper," behavior, Lutie walks directly into the demoralizing fate that awaits her on "the street." This
is so in spite of the fact that Lutie's decision to take the apartment has
already "happened" in the text by the time readers are given to understand her motivation; as Lindon Barrett's insightful reading of Petry's
novel points out, "The chronological sequence of *The Street* is exceedingly intricate," being, as it is, "excessively populated with flashbacks"

and "rehearsals of past events."[43] Barrett points to this jumbled chro-
nology in order to argue that "the street seemingly possesses no future,"
and that Lutie is trapped in a progression of equally oppressive present
moments.[44] Indeed, given that the novel begins with a scene representing Lutie's tour and acceptance of the ill-fated apartment, one might
argue that narratively, her character is always already on "the street,"
even when textual representations indicate that she has not yet arrived there.

On the other hand, it is certainly not impossible to consider Lutie's
story chronologically, as a series of events occurring in (admittedly re-
cursive) sequence. This is particularly true of Lutie's passage between
her father's apartment and the street—her brief and doomed journey
from the frying pan to the fire, if you will. Even Barrett describes
this moment of mobility in terms that recall traditional temporality:
"[T]he protagonist's *first* quandary—how to escape the unacceptable
atmosphere of Pop's seven rooms—*is resolved* by puzzling out whether
[the landlord]'s sign advertises two rooms or three."[45] The sense that
Pop, and Lil, are a "quandary" to be solved—Lutie's "first," *originary*
quandary, that is ultimately answered via her action—again suggests
that her character has been empowered to make a choice, and that this
choice precedes and enables her experiences on the street.

In light of that choice, we might begin, as readers, to see Petry's
purportedly naturalist approach in a new light. The narrative actually
implies a level of agency for Lutie, willingly exercised for the wrong
reasons. Even if it is possible to read Lutie as merely a "higher order
animal" shaped by heredity and environment, her attachment to the
social strivings of the salvific wish must be acknowledged as an equally
inevitable aspect of her character, especially given the influence of the
Chandlers on her thought processes—not just as models for success, but
because Lutie hopes to prove their racist assumptions about her character wrong. In either case, Petry's text suggests that Lutie's victimization on the basis of her race, gender, and class is more complex than
it initially appears, and has as much to do with Lutie's "internalize[d]
cultural assumptions" about gender and race as it has to do with external forces of oppression.[46] Vulnerable to a set of stereotypes about black

sexual and domestic character that violently collide with her sense of herself as "respectable," Lutie's own need for *ideological* self-protection, through the rigid armor of the salvific wish, materially endangers her life and all that she holds dear.

Critical Blindness and Cultural Vision: A Coda

Petry's novel comments upon the dire social consequences of reactionary ideologies such as the salvific wish, which hope to refute exclusionary racist dogma through the embrace of some of that dogma's most basic premises. In fact, the comment offered by Petry's work arguably is relevant not only to black women, but to black people, as black men are certainly implicated in narratives of black intimate degeneracy—and as we shall see in later chapters of *Private Lives, Proper Relations,* more than capable of espousing the values of the salvific wish. Insofar as Petry's text is a reminder of the dehumanizing consequences of racist dogma for even its perpetrators (witness the cruelty Lutie's white female employers must evidence in order to maintain their own social position *vis-à-vis* African American domestics), it also bears acknowledgment by the white majority culture. Given this, one might at least *argue* that Petry's work speaks broadly to its readers. It might be useful, then, to return to the "Symposium" section of *Phylon* 11, and reconsider Locke's oversight of Petry and other female authors in light of his ambitious hopes for a "universalizing" black literature at mid-century. We might now more accurately read Locke's position within a larger discursive context, taking into account the perils of representing the black intimate and Locke's likely unease with interpreting narratives so deeply immersed within it as "universal" narratives of blackness.

Part of the reason for Locke's oversight is his seeming inability to accept black domestic spaces, or representations of such spaces, as sites for the articulation and elaboration of a so-called "universal" experience; this is related, as well, to Locke's apparent discomfort with black artists' reliance upon "counter-stereotypes" and what he calls "falsely conceived notions of 'race respectability.'" In both cases, I would argue that Locke's uneasiness has to do with an unavoidable black *particularity* around intimate matters, one of the "special racial complexities" to which Locke dismissively alludes in this chapter's epigraph.[47] The peculiar vulnerability of the black intimate subject—which supposedly necessitates such "counter-stereotypes" as those advanced by proponents of the salvific wish—is itself a marker of black Americans' racial distinctiveness, and calling attention to such distinctiveness potentially invalidates any claims for "universality" that could arise from representations of the black intimate sphere. The intimate, the domestic, so rigidly aligned with femininity in prevailing Western ideology, yet so fraught with peculiarly racialized meaning for the black subject of either gender, might in fact be understood as one of the "tabus" of black representation, a reminder of black specificity that is better left unspoken. Thus, ironically enough, Locke himself becomes an arbiter of "race respectability" when he overlooks the writing of his black female contemporaries, due to that writing's inextricable link to the racial intimate.[48]

Locke's is not the only critical blindness around Petry's work, however, and while his limited vision might be excused by the political nuances of his moment, a later critical oversight is not so easily explained. I allude to the fact that few of the post-1970 critics of Petry's *The Street* (in fact, none that I have been able to identify) comment upon the crucial scenes that I read in the body of this chapter.[49] Given the number of scholars over the past several decades who have written about Petry's novel—and given that Lutie's decision to move onto 116th Street is what allows the rest of the narrative's events to take place, this critical oversight is certainly startling, if not downright astonishing. This is so even taking into account that Lil is a "minor" character in Petry's 400-plus page novel. Lutie's decision to move onto the street that becomes her downfall is so clearly motivated by her need to escape Lil that I would argue Lil's role in the text is pivotal, in spite of her putative "minor" status. Yet I am not pointing out this critical lapse in order to highlight my own originality in addressing these scenes—in fact, it was only after many rereadings of Petry's novel that such an analysis occurred to me. What I want to argue instead, here in the final pages of this chapter, is that Petry's readers, including myself, may be casualties of a peculiar critical blindness around black intimacy.

To make the point more plainly, I would suggest that most critics of Petry's novel—more riskily, I would include most readers of African American cultural texts in general—approach the narrative from perspectives informed by an understanding of how the black intimate subject historically has been stigmatized and degraded in the United States. They read with an understanding, in other words, of what I have already identified as an African American "doubled vulnerability" around issues of intimacy. Such a perspective may make it difficult for these readers even to *see* certain narrative moments when the salvific wish is at work, in that the salvific wish has for at least a century been understood in the African American cultural imaginary to be the necessary corollary to black intimate vulnerability. Scholars of Petry's work seem simply to take for granted that Lutie must leave her father's home and move into a space of her own—even those who ultimately question Lutie's motivations once she arrives on the street.[50] Such acceptance seems to indicate these scholars' complicity with what Sybil Weir names "a New England code of genteel behavior" and Bernard Bell calls an "urge to whiteness and [. . .] respectability"—an ideology that I would identify more simply as the salvific wish.[51]

Given that this salvific wish, a racialized desire to rescue the African American subject from stigmas around sexuality and domesticity through the embrace of bourgeois respectability, can be understood as a particularly middle-class response to the peculiar vulnerability of black intimacy, it may not be surprising that Petry scholars—by definition an educated and literate group, largely middle-class in *status* if not origins—would in some way, even if only covertly, embrace the values of the salvific wish. Indeed, such an embrace is one of a very few responses that have historically been available to African Americans around the subject of intimacy, because it is such a fraught issue in black U.S. culture.[52] Perhaps, then, the larger critical blindness that I have happened upon in relation to Petry's depiction of Lutie and Lil is the consequence of what we might read as a cultural *hyper*vision, an extreme sensitivity to intimate matters which is, of necessity (due to racism's invasiveness), skewed in the direction of self- and communal protection. I have invoked the concept of "vulnerability" here, and will continue to do so throughout this volume, because that concept most accurately captures the real *and* the imagined dangers that come with persistent narratives of black intimate pathology. Perhaps scholars with an understanding of these dangers read Lutie's fear of the sexual and domestic laxity that Lil represents as only "natural," as a part of the continual negotiations of circumstance and position faced by the doubly vulnerable black intimate subject in the United States.

As I conclude this chapter, however, I am left with the question of Lil's subjectivity, the subjectivity of poor and working-class women whose bodies become the allegorical repository for all of those mythologies of black sexual and domestic degeneracy from which women like Lutie hope to distance themselves. Here I mean neither to claim that poor or working-class women's sexuality provides the "authentically" black counter to the white-identified "artifice" of the black middle class, nor to argue that class distinctions among African Americans actually, necessarily, mark a difference in intimate values and behaviors. Instead, I want to suggest that certain all-too-common angles of vision make it impossible to consider these issues with any rigor—Lil simply must be reduced to a figure for "pathology" if readers are to naturalize Lutie's actions as a sensible response to black doubled vulnerability around issues of intimacy. The critic, the reader, can only account for Lil's subjectivity if he *sees* her in the first place, underneath the layers of stigma with which she has been invested, by Lutie, by the larger culture, perhaps by Petry herself. So much of what I try to elucidate in *Private Lives, Proper Relations* relates to this inability to see beyond stigma and beyond black Americans' very limited defensive reactions to it—and to how certain cultural texts alert us to these lapses in vision. In the next chapter, through a reading of Daniel Patrick Moynihan's 1965 report and Toni Morrison's 1973 novel *Sula,* I return to the ways that African American women have been pathologized in U.S. culture, in order to point out more directly the instability of those intraracial distinctions that are designed to protect certain blacks from stigma, but that rarely succeed and, in the process, dehumanize the community as a whole.

Chapter 2

Pathological Women

*Things were so much better in 1965. Or so it
seemed. You could go downtown and see colored
people working in the dime store behind the counters,
even handling money with cash-register keys around
their necks. And a colored man taught mathematics
at the junior high school.*
—Toni Morrison, *Sula*

*The most fundamental problem [. . .] is that of
family structure. The evidence—not final, but powerfully persuasive—is that the Negro family in the
urban ghettos is crumbling.* A middle-class group
has managed to save itself, *but for vast numbers of
the unskilled, poorly educated city working class the
fabric of conventional social relationships has all but
disintegrated.*
—Daniel Moynihan, *The Negro Family:
The Case for National Action* (my emphasis)

Toni Morrison's 1973 novel *Sula,* set in a small black neighborhood in
rural Ohio (the "Bottom"), concludes with a chapter simply entitled
"1965." The narrative actually spans forty-six or more years, beginning
with an undated story of the neighborhood's origins followed immediately by a chapter labeled "1919." In fact, all of *Sula*'s chapter titles are
dates: 1919, 1920, 1921, 1922, 1923, and 1927 in Part I; 1937, 1939, 1940,
1941, and 1965 in Part II. Yet by far the largest chronological jump in
the text is between the final two chapters, "1941" and "1965"—an incon-
gruity which leads to questions about the year's significance. Why did
Morrison skip ahead exactly 24 years, no more or less, when choosing
the temporal setting of her final chapter? Why not, for example, bring
the setting forward thirty-two years, to the book's actual contemporary
moment? Instead, Morrison's narrative stops fully eight years short of

Sula's 1973 publication date, although the number of years between 1941 and 1965 is still more than twice the number between the next largest chronological gap in the text (1927 and 1937).

It seems safe to assert that the year 1965 is in some way significant, situated at the end of this novel for a reason. Indeed, in this chapter I want to suggest that not only Morrison's final pages, but her novel as a whole comment upon the sociopolitical climate in the United States in 1965, a climate shaped by such events as the Watts race riots (August 1965) and the earlier appearance of a now-infamous government report, *The Negro Family: The Case for National Action*, written by former Senator Daniel Patrick Moynihan for the Office of Policy Planning and Research in the U.S. Department of Labor. My interest lies most specifically with this report (popularly known as the "Moynihan Report") and its pronouncements about the black American family—pronouncements to which Morrison's text seems to be responding. Questions about an emasculating black matriarchy, black family "disorganization," and exceptionalizing class differences among black people—all raised by Moynihan's writing—surface as well in Morrison's novel, and are fundamentally challenged by the narrative's characters and plot. Such ideas did not begin or end with Moynihan's report, however, and before attending more closely to Morrison's novel, it might be useful to look at a few of the many other voices in 1965's sociopolitical chorus.

Moynihan, and Others: Black Family "Pathology"

The pathology of the black family was a popular subject in the United States in the mid-1960s. In the previous chapter, I noted that black sociologist E. Franklin Frazier made arguments about the "Negro matriarchate" as early as 1939, but as the civil rights movement progressed in the following decades, numerous others echoed his pronouncements.[1] The most famous, and controversial, of these subsequent commentators was former Senator Moynihan, but he was not the only scholar to take up Frazier's ideas and expand upon them. For instance, another black sociologist, Kenneth Clark, suggested in 1965 (in a text released very close to the time of Moynihan's infamous "report") that female dominance of the black family was a carryover from slavery. Combined with postslavery discrimination, notes Clark, this carryover placed the black male in an "intolerable psychological position," one in which he could not appropriately express his *normal* desire for dominance."[2] Clark goes on to argue that in being "required to hold the family together," the "compensatory strength" of black women "tended to perpetuate the weaker role of the Negro male."[3]

Former director of the National Urban League, Whitney Young, made similar pronouncements in his 1964 monograph *To Be Equal*. Young writes, "[A]fter emancipation the Negro male was emasculated economically by the practice of keeping him in low-paying jobs, if any[.]"[4] He goes on to suggest that "the composition of the Negro family continued to be such that the father, if identified, had no established role, and the Negro male, his manhood weakened, suffered economically and psychologically."[5] On the subject of the black mother, Young writes, "As a major—if not the only—breadwinner in the family, she takes on responsibilities and duties far beyond her ability to perform well."[6] Both Young's and Clark's statements about the black family at mid-century are eerily similar to Daniel Moynihan's. In both cases, black scholars whose work was nearly simultaneous with Moynihan's argued that black men were inappropriately weak figures within the black family structure, and that black women were disproportionately strong, even emasculating—the same points that E. Franklin Frazier had made about the black family nearly thirty years earlier.[7]

Nonetheless, the Moynihan report differed in one central respect from the work of other scholars espousing similar arguments: namely, it seemed to emphasize the "pathology" of the black family, above all other issues, as the underlying cause of racial oppression—rather than as an unfortunate effect of it.[8] Civil rights leaders at the time perceived Moynihan's report as an indictment of the black community that simply blamed poor blacks for their situation—by intimating that black family "pathology" was somehow innate, rather than the direct result of centuries of discrimination. Because of this perception on the part of prominent blacks, responses to Moynihan's report both before and after its public release were passionate, and frequently critical.[9] To many of his critics, Moynihan had (perhaps inadvertently) created space for those hostile to black progress to argue that family pathology was more important than economic oppression, that indeed, poor blacks were themselves to blame for their situation.

It would be difficult not to notice the masculinist assumptions made by civil rights leaders' responses to Moynihan. All were quick to suggest that economic empowerment for black *men* was the real solution to the black family's so-called pathology. In the words of Bayard Rustin, "The Negro family can be reconstructed only when the Negro male is permitted to be the economic and psychological head of the family."[10] For Rustin and others, there was no question that black men's "rightful place" was as the leader of the black family unit, in a dominant position vis-à-vis black women and children. Indeed, most of Moynihan's critics seemed to agree with his assertion that black women were disproportionately "strong" in comparison with black men, that black women were rewarded in the economic marketplace in ways that black men had not been. Again, from Rustin, "When [the black man] married, he knew that his wife had much better chances economically than he did."[11] According to Patricia Morton, the underlying message of Moynihan's report seemed to be black women's inadequacy as mothers and/or wives—so "strong" they were emasculating, perpetuators of a "matriarchy" that worked to no one's benefit except their own—yet this censure of black women went largely unremarked upon by those who responded to Moynihan in an otherwise hostile fashion.[12]

In the decades following the report's publication, feminist scholars like Morton have pointed out this masculinist emphasis among Moynihan's critics, most of whom disagreed with Moynihan not about whether black "matriarchy" was a problem (it was), but only about Moynihan's apparent implication that the problem could be solved through psychological and emotional instead of socioeconomic reform.[13] Rather than repeat these feminist counterarguments, however, I would like to consider another, related but largely unexamined, issue raised by Moynihan's report—that is, the question of class distinctions among blacks. Few of Moynihan's contemporary critics commented di-

rectly upon this question; one notable exception was Whitney Young, whose column in the *St. Louis Argus* made the point that "the report isn't about the Negro family at all, it is about *some* Negro families."[14] Young noted, "What appear to be racial differences in regard to family stability are more probably *class differences,* which Negro lower-class families share with whites."[15]

Indeed, Moynihan himself made a point more than once in his report to distinguish between poor and middle-class blacks, in one instance suggesting that "there are indications [. . .] that the middle-class Negro family puts a higher premium on family stability and the conserving of family resources than does the white middle-class family."[16] At the start of his "Tangle of Pathology" chapter, Moynihan again notes that the black middle class "have managed to break out of the tangle of pathology and to establish themselves as stable, effective units, living according to patterns of American society in general."[17] But only a few paragraphs later, he suggests that because of continued housing segregation, "the children of middle-class Negroes often as not must grow up in, or next to the slums," and are therefore "constantly exposed to the pathology of the disturbed group and constantly in danger of being drawn into it."[18] As a result, Moynihan sees the lower-class-specific conclusions drawn in his study as having "a more or less general application."[19] Moynihan seems, then, both to distinguish between poor and middle-class blacks and to argue that the black middle class, no matter how successful, cannot escape its lower-class counterparts. In the second epigraph of this chapter, above, Moynihan's language (which I have italicized for emphasis) is indeed telling—his suggestion that a middle-class segment of the black population has "saved itself" implies that family structure among poor blacks constitutes a dangerous morass from which the black bourgeoisie must actively try to escape.

In fact, Moynihan's language unintentionally recalls the black middle-class ideology I have identified in previous portions of this book as the "salvific wish." Best articulated as a desire to rescue African Americans as a group from racist stigma through the embrace of bourgeois strictures of decorum and propriety, the salvific wish involves

precisely the kind of communal and self-recovery that Moynihan identifies among the stable families of the black middle class. Emerging
in the late nineteenth century among elite African Americans who
hoped to combat racial discrimination through their exemplary behavior, the wish has become a kind of unspoken cultural shorthand,
particularly for the black middle class—in spite of increasing evidence
that black moral rectitude has little ameliorative effect against racism.
Moynihan's emphasis on "family stability" also meshes with the concept of the salvific wish, for the stigma that blacks who espouse the
wish's ideology strive to escape is that of pathological black intimacy
and domesticity—what Rhonda Williams calls "racism's larger story
of black dysfunction," a story "both gendered and fraught with representations of black sexuality."[20] Here the idea that the blacks of the
middle class put "a higher premium on family stability" than whites
of the same status takes on a unique clarity, given that middle-class
blacks are believed to have (or believe themselves to have) much more
for which to compensate.

When read with a critical eye that takes the sociohistorical context of the salvific wish into account, Moynihan's references to class
difference in the African American community become a powerful
illustration of the human element of racial stigma, and the apparent urgency—for many blacks—of working to combat it. It is easy to
imagine how the "weakness of the [black] family structure" could become a proxy for alleged black deviance more broadly, especially given
that Moynihan explained this family weakness as "the principal source
of most of the aberrant, inadequate, or anti-social behavior" among
the black poor.[21] Indeed, it is even easier to imagine how impoverished blacks themselves could come to be viewed as the visual, physical
embodiment of such deviance, creating a concrete need for class distinctions that would set striving middle-class blacks apart from their
misbehaved lower-class counterparts. Another quote from E. Franklin
Frazier, ironically, provides insight into this point of view. Writing of
an "upper social class" of blacks post-Emancipation, he notes: "Often,
intensely conscious of their peculiar position with reference to the
great mass of the Negro population, they have placed an exaggerated

valuation upon moral conduct and cultivated a puritanical restraint in opposition to the free and uncontrolled behavior of the larger Negro world."[22] In other words, following the logic of the salvific wish, elite blacks adopted "puritanical restraint" in order to distinguish themselves from the morally "free and uncontrolled" black masses.

Yet Moynihan's work also seemed to suggest that this hard-won demarcation was tenuous, at best—for middle-class blacks continued to be dangerously proximate to the "pathological" underclass. Moynihan referred specifically to the large numbers of middle-class blacks who, as a result of housing segregation, were forced to remain in or near impoverished black ghettos. For black scholars, however, it was also easy to postulate a symbolic link, a sense that middle-class blacks could never quite overcome the dishonor of their color, the disgrace of their brethren. Like striver Lutie Johnson's uncomfortable nearness to Lil in Petry's *The Street*—nearness that was both physical and metaphorical— many middle-class blacks in 1965 perceived themselves to be "too close" to poor blacks both actually and figuratively. The sense of triumphant escape Moynihan's work initially implied is thus replaced with a sense of obligation and constraint. As Kenneth Clark noted in *Dark Ghetto*, "[I]n a society where wealth, aristocratic bearing, and talent are insufficient to overcome the stigma of one's skin, there is no [. . .] escape for any generation [of blacks]."[23] Whitney Young stated the issue even more directly: "The educationally privileged middle-class Negro will share the horrors and hardships of his more handicapped working-class brother as long as racism exists in our society."[24] Neither Clark's nor Young's words imply mere physical proximity—they move beyond Moynihan's literal notion that the nearness of the ghetto to the middle class could prove a bad influence, instead suggesting that it is the nearness of middle-class blacks to lower-class blacks *in the minds of whites* that most limited the former group's progress.

Moynihan's conclusions thus emphasize the seemingly urgent necessity of the propriety-minded salvific wish, without adequately articulating the ineffectual nature of its efforts. For the success of the salvific wish, like the success of that "stable middle-class group" identified by Moynihan, depends upon the binary opposition of two classes—an opposition that, given the totalizing nature of racial stigma, is untenable. Instead of acknowledging the figurative impossibility of such distinctions, however, and the larger threat of white racism underlying them, Moynihan's report implies that the real danger to middle-class blacks is the undue influence of poor blacks' "pathology." As such, Moynihan's work actually *encourages* an obsessive emphasis on what Kenneth Clark calls the "moral fiber" of other blacks. It encourages, in other words, the philosophical basis of the salvific wish—self-improvement and -protection through moral reform. This notion, dependent as it is upon the idea that some African Americans are or must strive to be "better" than others—indeed, that one group is so "bad" it has the potential to weaken, even to destroy the "good" group with its influence—is what Morrison's novel *Sula* ultimately undermines.

Beyond Moynihan: Binary Oppositions in *Sula*

More than one critic has noted that *Sula* constructs and then subverts a number of binary oppositions in order to challenge the reader's assumptions.[25] Usually these analyses observe a number of conventional dichotomies—in Hortense Spillers's words, "black/white, male/female, good/bad"—within *Sula*, pointing out the instability of such oppositions and the impossibility of gleaning useful meaning from the text while relying upon them.[26] While I agree with this critical assessment, I would also suggest that class status plays into the (admittedly unstable) binary oppositions within the text. Although class differences within the boundaries of the novel's central black neighborhood, the "Bottom," may be obscured because of the overall poverty of the community, perhaps it is worth recalling Kevin Gaines's suggestion that for African Americans, class status has always had as much to do with aspiration as with economic means.[27] In other words, the striving is the thing, and the Bottom certainly includes those who strive for bourgeois respectability and those who eschew it in favor of an apparent racial authenticity. Not coincidentally, the former group aligns roughly with the "good" side of those good/bad binary oppositions in *Sula*, the latter with the "bad."

This is particularly true for the black women in the text, especially those who are mothers. Indeed, in what might be read as the first coalescence between Morrison's novel and Daniel Moynihan's analysis of the black family, many of the families in *Sula* are headed by black women—matrifocal if not explicitly matriarchal (arguably, this is true even of those households in which a father is nominally present, like the one in which Nel Wright grows up). At first glance, Morrison's text not only takes up the question of "black matriarchy" raised by Moynihan's work, but seems to reinforce a class-based opposition between "bad" black matriarchs—or "bad" black women more generally—and those whose motherhood/womanhood more appropriately serves the patriarchy. Ultimately, however, Morrison's novel denies the stability of this opposition, in the process critiquing the class-based ideology of the salvific wish, which so futilely attempts to maintain a hierarchical distinction between middle-class and poor African Americans.

Sula, the novel's title character and a "bad" black woman in her own right, is the child of Hannah Peace, herself a woman who "simply refused to live without the attentions of a man, and after [her husband's] death had a steady sequence of lovers, mostly the husbands of her friends and neighbors."[28] Before Hannah's death in 1923, when her daughter is thirteen years old, young Sula learns from her mother that "sex was pleasant and frequent, but otherwise unremarkable" (37, 38). This sense of the quotidian nature of sexual activity, in addition to the frank appreciation of its pleasurable qualities, already runs counter to the sexual repressiveness encouraged by the salvific wish. Still, there is more to Sula's relationship with Hannah than this early lesson in sex education.

Perhaps most critically important about the relationship between Sula and her mother is what Sula does *not* learn from Hannah, namely, conventions in the Bottom about propriety and female behavior. Such conventions are traditionally transmitted from mother to daughter—as Adrienne Rich writes in her treatise on motherhood, *Of Woman Born*, "it is the mother through whom patriarchy early teaches the small female her proper expectations."[29] Yet Sula seems to grow up with no maternally taught lessons of propriety to guide her. In the Peace family, "the mother, Hannah, never scolded or gave directions" (25). Instead Sula, "wedged into a household of throbbing disorder constantly awry with things, people, voices and the slamming of doors" (44), is left seemingly unmothered. In fact, with its laissez-faire mothering and complete absence of a father figure, the Peace household seems to reflect precisely that black family "disorganization" identified by Moynihan and his predecessors as an unhealthy carryover from slavery.

Hannah Peace's careless style of mothering is counterpoised, in the novel, to that of Helene Wright, who in her mothering of Nel seems a model example of how a more traditional Western mother might train her daughter to be "obedient and polite." The homophonic connection between "Wright" and "right" is no coincidence here, for Helene's project in raising Nel is to make the child right, correct, in every way. Helene reduces Nel's "sparkle [and] splutter" to a "dull glow" (72), leaving Nel with no aggression and an imagination driven "underground." Unlike Hannah Peace, Helene Wright seems to have mastered conventional tenets of bourgeois feminine propriety, and to be more than capable of transmitting these to her only daughter. The differences between these two styles of mothering point out the role of intergenerational training in the progression of black women's sexual dissemblance. Morrison's text seems to suggest that the self-discipline required of black women by the salvific wish is a learned behavior, the logical extension of a prior, maternally imposed discipline.

Yet the easy binary between Hannah and Helene is quickly de-stabilized in the novel, as the text recasts each woman's identity in a manner that draws her closer to her narrative opposite. Hannah Peace, for example, was at one point legitimately married, and that marriage ended legitimately, in her husband's death. Thus, Hannah's later single status, and possibly even her continuous extramarital involvement, is "not by choice" (80). Oddly enough, then, even as Hannah neglects to educate Sula in the requirements of proper womanhood, she meets some of those requirements herself. In addition, patterns Hannah follows in her adulterous rendezvous show respect for other conventions of proper behavior. While Hannah brings her lovers into the cellar, the pantry, the parlor, or her bedroom, she "liked the last place least, not because Sula slept in the room with her but because her love mate's tendency was always to fall asleep afterward and Hannah was fastidious about whom she slept with. . . . [S]leeping with someone implied for her a measure of trust and a definite commitment" (37). Hannah's reluctance to share the bedroom, with its overtones of socially approved, committed sexual behavior—including the legitimate production of children—with just any lover, demonstrates that she has some measure of connection to bourgeois conventions around female sexuality.

Indeed, the "manlove" that Hannah shares with her mother, Eva, quite surprisingly aligns them both with patriarchal order. In another deft counter to the logic of Moynihan's theories about black "matriarchy," Morrison writes:

> With the exception of [Eva's absent husband] BoyBoy, those Peace women loved all men. It was manlove that Eva bequeathed to her daughters. Probably, people said, because there were no men in the house, no men to run it. But actually that was not true. The Peace women simply loved maleness, for its own sake. (41)

Rather than a defensive and desperate need for male attention born out of their home's lack of a patriarch, the Peace women value and affirm black manhood because they want to—and see no conflict between this affirmation and their own matrifocal home life. In fact, in a sly bit of irony, the rightful patriarch of the Peace household is the only man directly exempted from the women's "manlove," perhaps because (as his name all too obviously reveals) he cannot actually be understood as a man.

Apart from BoyBoy, the Peace women's manlove has an extremely wide reach; Eva even takes it upon herself to legislate how men in other relationships are treated, overseeing the newlywed couples that frequently stayed in her home with a practiced eye: "[Eva] fussed interminably with the brides of the newly wed couples for not getting their men's supper ready on time; about how to launder shirts, press them, etc" (42). Here a black "matriarch," ostensibly a source of black domestic "chaos," instead orders and regulates not only her own home, but the homes and families of others, according to very conventional values.

Moynihan's report rather comically asserts that "the very essence of the male animal, from the bantam rooster to the four-star general, is to strut[,]" and suggests that as a carryover from slavery, the black matriarchate prevents this.[30] Ironically enough, however, the Peace women allow for the male to "strut" while maintaining their own female-only household. The men who receive their attentions are well aware of this, acknowledging that "it was they who had won something" (41) from the experience.

In a similar reversal of the expected, Helene Wright's status as the only child of a "Creole whore" from Louisiana suggests that her "perpetual query about other people's manners" (16) has a great deal to do with her fear of her own potential "wild blood." Helene's efforts to subdue Nel seem to suggest the denial of sexuality that African American women have historically turned to in order to evade public accusations of black sexual pathology. Her need to travel "as far away from Sundown House as possible" (15), to escape the brothel in which she was born, indicate her fear of her own sexual expression. It is no coincidence that her birthplace displays red shutters that "haunt" both her and her grandmother, for red is a color that has continually been associated with illicit (female) sexual behavior.[31] In a sense, Helene's obsession with order and propriety can be read as consistent with the feminine self-repression demanded by the salvific wish, for she seems clearly to desire her own absolution from a maternal "lineage" of sexual degeneracy, through the embrace of conventionally appropriate behaviors. In addition, the hypervigilance with which Helene guards against sexual (and self) expression in both herself and her daughter suggests the tenuousness of this absolution; distance from Sundown House is necessary, presumably, because the lure of the sexual "wild" might be irresistible, otherwise.

This becomes evident during a scene in which Helene and Nel journey south for the funeral of Nel's great grandmother, the woman who raised Helene. Significantly, Helene first considers the trip south "with heavy misgiving," but then decides "that she had the best protection: her manner and her bearing, to which she would add a beautiful dress" (19). Although it will not become clear until later in the scene just from what Helene hopes to protect herself, her belief that "manner" and "bearing" provide adequate defense is telling. Helene's notion that behavior can shield her from the racialized dangers inherent in the journey south suggests the performative logic of the salvific wish. Yet with her inclusion of the adjective "beautiful," Morrison provides a clue even at this juncture that Helene's motivations are inconsistent, even contradictory. Surely outward appearance, including clothing, is a part of the bourgeois decorum for which devotees of the salvific wish strive, but Helene's insistence upon a "beautiful" dress—"beautiful" with its connotations of aesthetic pleasure, and, in the case of attire, visual and tactile excess in the form of sumptuous textiles like silk and velvet—indicates that decorum is not her only goal.

In fact, Helene's fashionable wool and velvet dress, and her diligent efforts to create it (sewing "late into the night" before the trip) recall another literary black female clotheshorse, Helga Crane, who in Nella Larsen's *Quicksand* (1928) is an outsider in the conservative educational institution of Naxos in part because of her opulent and luxurious costumes.[32] Those costumes mark Helga as an *erotic* figure in Larsen's text, a woman whose visceral pleasure in attractive clothing is viewed as evidence of her moral laxity. Similarly, Helene Wright's fashionable garment suggests a sensual undercurrent to her behavior that runs counter to the rigidity of the salvific wish. Helene, who expresses relief that her daughter did not inherit "the great beauty that was hers" (18), nonetheless deliberately cloaks herself in her beauty (as much as in her upright "manner" and "bearing") when she sets off to New Orleans.

That beauty, however, provides far less protection than Helene initially seems to have imagined. Rushing to board the train before it departs, Helene and Nel enter a whites-only car by mistake and are confronted by the conductor, a white man who addresses 35-year-old Helene as "gal" (girl). Helene's internal reaction is surprisingly swift: "So soon. She hadn't even begun the trip back. Back to her grandmother's house in the city where the red shutters glowed, and already she had been called 'gal.' All the old vulnerabilities, all the old fears of being somehow flawed gathered in her stomach and made her hands tremble" (20). It is unclear, here, whether Helene's reawakened frailties, her fears of being "somehow flawed," have to do with her shameful origins at Sundown House or with race (and gender) more broadly. Is her flaw her blackness, or her mother's "wild blood"? Perhaps it isn't necessary, or even possible, to distinguish between them. Indeed Helene's shame, conveniently signaled by the word "vulnerabilities," suggests the thorny racial vulnerability inspiring the salvific wish—the sense that the black intimate subject is always-already exposed to a sexualized racist scrutiny, scrutiny that assumes black sexual and domestic pathology.

Morrison tells us that "an eagerness to please and an apology for living" meet in Helene's voice as she responds to the conductor (19). If her knee-jerk apology—for being a black woman in a whites-only car, for being the illegitimate child of a "Creole whore," for some combination of the two—makes a disturbing kind of sense given Helene's own rigid moral hierarchies, and given the period in which the scene is set (1920), her eagerness to please is at the least more confounding. Rather than acquiesce to the conductor's insult with sullenness or hostility, or even the seemingly neutral apathy affected by the other blacks watching the scene, Helene literally serves up her defeat with a smile, "dazzlin[g] and "coquettis[h]" (21). Her flirtatious smile, like her "beautiful" dress, provides evidence that Helene is not so "wright" as she appears, but rather is, in the face of white patriarchy, all too capable of the sexual availability for which she despises and fears her mother.

Perhaps not surprisingly, then, the reaction of the black soldiers watching is an immediate coagulation of hatred; something Nel sees and Helene, appropriately, does not. This blindness on Helene's part is consistent with an earlier moment in the scene, when Helene is unable to read the faces of the blacks in the colored-only car, who observe her confrontation with the conductor. Writes Morrison, "Four or five black faces were watching, two belonging to soldiers still in their shit-colored uniforms and peaked caps. She saw their closed faces, their locked eyes, and turned for compassion to the gray eyes of the conductor" (21). Why are these faces "closed" and "locked," so unavailable to Helene that she turns to the wielder of her shame, the conductor who has just mis-named her "gal," for a modicum of sympathy? If Helene cannot recognize the danger within those gray eyes, it is reasonable to assume that what she sees within the soldiers' faces as "closed" is in fact something else, perhaps a kind of self-protective evasion—feigned impassiveness in view of the conductor's greater power over both the soldiers *and* Helene.

This racialized power differential may be invisible to Helene because she is only able to "read" intraracial class status; the proper manner and bearing that she has imagined would protect her (from disrespect and abuse such as that leveled at her by the conductor) depends upon distinguishing herself from other blacks, not on acknowledging her inescapable ties to them. In other words, Helene sees the soldiers, and all of the blacks in the car, as part and parcel of the alleged black deviance from which she strives to escape—the use of *shit* is a possible hint at the lack of value Helene ascribes to these, her "colored" brethren. Helene's passive disregard for the soldiers is understandably returned to her as hatred, hatred for the sexualized "custard" that Helene's dress hides.[33]

It is no wonder that Nel "resolves to be on guard—always" against a similar response: "She wanted to make certain that no man ever looked at her that way. That no midnight eyes or marbled flesh would ever accost her and turn her into jelly" (22). Joanne Gabbin suggests that in her mother's smile, "Nel recognized a vulnerability, an obsequious, smiling acceptance of caste that was obscene."[34] Yet these two things—acceptance of caste and vulnerability—are not one and the same. Yes, Helene's smile demonstrates the destructiveness of her slavish obeisance to social class—given that potential bonds between Helene and the soldiers, as well as between Helene and Nel, are broken by her choice to seek solidarity with the conductor—but her actions also reveal the danger Helene and all black women face simply because of their racial and sexual subject position.

This danger, the black subject's vulnerability to mental and physical *violation* by white patriarchal order, is what Helene's smile uselessly attempts to efface or mitigate. Her smile is meant to distinguish her from the other blacks in the car, to make the conductor see her as exemplary—thereby lessening her vulnerability in the face of his power. In other words, that smile is not an *acceptance* of Helene's own lower caste position with respect to the conductor, it is her attempted *resistance* to that position. Yet this resistance fails precisely because it is couched in sexual availability, an availability that highlights her lower caste position, along with the lower caste position of all blacks. This explains why her smile raises the soldiers' ire. In this moment, she who strives to be socially and culturally "Wright" abandons sexual dissemblance for a more direct currying of favor through sexual spectacle—a spectacle that literally plays upon the degradation she wishes to avoid. In this she embodies everything that the salvific wish most abhors, utterly giving the lie to her initial, oppositional characterization as the paragon of black propriety.

Erotic Stereotype, Erotic Power: Reading Sula and Nel

The setup and dissolution of binary oppositions in *Sula* continues in the second half of the novel, with Morrison's depictions of the adult Nel and Sula. Similarly to the opposition between their mothers, in this binary Nel seems to represent the "good" woman and Sula the "bad." The clearly class-based distinction that existed between Helene and Hannah is no longer so easily identifiable between Nel and Sula, however, in part because while Nel has stayed in the Bottom and become a wife and mother during the ten-year interval between Part I and Part II, Sula has traveled and attended college (Fisk University). In some senses the two women occupy opposite class positions than did their mothers, thanks to this disparity in life experience. Yet given the largely symbolic aspects of social class in this novel—i.e., Helene characterizes Hannah as "sooty" (29) and therefore beneath her and Nel in social standing, although this determination is based on a perception of Hannah's "slackness" (29) rather than any material difference between them—it is still possible to read Nel and Sula as classed in ways that parallel rather than counter Helene and Hannah.

This is particularly true given Nel's position as an upstanding married woman, one who had begun her conjugal life with "a real wedding, in a church, with a real reception afterward"—a rarity in an environment where most couples "just 'took up' with one another" (80). Her legitimate wedding, and subsequent marriage, mark Nel as particularly "respectable," implying a certain level of social status. By contrast, Sula's sexual escapades, beginning with her casual tryst with Nel's husband, Jude, imply precisely the "sootiness" that Helene saw in her mother, Hannah. Indeed, the text suggests that the townspeople see Sula's behavior as exponentially worse than Hannah's, because Sula beds each woman's husband "once and then no more" (115). Whereas Hannah "was complimenting the women, in a way, by wanting their husbands," Sula "tr[ied] them out and discard[ed] them without any excuse the men could swallow" (115).

If Nel has taken over her mother's elevated class position, Sula seems almost to have fallen beneath, or outside, her own mother's— literally "out-caste" because she operates with complete disregard for all measures of social convention. Sula "came to their church suppers without underwear, bought their steaming platters of food and merely picked at it—relishing nothing [. . .] They believed that she was laughing at their God" (114, 115). The Bottom's "God," here, seems unrelated to actual spiritual concerns—instead It/He is shaped by a rigid and dishonest social contract for which Sula's personality is unsuited. Notes Morrison, "When [Sula] had come back home, social conversation was impossible for her because she could not lie" (121). Unable to tell an acquaintance "girl, you looking good" when the statement is untrue, unable to perform a false respectability for the sake of social acceptance, Sula acquiesces to her status in the Bottom as "pariah" and outsider (122).

Nel, by contrast, is guided by this social contract, unthinkingly obedient to it and the safety it promises: "[A]live was what they, and now Nel, did not want to be. Too dangerous. Now Nel belonged to the town and all of its ways. She had given herself over to them [. . .]" (120). Part of what Nel gives herself over to is the belief in her own moral superiority and virtue. Nel's virtuous conviction extends to her decision to visit her former friend Sula on her deathbed. Internally rehearsing her interaction with Sula, whom she has not seen or talked to in three years, Nel reflects, "The sound of her voice as she heard it in her head betrayed no curiosity, no pride, just the inflection of any good woman come to see about a sick person who, incidentally, had such visits from nobody else" (138). Indeed, Nel's perception of herself as a "good woman" seems to be all she has left to cling to in the years following Jude's departure, even as the narration reveals that perception's flaws: "Virtue, *bleak and drawn*, was her only mooring. It brought her to Number 7 Carpenter's Road and the door with the blue glass; it helped her to resist scratching the screen as in days gone by; it *hid from her the true motives of her charity*" (139, emphasis added). As with the telltale "beautiful dress," revealing the lie in Helene Wright's immaculate comportment, the words "bleak" and "drawn" suggest that Nel's virtue is far from uplifting, nor purely "good." Instead, virtue cloaks Nel's "true motives," which will not become clear either to Nel or to the reader until much later in the text.

Upsetting the binary opposition of Nel and Sula in fact proves a more complicated effort in the novel than does upsetting the dichotomy between Helene and Hannah, perhaps because the former are both more complex and more enigmatic than the latter. Sula, for instance, has entirely different motives for her promiscuous behavior than did Hannah, who merely wanted "some touching every day" (44). Sula, instead of seeking such simple pleasure from her frequent (and frequently adulterous) sexual encounters, looks for "misery and the ability to feel deep sorrow. . . . a stinging awareness of the endings of things; an eye of sorrow in the midst of all that hurricane rage of joy" (106). In this she is hardly the black Jezebel that racist iconography believes it knows, and that the salvific wish endeavors to guard against. Nor does she fit neatly into the Moynihanian schema of bad black matriarch, as she outright refuses motherhood in favor of personal development: "I don't want to make somebody else. I want to make myself" (92).

Likewise, Sula seems interested in sex because of its consequences for her selfhood; after her orgasms, she enters a "postcoital privateness in which she [meets] herself, welcome[s] herself, and join[s] herself in matchless harmony" (107). Sula seems to crave a richer relationship with herself, a fuller sense of her own subjectivity, and she finds this in sexual intercourse. Contrary to what one might assume given Sula's seeming sexual and domestic "pathology," her interest is not in men, or the simple physical gratification they provide; in fact, all of the men in her past "had merged into one large personality" that "taught her nothing but love tricks, shared nothing but worry, gave nothing but money" (104). Sula instead craves a certain deep solitude, "a loneliness so profound the word itself had no meaning" (106). The pleasure Sula finds in sex is a self-referential pleasure, the pleasure of a powerfully intimate self-knowledge. She seeks a "version of herself" that she can "touch with an ungloved hand" (104). While these images have distinct overtones of masturbatory pleasure, I would also read the "ungloved" hand as a reference to the bourgeois gentility promoted by the salvific wish, the "ladylike" behavior that an immaculately gloved hand might symbolize. Sula's self-touch with uncovered fingers and palm mark her rejection of such propriety—and, in that the image of a glove also suggests the potential *masking* of both identity and actual sensation, the "ungloved hand" recalls the embrace of a fuller, more intense and honest experience of sexuality than that which her community would allow her.

Sula is thus not so simply categorized as a "bad" woman, given that her misbehavior is in service of her own growth. Yet there is little about her that can be read categorically as "good"—Sula instead defies categorization. As Hortense Spillers has noted, Sula's character walks a line between the assumed "heroism" of the respectable black woman (a heroism that is itself hardly stable, as Helene Wright's character demonstrates) and the presumed deviance of her opposite: "Sula attempts a correction of [. . .] uninterrupted superiority on the one hand and unrelieved pathology on the other; the reader's dilemma arises in having to choose."[35] For Spillers, a courageous reader "recognizes that the negating countermyth would try to establish a dialectical movement between the subperspectives, gaining a totally altered perspective in the process."[36] In other words, Sula's complex character forces readers to put the two sides of the binary into dialogue, in this way discovering something new about the meaning of black womanhood. Yet I would suggest that Sula is not the only character to create such "dialectical movement" in the text. I have already noted how false the

distinction is between Helene and Hannah, but Nel, Sula's immediate counter in the novel, contains her own similarity to Sula, one that
becomes more evident upon closer reading of key scenes in the text.

Sula's threat to the Bottom seems to lie in her will to place herself at
the center of her own life, exposing this most basic of desires that other
women in her community are hardly able to acknowledge. Sula's insistence on self-valuation recalls Audre Lorde's groundbreaking 1984
essay "Uses of the Erotic: The Erotic as Power." In it, Lorde writes,
"The erotic is a resource within each of us that lies in a deeply female
and spiritual plain, firmly rooted in the power of our unexpressed or
unrecognized feeling."[37] Yet Sula is most certainly not the only character to embody this erotic power in the novel. Nel, who as a girl had
stared into a mirror and whispered "'I'm me. I'm not their daughter.
I'm not Nel. I'm me. Me" (24) is a primary example of how Lorde's
principle might be more broadly applied, and how the seemingly easy
oppositions between women in *Sula* are far from stable. During her
childhood, Nel is open to the feelings of "power . . . joy . . . fear" that
course through her as she acknowledges herself, the self that exists
beyond her daughterly training, the self that exists even beyond naming. Nel's experience seems emblematic of the "measure between the
beginnings of our sense of self and the chaos of our strongest feelings"
to which Lorde refers in her work, "an internal sense of satisfaction
to which, once we have experienced it, we know we can aspire."[38] Nel
does not return to these feelings again as an adult until well after Sula's
death; only after her perceived difference from Sula is shattered can she
make that return.

Nel's visit to Eva Peace sparks the first part of her transformation,
for Eva suggests that the drowning death of Chicken Little, which Nel
had for years believed was Sula's sole responsibility, belonged to both
girls: "'You. Sula. What's the difference? You watched, didn't you?'"
(145). Here Nel recognizes, belatedly, that she and Sula both had felt
the pleasure of misbehavior: "[I]t seemed that what she had thought
was maturity, serenity and compassion was only the tranquillity that

follows a joyful stimulation. Just as the water closed peacefully over the turbulence of Chicken Little's body, so had contentment washed over her enjoyment" (146). In fact, the two girls have shared an erotic bond through the (phallic) body of the drowned child, an orgasmic release that is the culmination of earlier time spent together on the riverbank. As Lorde writes, "The erotic functions for me in several ways, and the first is in providing the power which comes from sharing deeply any pursuit with another person."[39] For Sula and Nel, this pursuit is a scene of intensely erotic play.

The play that Sula and Nel enact together as children is narrated several chapters prior to the adult Nel's acknowledgment of their connection, and provides insight into her later ability to reaccess her own erotic power through her memories of Sula. I quote the passage at some length, below:

> They lay in the grass, their foreheads almost touching, their bodies stretched away from each other at a 180-degree angle. . . . Nel leaned on her elbows and worried long blades of grass with her fingers. Underneath their dresses flesh tightened and shivered in the high coolness, their small breasts just now beginning to create some pleasant discomfort when they were lying on their stomachs.
>
> Sula lifted her head and joined Nel in the grass play. In concert, without ever meeting each other's eyes, they stroked the blades up and down, up and down. Nel found a thick twig and, with her thumbnail, pulled away its bark until it was stripped to a smooth, creamy innocence. Sula looked about and found one too. When both twigs were undressed Nel moved easily to the next stage and began tearing up rooted grass to make a bare spot of earth. When a generous clearing was made, Sula traced intricate patterns in it with her twig. At first Nel was content to do the same. But soon she grew impatient and poked her twig rhythmically and intensely into the earth, making a small neat hole that grew deeper and wider with the least manipulation of her twig. Sula copied her, and soon each had a hole the size of a cup. Nel began a more strenuous digging [. . .] Together they worked until the two holes were one and the same. When the depression was the size of a small dishpan, Nel's twig broke. With a gesture of disgust she threw the pieces into the hole they had made. Sula threw hers in too. Nel saw a bottle cap and tossed it in as well. Each then looked around

for more debris to throw into the hole [. . .] until all of the small defiling
things they could find were collected there. Carefully they replaced the
soil and covered the entire grave with uprooted grass.

Neither one had spoken a word.

They stood up, stretched, then gazed out over the swift dull water
as an unspeakable restlessness and agitation held them. (49, 50)

This is the scene that directly precedes the drowning of the young
Chicken Little—whose body Houston Baker links to the Lacanian
phallus in his interpretation of Morrison's novel—and the "contentment" that subsequently washes over both girls.[40] The language of the
scene, both literally and figuratively ("tightened," shivering flesh; the
stroking of grass blades "up and down, up and down"; twigs penetrat-
ing "rhythmically and intensely" into the earth), certainly suggests
sexual exploration. But because the play includes both phallic imagery,
in the long blades of grass as well as the thick twigs, and vaginal/womb-
like imagery, in the "small neat hole that grew deeper and wider," the
meaning of such play for Sula's or Nel's own sexual character cannot
easily be discerned. Do the girls identify with the twigs or the holes
they create? The eventual union of the holes seems to signify a sexual
union between the girls, but also might be read as the mutual rejection
of their homosocial childhood innocence for the "pleasant discomfort"
of separate, adult sexual development—particularly since the hole in
the earth becomes a "grave" by the end of the scene. Certainly, too,
the "smooth, creamy innocence" of the twig as easily suggests the un-
hooded clitoris as the circumcised penis, and the digging of the holes
seems both masturbatory and intercursive.

Barbara Smith's early reading of *Sula* as a lesbian text (which, curi-
ously enough, omits a reading of this scene) might have found more
critical support if it had included the language of homoeroticism,
which is certainly at play in Nel and Sula's interaction.[41] The girls' play
does, ultimately, suggest the fluid sexual expressiveness that the term
"queer" is often meant to convey, and it is also suggestive that the scene
takes place in silence, for queer sexuality frequently resists the restric-
tiveness of putting acts into language, "naming" them as one thing or
another so as to categorize them neatly. As Eve Sedgwick writes in the

introduction to *Tendencies*: "[O]ne of the things queer can refer to [is] the open mesh of possibilities, gaps, overlaps, dissonances and reso-nances, lapses and excesses of meaning when the constituent elements of anyone's gender, or anyone's sexuality aren't made (or *can't* be made) to signify monolithically."[42] This kind of ambiguity is precisely what is at stake in the girls' play on the riverbank.

What *is* unambiguous about the scene is Nel's leadership in the erotic performance—she is first in the grass play, the digging, and the transformation of the hole into a grave, "copied" by Sula at every turn. As Nel recalls the scene from her adult standpoint, she real-izes that while "[a]ll these years she had been secretly proud of her calm, controlled behavior when Sula was uncontrollable[,]" her pride had been misplaced. Nel's feelings of genteel superiority to Sula have instead long masked a correspondence between the two women. As Rita Bergenholtz notes, "[A]lthough Nel and Sula appear to be quite different—one the epitome of goodness and the other the embodiment of evil—they are also quite similar."[43] To genuinely understand who she is, Nel is forced to acknowledge her debt to Sula, the community outcast who flouts, for most of her life, bourgeois conventions of femi-nine behavior that Nel has been trained to hold dear. In Lorde's words, "[Women] have been taught to suspect this resource [the erotic], vili-fied, abused, and devalued within Western society. . . . It is a short step from there to the false belief that only by the suppression of the erotic within our lives and consciousness can women be truly strong. But that strength is illusory[.]"[44] Such a false belief thoroughly encapsulates the salvific wish—an embrace of propriety and a rejection of the erotic that is believed to be a source of personal and communal strength, but which instead offers only limitation and a self-imposed repression.

Return to 1965

The complicated oppositional relationship between Sula and Nel's char-acters does not end with Nel's emotional shift, however. If Nel tries Sula's erotic autonomy on for size near the end of the text to liberating, if overdue results, Sula, at an earlier point in the novel, also tries on

Nel's sexual repression, with far more disastrous consequences. In the midst of her radically egalitarian relationship with Ajax, a man who not only "seemed to expect brilliance" from Sula, but who "refus[ed] to baby or protect her" and "assum[ed] that she was both tough and wise" (128), Sula begins "to discover what possession was" (131). Ajax recognizes her subsequent actions—tying a green ribbon in her hair, undertaking household efforts that leave "the bathroom [. . .] gleaming, the bed [. . .] made, and the table [. . .] set for two" (132)—as a prelude to the "death-knell question, 'Where you been?'" (133). His departure from Sula's life is swift and complete, and seems clearly tied to Sula's uncharacteristic performance of domestic labor, which Ajax rightly assumes will bring with it a desire to control his behavior.

As Houston Baker notes in his reading of *Sula*, "the same materially possessive drive that makes Nel unable to forgive Sula [for sleeping with Jude] forces Sula herself to transmute egalitarian flights of pleasure into a plan to 'nail' Ajax."[45] This "drive," which Baker credits with the failure, in the novel, of a "potentially redemptive heterosexuality," seems to be the same disciplinary force motivating both the salvific wish and the moralistic judgment of the Moynihan report. Sula's remarkable relationship with Ajax ends in his departure because through her increasing desire for domestic "possession," culminating in dust-swept floors, neatly made bed, and sparkling kitchen (all exuding "the scent of the nest" [133]), Sula is temporarily transformed from a woman in control of her own pleasure to a willing participant in the conventional domestic/patriarchal order—the same order, ironically, that Moynihan's report suggests is woefully "reversed" in African American culture, the same order to which the salvific wish demands a self-protective allegiance.

Sula's compliance with this order is certainly a surprise in the text, one that a number of critics see as a failure on Morrison's part. Madhu Dubey argues, for example, that Sula's "laps[e] into the expected role of the black woman as nurturer" is as good as a textual "capitulation to heterosexual conventions."[46] I might suggest, however, that Sula's lapse is more nuanced than this. She does not simply become a nurturer—she follows, for the first time in her character's experience in this novel, the rules of patriarchy as laid down by the salvific wish and/or Moynihan, and the healthiest heterosexual relationship in the text is shattered as a result. Rather than capitulating to heterosexual convention, Morrison's text seems to point out that convention's ultimate destructiveness. If, in fact, the push of the salvific wish toward an orderly, patriarchal domesticity mirrors Moynihan's critique of the black family, then *Sula* must be understood as a corrective to that push, in that the novel's continually shifting hierarchical oppositions undercut both the alleged dangers *and* the assumed safety of "bad" versus "good" black domesticity.

Which brings us, again, to 1965. As the first epigraph of this chapter, drawn from the final chapter of *Sula*, suggests, things were "so much better" for black people in 1965. Or at least they seemed to be, as evidenced by the incremental dismantling of segregation—a black teacher in a school, a black sales clerk at a store. Granted the school is a "junior" high school, the store merely a "dime" store, but blacks are clearly making economic progress. Yet does this progress come with a price, a shift in attitudes and values? As Roderick Ferguson notes, referring to a scene in the same chapter that suggests "even the whores were better" forty years earlier:

> 1965 has brought with it not only a new class formation [. . .] but a new
> sensibility, one organized around shame and embarrassment for non-
> heteronormative subjects. This shame, this embarrassment, we may
> read as the evidence of disciplinary techniques that were simultaneous
> with a new class emergence among the people in the Bottom.[47]

While I agree with Ferguson's emphasis on class as the source of the "disciplinary techniques" employed against the nonheteronormative in *Sula*, I would argue that these techniques exist throughout the novel's chronological setting, not merely in 1965. Ferguson points to Morrison's portrayal of a whore's forthright shamelessness in 1925 (contrasted, in the text, with the perpetual embarrassment of those forty years later) as evidence that social mores have changed, shifted into a system for "regulating and differentiating" among the Bottom's residents.

Lack of shame does not necessarily indicate lack of regulation, however. The salvific wish—traceable, historically, to the turn of the twentieth century—is one powerful example of how intraracial regulation or differentiation on the basis of class and (non)heteronormative practice has existed in the black community for decades. Morrison's character Helene Wright, thirty-five years old in 1920, is the text's chief representative of this ideology, evidence of its longstanding temporal relevance—and Helene's story is also evidence that "shame" is not new to 1965. The idea of that year as a metaphorical turning point within African American cultural history still makes sense, however, if we once more recall the Moynihan report, which appeared in 1965. As I have previously noted, a number of Moynihan's theories added to an already existing cultural ideology that posited black poverty *as* black intimate deviance, a sociocultural morass wisely avoided by the middle class. *Sula* responds to and critiques that ideology, and depends upon the significance of the year 1965 to do so.

Following Houston Baker, Phillip Novak notes that Morrison's novel "unfolds within absence," the absence of a neighborhood that has already been lost: "It is called the suburbs now, but when black people lived there it was called the Bottom" (3).[48] Although the "now" of this line is never attached to a date, the final chapter of the text returns to a fuller explanation of how what once was the "Bottom" has become something else:

> Nobody colored lived much up in the Bottom any more. White people were building towers for television stations up there and there was a rumor about a golf course or something. Anyway, hill land was more valuable now, and those black people who had moved down right after the war and in the fifties couldn't afford to come back even if they wanted to. (166)

The tone of this passage, as well as the period in the Bottom's history that it describes, is quite similar to that of the undated section that begins the novel—both the chapter "1965" and the opening section of the book describe the Bottom from a latter-day vantage point, and imagine it as a place already essentially lost. In other words, both seem to be speaking to readers from the same temporal space—and since the final chapter is dated, we know that that space is 1965. In a sense, then, we might say that the novel begins and ends with that year, is ultimately *framed* by 1965's sensibility. The salvific wish was newly relevant in 1965 because of Moynihan's highly publicized report, and as such not just the final chapter of *Sula*, but the entire text, can be read through 1965's heightened attention to black intimate behavior, the sexual and domestic practices that, according to Moynihan, made "black family stability" so culturally anomalous.

This is certainly one plausible justification for Morrison's otherwise unexplained choice to title the book's final chapter as she does. More importantly, it may explain the narrative's obsessive attention to binary oppositions between women, and between classes. Such oppositions have a peculiar resonance in African American culture precisely because distinctions between "good" and "bad" black people have so frequently been couched in class-based characterizations of black intimate character. *Sula* highlights the defensive intraracial classism behind assertions of black family "pathology," and continually works to shift cultural emphasis from this classism back to the persistent danger of racist hierarchy—hierarchy that refuses to distinguish between black people on the basis of class or anything else, instead seeing only the stigma of color.[49] In the process, *Sula* offers a critique of the salvific wish informed by the sociopolitical environment of the mid-1960s, one which differs from the discursive blindness of a decade earlier but only partially anticipates shifts in the decade to come.

That period, beginning in the latter half of the 1960s and continuing through the late 1970s, would be more focused on black patriarchal power than had any previous period in the twentieth century. The Moynihan report almost inadvertently tapped into a larger cultural discourse that would come to full fruition in the years following its publication—the thinly veiled misogyny of suggestions that black women, occasionally in collusion with or as proxies for white racism, stand in the way of (black) patriarchy's success. Notes Robert Reid-Pharr, "[O]ne of the most often executed maneuvers in the production and reproduction of discourses of black family crisis is the articulation of a strange, even uncanny, hostility to black women[.]"[50] Yet the black woman's disappearance from this discourse is impossible; even in her "failure," her presence is necessary on the ideological scene. As Reid-Pharr goes on to suggest, "The bad black mother does important work in the maintenance of the black community. She is the figure who takes up the management of the crisis that is the black family."[51] This sense that the "bad black mother" is ultimately *responsible* for the black family's political and ideological meaning remains consistent even with respect to the dreamed-of black patriarch, always on the verge of heroic (re)appearance. Who, after all, need "permit" (recalling Bayard Rustin's words) black men to take their rightful places at the "head of the family," except the black wife and mother, usurper at the table of intimate power? In the next chapter I will consider how and why Alice Walker's 1982 novel *The Color Purple,* published just after the end of this "Masculine Decade"—or *decades,* if one considers the 1970s in that appellation—challenged a politicized vision of black patriarchal power, and question the relation of that power to the logic of the salvific wish.[52]

Chapter 3

Queering Black Patriarchy

Family has come to stand for community, for race,
for nation. . . It is a kind of short-cut to solidarity.
The discourse of family and the discourse of nation
are very closely connected.
—Paul Gilroy, "It's a Family Affair:
Black Culture and the Trope of Kinship"

In her 1989 essay "Reading Family Matters," Deborah McDowell examines a pattern of hostile critical responses directed toward a "very small sample" of contemporary black women writers by some black reviewers and critics, mostly male.[1] McDowell describes the critical narrative employed by these figures as a black "family romance," the creation of a "totalizing fiction" of community wholeness—a fiction that, if realized, could rehabilitate a fragmented and painfully complex racial past. Gesturing toward the overwhelmingly masculinist ideology of black cultural nationalism, whose disciples she posits as the most powerful proponents of this family fiction, McDowell writes: "[T]his story of the Black Family cum Black Community headed by the Black Male who does battle with an oppressive White world, continues to be told, though in ever more subtle variations."[2] Indeed, part of the increasing subtlety of such narratives is their extension into broader spheres of cultural influence than the putatively "political" arena, including the space of black literary production and analysis.

As McDowell goes on to note, Alice Walker has received more than her share of black (male) critical attack for disrupting this notion of family romance in her fiction; at least in part, that attack has been in response to the 1985 film adaptation of Walker's novel *The Color Purple* by Steven Spielberg, which brought a great deal of additional publicity to Walker and her work. Walker, accused by various critics of being unduly influenced by white feminists and of harboring animosity toward black men, seems to have written herself out of the so-called black family embrace, even out of the black community as a whole, by "expos[ing] black women's subordination within the nuclear family, rethink[ing] and configur[ing] its structures, and plac[ing] utterance outside the father's preserve and control."[3] In other words, Walker's work (along with the work of writers like Ntozake Shange and Gayl Jones, who have been similarly criticized) *deconstructs* a black family romance, and represents unequivocally the ways in which "traditional"—and traditionally idealized—family structures can endanger black women both physically and psychically, largely because of the patriarchal power that such structures grant to black men.

Perhaps even more significantly, however, Walker's writing, and particularly her 1982 novel *The Color Purple*, also engages in a project of "queering" the black family, reshaping it in unconventional ways that divest its black male members of a good deal of power, thereby reconfiguring the very meaning of kinship for black sons, brothers, and especially fathers.[4] Indeed, I invoke McDowell's essay, and the generally masculine critical furor to which it refers, at the opening of this chapter on Walker's *The Color Purple* because I believe there are crucial connections to be made between the ways in which Walker's text calls for a queering or refashioning of family dynamics and the manner in which Walker herself, as author, has been scripted by a black (male) critical establishment as a delinquent daughter who has strayed from the black family fold. Not only do Walker's characters repeatedly find ways to subvert the shape and order of the heteronormative, patriarchal family, but in many ways Walker's authorly body functions as an apparent source of subversion or betrayal in its own right, imagined by her critics to be waging treacherous assault upon a mythologically unified black community.

"Imagined" is, of course, the operative word in the foregoing sentence; nothing in Walker's published reflections on the filming (and resulting criticism) of *The Color Purple* suggests that her intention in writing this novel was to betray the black family/community.[5] Instead, what is at stake here is the behavior assigned to Walker by her critics, the motivations and loyalties she is assumed to hold; in short, the writerly persona grafted onto Walker's not-so-willing body by an act of critical storytelling. We might say, in fact, that Walker's writerly body is subject to *interpretation* in the same way that the narrative body of her fiction is. Indeed, the conclusion of "Reading Family Matters" cautions against the ways in which black women's "bodies" (in both senses of the term) might be reduced to the terrain upon which white and black men enact a struggle for power and control of the literary landscape.

While McDowell's point is well-taken, my interest in drawing such a link between Walker's authorly body and the textual body of her novel is to call attention to a different set of issues entirely—namely, the gendered and sexualized complexities that underlie the black drive toward a patriarchal "family romance." The power of this drive, and the particular vehemence of critical responses to Walker, has to do with the manner in which patriarchy's hierarchalized kinship structure has generative consequences for black (hetero) sexual subjectivity— and particularly black masculinity. Disruptions of this kinship structure such as those effected in Walker's novel thus have the potential to unsettle black gender difference, even to render it incoherent. If, as Michael Awkward has suggested, "monolithic and/or normative maleness" is conventionally defined by the "powerful, domineering patriarch," then a family in which men no longer dominate is a family in which masculinity itself is called into question.[6]

This challenge to heteronormative masculinity is precisely why Alice Walker herself is imagined as a kind of racial turncoat for her portrayals of black men—not merely, as McDowell suggests, because these portrayals present black manhood in a so-called "negative" light, or simply shift the focus of black fictional narrative away from the black male. In fact, it is the radical *reshaping* of the family effected in Walker's novel that leads to her rejection by the black (male) critical establishment; Walker's transformative revision of black domesticity in *The Color Purple* accomplishes no less than the emptying of "black masculinity" as a term, insofar as that term has been dependent upon an assumption of black men's authoritative role in the family sphere.

In other words, Walker's refashioning of the black family "queers" the very notion of the potent black patriarch. Her text goes beyond simply representing an absent father, one who has abdicated the legitimate seat of patriarchal rule; nor does it portray merely a father inadequately fulfilling the requirements of his (again, assumed rightful) authority. Indeed, both of these possibilities evoke what Sharon Holland, following Hortense Spillers, identifies as "fatherlack": "the idea of a dream/nightmare deferred . . . an inevitable and unattainable fatherhood."[7] For Holland, the cultural trauma of this lack—or the difficulty of fulfilling what Spillers names the "provisions of patriarchy"—is a "founding and necessary condition/experience of what it means to be black."[8] In this schema, the very concept of black patriarchy becomes a conceptual impossibility, precisely because of a fatherly absence contained within the cultural signifier "black."

I would differentiate the queered black father of Walker's novel from Holland's idea, however. Walker's subversive transformation of the black family, and of the black father, responds more to ahistorical *fantasies* of black patriarchy (erected, perhaps, as a defensive response to fatherlack), of which the black community harbors many. As Ashraf Rushdy notes in *Remembering Generations,* "African American intellectuals espousing black nationalism have long argued that the family represents the site for the development of the black nation"; for nationalists, "those families representing the race can form a nation only when . . . patriarchal power is evident."[9] Ultimately, in playing with, literally queering, such patriarchal fantasies, Walker's novel invites hostile critical scrutiny. By the conclusion of the text, Walker's black family contains a possibility far more bewildering than the father's absence: a father who is *present,* but nonetheless no longer dominant or even interested in domination. It is no wonder, then, that Walker's narrative is viewed by many critics as an affront to black community wholeness, for it posits a community without a (male) leader, a mascu-

linity without even the desire for what has traditionally been understood as masculinity's hallmark: power.

Contexts: The Salvific Wish and Patriarchal Tyranny

Crucial to my argument in the remainder of this chapter is a closer
examination of the recurrent black drive toward a patriarchal family
romance. I believe this drive can be understood as part of the pattern of black desire that I have already identified as the "salvific wish."
Best understood as an aspiration, most often but not only middle-class
and female, to save or rescue the black community from white racist accusations of sexual and domestic pathology through the embrace
of conventional bourgeois propriety, the salvific wish began in large
part as a response to moral defamation of black women in the U.S.
public sphere, and is closely related to the philosophy of middle-class
racial responsibility that began near the turn of the twentieth century. W. E. B. DuBois's notion of the "Talented Tenth" is a particularly illustrative example of this philosophy of "uplift": a small group
of economically and culturally privileged African Americans poised
to lead the masses of blacks "away from the contamination and death of
the Worst, in their own and other races."[10] In other words, middle- and
upper-class African Americans in the late 1800s and early 1900s sought
to improve the reputation and status of the race as a whole through
their "respectable" actions and influence, and the measure of respectability for these bourgeois blacks consisted chiefly in "conformity to
patriarchal family ideals."[11]

As I have argued throughout this volume, the logic of the salvific
wish continues to be both interrogated and reinscribed in black wom-
en's fiction of the twentieth century. In these narratives, female characters who refuse to behave according to the tenets of the salvific wish,
such as Toni Morrison's Sula Peace and Walker's own Shug Avery,
threaten a narrative of black community sanctity which, due to the
historic influence of white racism on black intimate life, has larger political meaning for black people. I contend, however, that in Walker's

case, more than her characters can be read as culturally threatening. As I have already noted, Alice Walker herself has been represented as such by a host of hostile critics, and I believe the reason for this representation is the way that Walker appears to defy the salvific wish *through* the shape taken by her narrative. In other words, her textual body operates (or is believed to operate) as a proxy for her authorly body, and the symbolically queer, or queer*ing* behavior of this proxy enacts a kind of intolerable threat to black community sanctity as it is defined by the salvific wish.[12]

Perhaps not surprisingly, the definitions of and contexts for the salvific wish outlined in previous chapters asume more complex contours in Walker's novel, *The Color Purple,* for several reasons. The first of these is the relationship to whites effected by the rural southern setting of the text. Because the novel takes place in the South during the Jim Crow era, the presence of whites in or around the community has more immediate (and immediately painful) consequences than in many other black women's texts. This is significant in part because the efforts of the salvific wish to protect black people's public *reputation* from racist assumptions about black character seem, in an environment in which blacks have little physical protection from white attack, to be far less urgent than the protection of black people from direct bodily harm at the hands of whites. Walker's text represents whites as a concrete and continual threat to black characters' lives, a shift that might alter the very meaning of "protection" for the black community.

The second complicating aspect of Walker's text is that the bulk of its characters cannot be understood as conventionally bourgeois or middle class. I say "conventionally" because in part, the apparent difference between Walker's characters and those of writers such as Toni Morrison or Ann Petry is one of rural versus urban expressions of bourgeois status. This is particularly true when one considers that Celie and Nettie's biological father is a wealthy man in the community, and that it is his wealth, which surpasses that of many whites, that leads to his lynching.[13] Indeed, many of Walker's characters are land and homeowners, some even business owners—hallmarks of bourgeois status for black people, especially in the period during which the novel is set. Although it is possible to identify certain of Walker's characters as poor or working class, it would be a mistake to assume that the salvific wish, with its strategic embrace of bourgeois propriety, would thereby have less of a hold in the community Walker describes. In fact, as Kevin Kelly Gaines's text *Uplifting the Race* reminds us, the embrace of uplift ideology historically has served as a crucial marker, among poor and working-class blacks, of aspirations toward "respectability," in spite of actual economic status.[14] It is perhaps not surprising, then, that Walker's characters, although rural or working class, are concerned with uplift-based issues of propriety, since such concern would in fact help to mark them as respectable.

Ironically enough, however, given the presumably *female* emphasis of the salvific wish, in Walker's text many comments about black respectability are voiced by male characters. This connection between the ostensibly feminine salvific wish and the interference of men is one means by which Walker's work critiques the wish and the patriarchal values that motivate it, a point to which I will return later. Many of the men who express concern with feminine behavior and reputation in *The Color Purple* behave (or attempt to behave) as oppressive tyrants toward women, pointing to an obvious link between repressive social strictures around female character and abusive actions designed to force women into specific patterns of behavior. And what remains consistent, in Walker's novel, among these male characters' attention to black women's respectability, their seemingly masculine expression of aspects of the salvific wish, is that such attention repeatedly concerns pregnancy, marriage, and appropriate (female) behavior in the domestic sphere. Indeed, these masculine assertions of the salvific wish are nearly always accompanied by direct expressions of patriarchal power over the domestic sphere: a father refusing to allow a son or daughter to marry, refusing to extend support to a mother or child, or insisting upon specific behaviors from a wife or daughter.

That this power to restore propriety and order is expressed in relation to marriage, children, and family is not surprising, since the privatized space of the domestic is precisely where a traditional patriarch wields unchecked power. As Catharine MacKinnon has written, "In private, women are objects of male subjectivity and male power. The private is that place where men can do whatever they want because women reside there."[15] While MacKinnon speaks of the "private" in a legal sense, her words are certainly relevant to the space of the household or the domestic, since this space is traditionally assumed to lie within the realm of the private. The home, the family—all are a part of the world to which men are expected to retreat for comfort after their forays into the "public" sphere of commerce and paid work.

Of course, as Patricia Hill Collins notes, "Black women's experiences . . . have never fit this [public/private spheres] model."[16] Indeed, Collins goes on to suggest that "Because the construct of family/ household . . . is rooted in assumptions about discrete public and private spheres, nuclear families characterized by sex-segregated gender roles are less likely to be found in African-American communities."[17] Since black women have always labored in what could be considered the "private" sphere—either through domestic work for whites both during and after slavery, or in order to maintain their own black household spaces—the distinction between a public sphere reserved for work and a private sphere reserved for leisure and intimacy has often been of little consequence in real black women's lives. In Walker's text, however, perhaps because of the novel's focus on a male-driven notion of patriarchy, this concept of separate and opposing spheres is not entirely ineffectual, particularly for male characters. For these characters, enforcing a public/private distinction is one way of ensuring masculine power over women.

The rural setting of Walker's narrative does further complicate this notion of a public versus a private sphere, however, since the work of maintaining the farm and homestead mean that no domestic space is solely for "relaxation." Still, as Walker's text suggests, the work that takes place on Mr.——'s land is rarely done by the patriarch himself, which means that the space of the "private" in *The Color Purple* maintains some coherence as a space in which men are empowered to behave as they please. Indeed, MacKinnon's sense that the space of the "private" or the domestic is a space in which men wield power

over women might, in the case of *The Color Purple*, also be understood
to imply two other potential objects of privatized masculine control:
children and less powerful males.

In fact, in Walker's text, men who are dominated by their own
fathers seem determined to dominate their sons (as well as any women
in their lives) in equal measure within their own "private" realms.
This phenomenon is made clear by Mr.——'s subordinate relationship to his own father, and his (consequently) dominant relationship
to Harpo; Harpo's resultant efforts to dominate his own family can
thus be read as gestures toward the same sort of defensive patriarchal
control. Harpo's inability to challenge his father—Celie remarks that
"Harpo no better at fighting his daddy back than me" (29)—points
out the way in which a dominant male, in this case Mr.——, exercises
power over not only the women in his control but also the male and
female children. Celie's description of Harpo working for his father in
fact provides a subtle comparison between a subordinated male and a
woman (already subordinated simply because of her gender):

> Harpo nearly as big as his daddy. He strong in body but weak in will.
> He scared. Me and him out in the field all day. Us sweat, chopping and
> plowing. I'm roasted coffee bean color now. He black as the inside of a
> chimney. His eyes be sad and thoughtful. His face begin to look like a
> woman face. (29)

That Harpo is "nearly as big" as Mr.—— reminds the reader that
his father's ability to dominate him does not stem from sheer physical prowess. Instead, Harpo is "weak in will," controlled by fear of
his father's power. It is this fear that turns Harpo's eyes "sad and
thoughtful," and that leads Celie to describe his face as feminine—the
comparison points up the ways that all those subordinate to a family
patriarch are feminized, because they are all subject to the same hierarchical relationship.

In addition, however, the narrative's juxtaposition of Harpo's "sad,"
"thoughtful" eyes with the claim that he has begun to resemble a
woman reminds readers of the rigidity of conventional gender norms.
Clearly, neither melancholy nor reflection are behaviors expected of

men, so much so that when a man exhibits them, he is immediately feminized. Here Walker's text begins its commentary on the limitations patriarchy imposes upon both women and men—anticipating the more radical project of "queering" patriarchy that will take place later in the novel through the character of Mr.——. Harpo's case, however, falls short of this radical revision precisely because, while he is feminized by his father's control, he maintains a conventionally masculine determination to control the subjects of his own patriarchal domain.

In fact, Harpo provides one of the novel's major conflicts (and major sources of comic relief) in his own efforts to dominate his wife, Sofia. Described as "a big strong girl. . . . Solid. Like if she sit down on something, it be mash" (36), Sofia never acquiesces to her husband's patriarchal authority, though he continually attempts to dominate her. In stark contrast to Celie's silent obedience in Mr.——'s home, Sofia demands to be treated as an equal by Harpo, to his surprise: "Harpo want to know what to do to make Sofia mind. He sit out on the porch with Mr.——. He say, I tell her one thing, she do another. Never do what I say. Always backtalk" (37). And, Celie adds, "To tell the truth, he sound a little proud of this to me." It is crucial to acknowledge this pride of Harpo's, for it marks one of several instances in Walker's text when characters take a particular pleasure in behaving (or in interacting with others who behave) counter to gendered expectation. This pleasure is often short-lived in early portions of the novel, however, because the hegemony of the patriarchal family structure, what Kaja Silverman has called the "dominant fiction," repeatedly reimposes itself, reminding those characters of the appropriate manner of behavior.[18]

In Harpo's case, the reimposition of patriarchal order comes, not surprisingly, from his own father, who strikes immediately upon the "problem" with Harpo and Sofia's relationship:

> You ever hit her? Mr.—— ast.
> Harpo look down at his hands. Naw suh, he say low, embarrass.
> Well how you spect to make her mind? Wives is like children. You have to let 'em know who got the upper hand. Nothing can do that better than a good sound beating. (37–38)

That Harpo is embarrassed to admit to Mr.—— that he doesn't hit Sofia indicates not simply discomfort with his lack of power over his wife, but shame at being exposed, in front of his own father, as an inadequate patriarch. Rather than being able to interact with his father as an equal, now that he has his own household to dominate, he proves himself incapable of the requisite authority. His low-voiced, eyes-averted response to Mr.——, replete with the previously absent "suh [sir]," thus signals Harpo's return to a subordinate position relative to his father—a position ensured by the fact that he has admitted he is unable to make his own wife "mind." Indeed, Mr.——'s assertion that "wives is like children" functions as a veiled reminder of the feminized subjugation that Harpo has endured as Mr.——'s child, the blanket patriarchal control that disciplines wives, children, and anything in between.

This widespread, violence-enforced tyranny, in which women are no more autonomous than children and children, even adult children, are feminized by their subordinance, recalls the resented black father figure that David Marriott points to in Richard Wright's writing:

> Deeply suspicious of his father's inheritance—in which all white men were "Misters", and all black men "boys"—Wright gives voice to his ambivalence towards a father, and towards father-figures, who, trapped in a time-warp, want to be called "Mister." These are fathers who identify with the racist violence of (white) culture in the South by miming that violence in their relations with their black sons.[19]

This description is stunningly reminiscent of father-son interaction in *The Color Purple*—black fathers who, in a social sphere shaped by white racism, gain access to manhood through the recreation of a violent (white) patriarchy in their own homes. While Marriott's reading of Wright's autobiographical universe posits a straightforwardly mimetic relationship between black and white masculinity, such a relationship is less directly visible in Walker's narrative. Instead, Marriott's analysis is useful because it highlights the way that whiteness can be understood as a *backdrop* for these intraracial, masculine assertions of power. After all, except for the lynching of Celie and Nettie's biological father,

Walker's text masks the actual interactions that black men have with white, focusing instead on the various assaults (literal and figurative) that black women like Sofia and Mary Agnes ("Squeak") experience at white hands. Even the aforementioned lynching is, arguably, hidden from view throughout much of the novel, a communal secret that is only revealed well into Celie's adulthood.

Still, the violent relationship that exists between black and white men in *The Color Purple*'s rural, southern setting is never far from the surface in the text. It is evident, for instance, in the statement from Celie's stepfather (Alphonso) that "[Y]ou got to give [whites] something. Either your money, your land, your woman, or your ass" (188)—and this particular collocational set presents disturbing, though hardly surprising, correlations between black (female) bodies and property that are consistent with the patriarchal tyranny otherwise expressed by Alphonso throughout the novel. The appellation "Mister" is perhaps a more subtle reminder of white controls over black life, however. For if, as Marriott suggests, every southern white man is "Mister" and every black man "boy," then the black men in Walker's text are scripted into a pattern of titular naming that even without direct reference to whiteness is informed by racial hierarchies. This scripting takes place through Celie's narration; Celie describes almost all the men in the text as Mr.——, even making it difficult to distinguish between male characters at times. Indeed, when Shug Avery first refers to Celie's husband, previously called only Mr.——, as "Albert," Celie notes, "Who Albert, I wonder. Then I remember Albert Mr.—— first name" (49). Shug, who is uninterested in maintaining artificial language tags meant to signify respect—"[D]on't you yes ma'am me, I ain't that old" (51)—is here as elsewhere starkly contrasted with Celie, who as arguably the most subordinated character in early portions of the novel is required to think of the men who surround her only as "Misters."

To return, then, to the salvific wish: I have suggested that men are frequently the characters in Walker's text who give voice to tenets of the salvific wish, and that these articulations are often linked to masculine expressions of control over the feminized spaces of domesticity with which the salvific wish is ultimately concerned. I want now briefly to reexamine the ways in which masculine and feminine articulations of concern over respectability in Walker's text might be differentiated, and what significance this has for the "treacherous" project of queering the patriarch in *The Color Purple*. For while it may be true that both men and women in the novel hope to control the appearance and actuality of the domestic sphere for the sake of propriety, only female characters link this control to the idea of recuperation or rescue for the community (or even for themselves). Celie's attempt to push her sister Nettie into marriage is only one example: "Sometime he still be looking at Nettie, but I always get in his light. Now I tell her to marry Mr.——. I don't tell her why" (6). In stark contrast to the behavior of most male characters in Walker's text, who orchestrate domestic behavior by forbidding marriage rather than encouraging it, Celie hopes to protect Nettie from a fate similar to her own by encouraging her sister to marry and leave Alphonso's house. What might be perceived as an effort at controlling the events of the household is quite literally in the service of protecting one of its members, from psychic as well as physical harm.

Male characters, on the contrary, seem to desire control for its own sake—to make a statement about their own capacity to rule in the private sphere. Of course, one reason that this distinction exists is that men's gestures toward respectability through "proper" behavior are always externalized—since the behavior that needs reform is always assumed to belong to women. This is true, for example, when Mr.—— protests Celie's inclusion in an outing to Harpo's juke joint: "Mr.—— didn't want me to come. Wives don't go to places like that, he say" (76), or when Harpo himself reacts with horror at seeing Sofia in the same place: "It just a scandless, a woman with five children hanging out in a jukejoint at night" (86). In neither of these instances do Mr.—— or Harpo consider their own behavior to be potentially improper—Mr.—— doesn't question a husband's right to go a "place like that," and Harpo, the father of Sofia's five children, finds nothing unusual about his own presence in (and ownership of) a juke joint.

The irony of this double standard is pointed out by Sofia herself, in an exchange with Albert/Mr.——:

> Mr.—— whisper to Sofia. Where your children at?
> She whisper back, My children at home, where yours?
> He don't say nothing.
> Both the girls bigged and gone. Bub in and out of jail. If his grandaddy wasn't the colored uncle of the sheriff who look just like Bub, Bub be lynch by now. (85)

Sofia's response to Mr.—— silences his question about her behavior, by calling attention to his own neglected responsibilities, and to the irony that while he finds it within his rights as a man to question the whereabouts of Sofia's children, his own family is significantly troubled (something Sofia may or may not have been aware of when she made her retort). The silence that Sofia's question elicits from Mr.—— is filled by Celie's narration, however, which informs the reader, at least, that Mr.——'s daughters had both gotten pregnant and left home.[20] Celie also reveals that Mr.——'s son was hardly well-behaved, and that only his physical resemblance to the town's sheriff prevented his untimely death.[21]

Thus it seems that male articulations of the salvific wish in Walker's novel ultimately eschew the project of communal recuperation in favor of self-aggrandizement—a self-aggrandizement that more often than not is undeserved. Still, these masculine articulations of externalized control over domestic life, and feminine gestures toward domestic self-discipline in the service of group safety, are aligned in the novel for good reason—it is only through this alignment that Walker is able to point out the pitfalls of the ostensibly feminine salvific wish, that drive to protect the community through self-control and sacrifice.[22] When voiced through the bodies of male characters, these ostensibly noble behaviors become something disturbingly close to tyranny, creating not community safety but a hyper-powerful masculinity that lays down the law of propriety solely in pursuit of the authority to enforce that law.[23] And it is this patriarchal authority, so spotlighted in early portions of Walker's narrative, that subsequently becomes the object of not only critique but creative and queer revision in the latter part of the text.

Tailoring Mr.——'s Masculinity: Rewriting the Black Patriarch

The term "patriarchy," as defined by feminist scholars, is "the rule of the father, including the rule of older men over younger men and of fathers over daughters, as well as husbands over wives."[24] This concept, so defined, seems to be precisely the prevailing system of male-female interaction in the beginning of *The Color Purple*. Certainly, Albert/ Mr.—— functions as a traditional patriarch in early portions of the novel, dominating both Celie and his grown children. He undergoes a transformation by the conclusion of the novel, however, from head of household wielding near-absolute power to a more subdued and philosophical friend and companion to Shug and Celie. In other words, Albert is displaced as patriarch, divested of his former dominance. Ironically enough, this transformation takes place in part because of Celie, who puts a curse on Albert as she leaves his house with Shug. While Albert's initial response is quintessentially patriarchal: "Who you think you is? [. . .] You can't curse nobody. Look at you. You black, you pore, you ugly, you a woman. Goddam . . . you nothing at all" (213), he soon discovers that the person he had assumed to be most powerless is, in the first of many reversals in Albert's life, in fact the one most capable of transforming his existence.

Indeed, by the time Celie returns, Albert is a different person; after the hardship he suffers under Celie's curse, his behavior begins to move away from the traditionally "masculine," in part because there is no one else in his household to dominate and coerce into working for him. As Sofia and Harpo inform Celie:

> I know you won't believe this, Miss Celie, say Sofia, but Mr.—— act like he trying to get religion. . . .
>
> He don't go to church or nothing, but he not so quick to judge. He work real hard too.
>
> What? I say. Mr.—— work!

He sure do. He out there in the field from sunup to sundown. And clean that house just like a woman.

Even cook, say Harpo. And what more, wash the dishes when he finish. (229)

Celie's disbelief is to be expected, since no one, least of all she, has ever seen Albert work to maintain his own household. Perhaps more importantly, however, the claim that he is "not so quick to judge" suggests that Albert/Mr.——'s transformation is more than simply an external one, wrought by necessity. Instead, the shift extends to his sense of morality. Rather than taking it as his prerogative to pass judgment on the world around him (as he did when he was more clearly functioning as patriarch), Albert assumes a more open-minded position. This is only the first of several changes in Albert that serve to "soften" him—he begins to collect shells, for example, displaying a tenderness for them that hardly resembles his former self: "He don't say that much about them while you looking, but he hold each one like it just arrive" (260). Later, he begins to sew alongside Celie, helping her to assemble her pants; sewing becomes an activity that the two share as friends: "Now us sit sewing and talking and smoking our pipes" (279).

It is no coincidence that the title of this section is a reference to both Albert's sewing and his gender; I read his participation in this traditionally "female" activity as an indication, perhaps the most striking, that his character has diverged from the patriarchal behaviors that marked him as a tyrant in earlier portions of the novel. In other words, his acceptance of a less traditional gender comportment goes along with his humanization in the text. This change is related to the distinction Karla Holloway identifies between destruction (gendered masculine) and creation (gendered feminine) in black narrative; Albert's transformation in Walker's text indicates his newfound ability to access the "spiritual creativity" that has traditionally been assumed the province of black women.[25]

The change in Albert/Mr.—— also, however, comes along with a shift in actual family dynamics—Albert becomes softer and more accommodating as he is displaced from the role of father and husband, as his family is "queered" by Celie and Shug's romantic involvement.

As Celie says to a disheartened Albert, still disappointed that Shug is
no longer his lover: "She still feel for you, I say. Yeah, he say. She feel
like I'm her brother. What so bad about that, I ast. Don't her brothers
love her?" (278). Celie's comment is important because it points out the
way in which Albert's connection to Shug (and to Celie herself) has
become a connection based in egalitarian affection, rather than hierarchy. The difference between "brother" and "lover/husband" points to
this transformation. In addition, Celie's question, "Don't her brothers love her?" again shifts the focus from Albert to the women in his
life—by asking about Shug's brothers' love for her, rather than her love
for her brothers, Celie reminds Albert of the potential for intimate
connection based not in a woman's devotion to a man, but in a man's
devotion to a woman, no matter what her feelings for him.

Indeed, this shift of focus from Albert/Mr.—— to the people,
largely women, who surround him, is a part of a larger pattern of family
reconfiguration in the novel, which decentralizes the patriarch and
calls for a more democratic distribution of kinship ties. For example,
Harpo and Sofia's family eventually includes the child of Harpo's former mistress, Mary Agnes ("Squeak"), who leaves with Shug and Celie
to go sing, and eventually moves away from Memphis with Shug's
(ex-)husband, Grady. Throughout the text, the concept of family moves
further and further toward a kind of unruly and unregulated jumble
of intimacies, many of which begin as sexual dyads but end up as more
platonic kinship relations. Shug's young lover Germaine, for example,
eventually takes on a more consanguine role in Shug's life: "He feel just
like family now. Like a son. Maybe a grandson" (291). In this move toward extended rather than strictly nuclear family, Walker's text ironically gestures toward familial patterns that, as Hortense Spillers notes,
were common among enslaved blacks:

> [T]he laws and practices of enslavement did not recognize, as a rule,
> the vertical arrangements of . . . family [for blacks]. From this angle,
> fathers, daughters, mothers, sons, sisters, brothers spread across the
> social terrain in horizontal display, which exactly occurred in the dis-
> persal of the historic African-American domestic unit. In this move-
> ment outward from a nuclear centrality, "family" becomes an extension

> and inclusion—anyone who preserves life and its callings becomes a
> member of the family, whose patterns of kinship and resemblance fall
> into disguise.[26]

This relationship to kinship ties among captive blacks is important because it may indicate, at least in part, why Walker's extensive "queering" of the family has received such hostile black critical responses. A
major project of the salvific wish, the aforementioned desire to recuperate black people from accusations of racist pathology around family
and sexuality, is the *repudiation* of unconventional family relations
such as the ones Spillers outlines, and the embrace of more traditional
bourgeois patterns of "proper" domestic and sexual behavior.

While the salvific wish is perhaps most deeply interrogated and critiqued within black women's fiction, it would not be inaccurate to suggest that the wish, as part of an African American cultural imaginary,
also affects external critical responses to black women's literature. This
is particularly plausible in light of what Evelynn Hammonds notes about
black women who undertake feminist work; in a conflation of feminist and female, she writes: "Black feminist theorists are themselves
engaged in a process of fighting to reclaim the body—the maimed,
immoral, black female body—which can be and is still being used by
others to discredit them as producers of knowledge and as speaking
subjects."[27] I would argue that the same is true, in different ways, of
all black theorists, not simply black women, even if women's bodies
are sometimes forced to assume a disproportionate share of pathologizing scrutiny. Thus black critics of either gender might fall sway to
the discourse of the salvific wish, enacting patterns of repression and
silence in the hopes of protecting themselves or the communities they
represent.

This was true in particular ways in 1982, when *The Color Purple* was
published. In the wake of Ronald Reagan's election to the presidency,
"Civil rights gains [were] being rolled back, [and] Black communities and families [were] in disarray."[28] Perhaps ironically, in this same
period black women's writing, particularly fiction, was undergoing a
renaissance of sorts, with authors like Gayl Jones, Toni Morrison, and

Gloria Naylor receiving a great deal of popular and critical attention. If the sixties and early seventies were what historian Paula Giddings called "The Masculine Decade," focused on the advancement of a militant, hyperpowerful black manhood, the late seventies and early eighties were characterized by the rise of Women's Liberation—a movement which, at least initially, centered on white, middle-class women—and the increasing presence of these women's concerns in public debate. This increased public interest in women's issues, coupled with the growing presence of women in publishing (Toni Morrison herself was an editor at Random House), may have contributed to the flowering of black women's fiction, though to many, that flowering came at the expense of black men.

Indeed, following the rise of "American feminism," suggested one critic in 1987, "[b]lack women writers seemed to find their voices and audiences, and black men seemed to lose theirs."[29] This perception is part of what fueled critical conflicts around black women's writing; coupled with it was the sense among some critics that black women writers such as Ntozake Shange and Michele Wallace were gaining notoriety by "[choosing] black men as. . . target[s]."[30] This perceived "targeting" of black men had to do with what the same critic called "the proliferation of scenes of violent interaction between black males and females, and of increased portrayals of black males as oppressors and brutalizers of black women."[31] Alice Walker's *The Color Purple* was accused by more than one reviewer of being the nadir of negative portrayals of black men; in just one example, Darryl Pinckney suggests that while other black women's writings contain "offhand scenes of domestic violence. . . . in *The Color Purple* this violence is on virtually every page."[32] As I have argued throughout this chapter, however, in the case of Walker's text, more may be at stake than simply "negative portrayals" of black men—and might explain why her novel is viewed as so much worse than others released during the period.

In rereading critics of Walker's novel twenty years later, it seems clear that the furor surrounding *The Color Purple* was driven at least in part by the propriety-seeking salvific wish. Discussing Walker's activist work with female clitoridectomy in Africa, Gina Dent has written that "Walker locks the proverbial feminist personal-is-political into battle with that notorious black manifesto—we will not have our business put in the streets—and cuts close to the communal nerve."[33] This description might just as easily apply to Walker's *The Color Purple*, given the defensive and moralistic tenor of (male) critical responses to the book. While all of the most unsympathetic reviewers and critics seemed to agree that Walker held "a high level of enmity toward black men," many also intimated that Walker, along with some other black women writers, had ignored conventions of black decorum by publishing her work.[34] One critic, asserting that "[b]lack women's concerns had earlier belonged to what was considered the private, rather than the public[,]" seemed disturbed to find that "the concerns of the kitchen" were now finding a wider audience.[35] Philip Royster, writing an extensive analysis of Walker's "persona" in *Black American Literature Forum,* insinuated on the one hand that Walker's "accepting attitude" toward lesbianism served to "aggravate the already troubled waters with a large number of black folk who possess more conservative . . . values," while in nearly the same breath dismissing Walker's own acknowledgment of such potential community sanction as a figment of her imagination: "Walker rejects the concepts of appropriateness and correctness . . . in her fiction . . . because *she believes* they have been used to keep black women down."[36]

In another ironic twist, Mel Watkins suggests that Walker and other black feminists have sidestepped "unspoken but almost universally accepted" rules of black literary production, by forgetting that "one of the major forces shaping black literature has been the commitment to rectify the antiblack stereotypes and propagandistic images created by nonblack writers."[37] Watkins goes on to argue that "fiction . . . produced by the Talented Tenth school of writers of the late nineteenth and early twentieth centuries. . . were *[sic]* characterized by their emphasis on establishing humane, positive images of blacks."[38] In this, at least, I would agree with Watkins. Part of what seemed to necessitate a focus on "positive images" at the turn of the century was

the repeated circulation, in mainstream American culture, of pathologizing invective about blacks. It is no coincidence that Watkins cites
DuBois's Talented Tenth as the source of propriety-driven resistance to
this invective; I have already noted that middle-class blacks such as the
ones DuBois describes in his famous essay were the originators of the
salvific wish, and its attempts to rescue blacks as a whole from accusations of pathology through the embrace of conventional moralisms.
The irony of Watkins' comments about Walker lie in his assertion that
by portraying black men in a negative light, she and other black women
writers "have, in effect, shifted their priorities from the subtle evoca-
tion of art to the blunt demonstration of politics and propaganda."[39] A
blind determination to "present positive images of blacks" is certainly as
political and as propagandistic as any other artistic choice, however—a
point that seems to elude Watkins. Walker's novel seems to have been
read as particularly political because it disturbs certain "unspoken but
almost universally accepted" markers of black *respectability.*

Trudier Harris's 1984 essay, "On *The Color Purple,* Stereotypes, and
Silence" is also important to consider here, precisely because the objections to the novel that Harris outlines bear striking resemblance
to the calls for black propriety fundamental to the salvific wish. In
fact, I read her piece quite closely, below, in part because the assumptions that seem to underlie it are so germane to my argument about
criticism of Walker's text, and in part because other scholars who have
commented upon the controversy surrounding Walker's work (such as
Deborah McDowell) have given surprisingly little attention to Harris's
essay. This lack of attention may be because Harris's piece precedes and
even anticipates the black male critical furor of the late 1980s, and has
thus been somewhat eclipsed by its successors.[40] As such, my intention
in reading Harris's article more closely here than I do reviews by male
writers such as Watkins or Pinckney is partially to acknowledge its
significance, and Harris's presence, in the larger debate.

In the essay, Harris recounts her unease with the way that the novel
has been "canonized," suggesting that Walker's text participates in racist mischaracterizations of black intimate life:

> The book simply add[s] freshness to many of the ideas circulating in
> the popular culture and captured in racist literature that suggested that
> black people have no morality when it comes to sexuality, that the black
> family structure is weak if existent at all. . . . The novel gives validity
> to all the white racist's notions of pathology in black communities. . . .
> Black males and females form units without the benefit of marriage,
> or they easily dissolve marriages in order to form less structured, more
> promiscuous relationships.[41]

Harris's reading of the novel begins with the assumption that Walker's depictions of such fluid and amorphous intimate relationships must be interpreted as categorically negative, and as unwittingly (rather than consciously) participating in a cultural narrative of pathology. What I read, for example, as a deliberate attempt to challenge the hegemony of the "traditional" family, by showing how that family has conventionally been based in hierarchical and oppressive relations between men and women, Harris reads as a confirmation of stereotype. The language of "benefit" used, *sans* irony, in relation to "marriage," as well as the indirect parallel of marriage with "morality" (i.e., Harris's claim that black people in Walker's text have "no morality when it comes to sexuality" might easily be related to her distaste for the "promiscuous relationships" Walker's characters form extramaritally) seem to reveal underlying investments in domestic and sexual orthodoxy highly similar to those supported by the salvific wish.

This apparent adherence to the tenets of the salvific wish, which insists that black people, particularly black women, should behave according to traditional definitions of sexual/domestic "propriety" in order to protect themselves, and other blacks, from "the white racist's notions of pathology," is not the only conservative turn in the essay, however, since Harris also critiques Walker's portrayal of black men. In fact, she describes in detail the hostile response of a black male student of hers to Walker's novel. Though it is unlikely that Harris herself agrees fully with her student's sometimes overstated opinions, they are worth examining precisely because, in spite of their excesses, Harris gives them a good deal of prominence within her essay. The student's complaint about Walker is that the author "had very deliberately deprived all the black male characters in the novel of any positive identity. From giving Albert a blank instead of a name, to having the only supportive males be young and potheads or middle-aged and henpecked (as is the husband of Sophie's [sic] sister, for whom Celie makes a pair of pants and whose only goal in life seems to be to please his wife—because she can beat him up?) [. . .] this student thought black men had been stripped of their identities and thus their abilities to assume the roles of men."[42] While I have already suggested that the use of "Mr.——" to describe not just Albert, but most of the men in Celie's life, is far more complex than simply leaving male identity "blank," and indeed has a great deal to do with Celie's own sense of herself as subordinate to all men, what is most striking to me about these assertions is the manner in which they describe Jack, Odessa's husband.

The student's parenthetical insertion of descriptors "middle-aged" and "henpecked" to describe Jack is alarmingly misogynist, since the only basis given for dismissing Jack as unable to "assume the rol[e]" of a man is his profound devotion to his wife. Her student's views are certainly ironic, given Harris's prior celebration of the "benefit" of marriage, but the unanswered addition "because she can beat him up?" reveals precisely the "flaw" in Jack's performance as Odessa's husband: he stays loyal to his wife not from a stoic sense of duty, nor as a result of iron-willed discipline or a vaguely defined "morality," but out of simple devotion to Odessa, and a single-minded willingness to please her. For Harris's student, such devotion must signify cowardice or weakness, indicating the extent to which traditional "manliness" or masculinity has in this view been divorced from emotional vulnerability. That Jack is interested in pleasing his wife because he values her as a human being seems an impossibility in such a rigidly gendered universe.

Such an interpretation of Jack is all the more troubling when one compares it to Walker's actual description of the character. Celie's two-paragraph discussion of Odessa's husband, including her sense of what his pants should be like, sounds much more like a man who is self-assured but unwilling to dominate with his body or his voice, a man very far from the fearful, "henpecked" object of ridicule outlined in the essay:

I sit looking out across the yard trying to see in my mind what a pair of pants for Jack would look like. Jack is tall and kind and don't hardly say anything. Love children. Respect his wife, Odessa, and all Odessa amazon sisters. Anything she want to take on, he right there. Never talking much, tho. That's the main thing. And then I remember one time he touch me. And it felt like his fingers had eyes. Felt like he knew me all over, but he just touch my arm up near the shoulder.

I start to make pants for Jack. They have to be camel. And soft and strong. And they have to have big pockets so he can keep a lot of children's things. . . And they have to be washable and they have to fit closer round the leg than Shug's so he can run if he need to snatch a child out of the way of something. And they have to be something he can lay back in when he hold Odessa in front of the fire. (220)

Jack is here associated with kindness and gentleness toward adults he encounters, as well as with a generous paternal affection for children and a genuine respect and love for his wife. That this particular character in *The Color Purple*, almost idealized in his positivity, can be dismissed as "middle-aged and henpecked" suggests that there is more at stake than "negative portrayals of black men" in critiques such as the one outlined in Harris's essay. In fact, what seems to underlie this misleading emphasis on "negative portrayals" is a rigid adherence to gender norms—norms that Walker's narrative challenges, norms without which the very boundaries of feminine and masculine subjectivity become dangerously indeterminate.

This reliance upon strict gender regulations, as well as upon the heteronormativity that gender binaries make possible, is clear in the student's subsequent dismissal, as described by Harris, of Albert's transformation from patriarchal tyrant to thoughtful and generous companion for Celie and Shug; rather than read this shift as a "positive" redemption, Harris notes, the student continues to insist that "[n]o man in the novel is respectable . . . not even Albert (because he can only change in terms of doing things that are traditionally considered sissified, such as sewing and gossiping)."[43] In another parenthetical interjection, Albert's reformation is here trivialized through its association with feminine, or effeminate, behaviors. It is hardly surprising that Harris (through her student) uses the language of respectability to describe Albert's alleged failures, since that language is consistent with the terms of the salvific wish, dependent as it is upon the black community's sexual and domestic repression in the service of appearing "respectable." Neither is the use of the term "sissified"—often understood to be a synonym for male homosexuality—a coincidence here, since gender-bending and queerness are so closely associated in Walker's text. That the student uses the term so uncritically, however, again points to a disturbing undercurrent of misogyny and homophobia, because it openly assumes that gay men, or straight men who behave in nontraditional ways, are somehow emasculated, "stripped" of their (assumed static and naturalized) abilities to be "real men."

As I note above, this rigidly heteronormative critique has been echoed in articles by male writers such as Mel Watkins, Philip Royster, Darryl Pinckney, and David Bradley. In uncanny agreement with Harris's student, for example, Bradley writes, "Black men in Alice Walker's fiction and poetry seem capable of goodness only when they become old . . . or paralyzed and feminized."[44] In either case, such men are, in Bradley's view, "symbolically impotent," and thus poor candidates for the title "positive black man." But as one more contemporary scholar of Walker's work asks, "Why do critics denigrate brutal characters who become nurturing?"[45] I would answer her question with a few of my own—why are patriarchal dominance and masculinity so closely aligned? Can a man remain "really" a man if he no longer possesses—or claims—the power to command? Who might a father become once he is no longer a patriarch? And if, as Martha Fineman suggests, "control, dominance, and independence are quintessentially masculine,"[46] then how might we—as writers, as literary scholars, as cultural critics, as a community of African Americans—reconceive manhood in a way that is not so dependent upon parallel binaries of male/female, strong/weak, potent/impotent, straight/sissified?

Walker's reply to such questions can be found in her novel, in characters such as Shug and Sofia, who challenge a traditional and submissive femininity, as well as Albert/Mr.——, who learns to relinquish his power to dominate in order to engage in more human and egalitarian relationships with everyone around him. Indeed, Walker's depiction of a family whose boundaries are indistinct and constantly shifting *relies* upon the decentralization of patriarchal figures such as Albert, for as long as the traditional father, empowered to dominate all younger men and all women, remains at the center of the family, rigid hierarchies will remain in place. As Barbara Ehrenreich notes in another context, patriarchy's dissolution "creates an opportunity for men and women to begin to meet as equals without the pretenses involved in gender roles, and to get together against our common sources of oppression. . . . Potentially, we can be brothers and sisters, comrades and lovers."[47] The radical symmetry between genders that this vision implies is certainly inspiring, though if Walker's critics are to be believed, it is also deeply frightening, verging on impossible to contemplate. For Walker demands an entirely new way of defining and understanding gender and male-female interaction, one that begins with men who are men *in spite of* patriarchal power, not because of it. In fact, Walker's text remains a bit enigmatic about the role that men can or should play in the "new" black family—rather than clearly delineating a man's place, she leaves several alternatives open, as evidenced, for example, by the difference between Jack's quiet confidence, Harpo's grudging acquiescence, and Albert's philosophical companionship. By the end of the novel, gender binaries seem no longer to apply to these characters; none of Walker's men, despite the claims of Harris's student, merely become "feminine" or reverse the gender hierarchy. Instead, they behave in ways that seem to transcend traditional notions of gender, leaving room for a multitude of pleasurable possibilities.

Indeed, *The Color Purple* presents precisely the kind of "open future" articulated by Judith Butler in her essay, "The End of Sexual Difference?" Writing about why such an unresolved eventuality is so difficult for some to accept, Butler suggests:

> The desire not to have an open future can be a strong one, threatening one with loss, loss of certainty about how things are. . . . This is one reason that asking certain questions is considered dangerous. Imagine the situation of reading a book and thinking, I cannot ask the questions that are posed here because to ask them is to introduce doubt into my political convictions, and to introduce doubt into my political

convictions could lead to the dissolution of those convictions. At such a moment, the fear of thinking, indeed, the fear of the question, becomes the moralized defense of politics. And politics becomes that which requires a certain anti-intellectualism. To remain unwilling to rethink one's politics on the basis of questions posed is to opt for a dogmatic stand at the cost of both life and thought.[48]

If we replace the words "political convictions" with the words "sexual (or gender) subjectivity," and the word "politics" with "oppositional gender roles" (or "heteronormativity"), it is clear that Butler's indictment of such fear has much relevance in the case of Walker's text. For Walker's is a novel that poses "dangerous" questions about the black family, and by extension the black community—since as Gilroy notes in this essay's epigraph, family has come to serve as the central metaphor for community and nation in black political discourse (even as that discourse has dismissed actual families and family dynamics as outside the realm of the political precisely because struggles that take place within families primarily concern women). By challenging conventional definitions of the black family, indeed, by challenging the very figure of the black patriarch, Walker challenges the very structure of the black community, inasmuch as that community is considered a kind of black patriarchal family-writ-large.

In the same essay from which the epigraph is drawn, Gilroy rails, and rightly so, against the way in which a discourse of race-as-family has repeatedly been used "to interpret the crisis of black politics and social life as a crisis of black masculinity alone"; he goes on to argue that "disastrous consequences [will] follow when the family supplies the only symbols of political agency we can find in the culture and the only object upon which that agency can be seen to operate."[49] While I agree with the potential dangers of this discourse, I am just as convinced that the hegemony of such discourse allows for sustained critique of both traditional family structures and the nation or community of which they are assumed to be microcosms. Rather than simply taking the family (and the gender binaries that underlie it) as a static, naturalized entity that cannot help but limit our conception of politics, it might be useful to consider how, within a culture that already takes family as the model for nation, the family itself can be redefined, and in the process can unsettle political "givens" that might otherwise remain equally fixed. In other words, by reexamining the ways that Walker's queering of the black patriarch, and disruption of oppositional gender roles within the black family, cast her as a kind of authorial "traitor," scholars of her work might better understand how the rigid sexual and familial hierarchies upon which the salvific wish is based foreclose a whole host of alternative familial *and* national possibilities.

In the next chapter, I further interrogate black nationalism, this time considering how the black "national" subject in the final decade of the twentieth century was shaped by histories of cross-racial intimate involvement. Through a reading of racial identity in Toni Morrison's 1997 novel *Paradise,* I suggest that there is a parallel between the strict policing of group borders, increasingly necessary in the ideological construction of a rigidly "pure" black nationhood, and the salvific wish's policing of moral boundaries. Individual transgressions cannot exist unchallenged in either case, for they pose a material and metaphorical threat to fictions of community sanctity. Such fictions take on particular urgency, I argue, when the multiracial origins of putatively monoracial black bodies are made visible—such that one way of understanding the doubled vulnerability of "blackness" is to acknowledge the category's complex racial origins, origins that have been masked by the disciplinary labors of both black nationalism and uplift ideology.

Chapter 4

Intimate Borders

*These telltale green eyes and that never quite dark
enough skin create a rather precise index of the traditions of racial commingling that exist more or less
comfortably under the sign of blackness. The black
in America has the maddening tendency to reveal
in her eyes, skin, hair, in her body a history of contact and conquest, of slavery and rebellion, in which
the African is certainly central, but never alone.*
    —Robert Reid-Pharr, "At Home in America"

*The future belongs to the impure. The future belongs
to those who are ready to take in a bit of the other, as
well as being what they themselves are.*
    —Stuart Hall, "Subjects in History:
    Making Diasporic Identities"

In October 1997, the U.S. Office of Management and Budget (OMB)
announced the results of several years of deliberation regarding the
addition of a "multiracial" category to federal guidelines for classify-
ing race and ethnicity. Adding such a category would have altered not
only the U.S. Census, a major focal point of the preceding debate, but
also federal civil rights compliance monitoring, which evaluates civic,
employment, and educational programs for their adherence to anti-
discriminatory law. Since the mid-1960s, such monitoring has relied
upon standardized data on race and ethnicity for accuracy.[1] Although
multiracial activists, including leaders of Project RACE (Reclassify
All Children Equally) and the AMEA (Association of Multi-Ethnic
Americans), had proposed that the federal guidelines be altered to include a separate box for "multiracial" status in addition to a "mark-all-
that-apply" option, the OMB ultimately accepted only the latter as an
actual alteration to the federal categories.[2]

For many African American leaders, this decision must surely have come as somewhat of a relief, given the numerous concerns raised by organizations such as the NAACP and the National Urban League about the possible institution of a "multiracial" category—concerns which, in addition to understandable apprehension about potentially adverse effects on civil rights compliance monitoring, also included speculation that such a category could lead to a racialized caste system in the United States, or a shift to a system more like apartheid South Africa, in which mixed-race individuals form a "colored" buffer class between blacks and whites.[3] Even more extreme alarmist arguments were made against the idea of a multiracial category among some high-ranking African American officials; for instance, civil rights leader and former executive director of the United Negro College Fund, Arthur A. Fletcher, testified before a House subcommittee that

> [A] whole host of light-skinned Black Americans [will run] for the door the minute they have another choice. And it won't necessarily be because their immediate parents are Black, White, or whatever, but all of a sudden they have a way of saying, "I am something other than Black." . . . I am ready to bet that if that category were added you would see a significant diminution in the number of Black Americans who under the present set of circumstances are identified as Black.[4]

In other words, simply having the option of self-identifying as "something other than Black" would have been likely to drive certain "light-skinned" individuals right out of the race, in a sort of mass exodus from blackness—an escape to the "multiracial" promised land.

The irony of Fletcher's remarks is how wrong they proved to be—in the 2000 census, the first in which Americans had the opportunity to "mark all that apply" among racial categories, the percentage of the population that identified themselves *solely* as "Black or African American" remained steady, at right around 12 percent (in fact, the fraction of respondents who identified themselves solely as black was slightly *greater* in 2000 than in 1990).[5] A part of the reason I am interested in Fletcher's comments is precisely that they turned out to be so far off base—the 2000 census results suggest that far from looking for an escape from the stigma of "blackness," most African Americans are intent on maintaining that racial status, in spite of their actual historic ties to multiraciality. The reasons for this are complex, and have much to do with both class politics and the social and cultural history of "blackness" in the United States.[6]

Fletcher's comments assume that fair-skinned blacks would have little motivation for accepting African American identity beyond the restrictive logic of hypodescent (the one-drop rule), a logic that makes it difficult, in the United States, to claim an identity other than black if one has any African ancestry.[7] His words may seem to boil down to skin color, but I would argue that they also imply class privilege, and that this unspoken implication gives the comments their sociopolitical weight. More than one scholar has suggested that historically, large numbers of the black bourgeoisie have been fair-skinned and/or of multiracial ancestry.[8] Indeed, literature from the late nineteenth through the mid-twentieth century has portrayed the black elite as overwhelmingly fair-skinned, with dark-skinned middle-class black characters notable enough to merit astonishment in some cases.[9] Yet as recently as 1998, scholar Kathleen Korgen noted that "Light-complected blacks dominate the middle and professional classes of African Americans."[10] Sociological studies repeatedly confirm the fact that even for contemporary blacks, lighter skin color means a much greater likelihood of high socioeconomic status relative to other black Americans.[11] Thus it is possible, even likely, that when Fletcher suggests that "light-skinned" blacks would run for the door when presented with the first opportunity, he really is attempting to identify a kind of *class*-based racial alienation, one which only appears to be driven by skin color.[12]

Indeed, I raise this anecdote here, in a chapter focusing on representations of race-based intimacy in Toni Morrison's 1997 novel *Paradise*, because related questions about skin color and class, racial belonging, and the meaning of multiraciality to the so-called monoracial are at the very heart of Morrison's text, written during a decade fraught with intraracial ambivalence and confusion about what it meant to be "black" in the post–civil rights era. In 1991, for instance, an article appeared on the front page of the *New York Times* declaring that "intense doubts and disagreements" prevailed in contemporary discussions of black identity.[13] The article reported that "The ever-changing black experience in America is being assessed with a new intensity[. . . .] Not since the 1960s has there been such an intense focus on [the meaning of] blackness."[14] Interracial contrasts and disputes were hardly inconspicuous during the period—witness, for example, the differing views of many whites and blacks on the 1995 O. J. Simpson verdict[15]—but contrary to earlier moments in American history, there seemed to be equal emphasis on what African Americans could or should do among themselves to effect sociopolitical change. Intraracial atonement and responsibility was the theme, for example, of Louis Farrakhan's Million Man March, which also took place in 1995.[16]

Morrison's 1997 novel takes up some of this contemporary concern with African American identity, in a narrative depicting an all-black Oklahoma town in the 1970s. It should come as no surprise that Morrison's text looks back to an earlier moment in order to discuss these issues, since intraracial debate in the 1990s can be traced to changes that took place more than twenty-five years prior. In chapter 2 of this volume, I argued that Morrison's novel *Sula* uses the year 1965 as a temporal touchstone for the shift to a more public vilification of black intimate conduct in American cultural parlance—a vilification in which many bourgeois blacks attempted to participate as a means of distinguishing themselves from the so-called "pathology" of black poverty. Yet 1965 ultimately marks only the beginning of an increasingly powerful rift between impoverished and well-off blacks, because of the numerous civil rights gains that came before or during that year, and which launched unprecedented numbers of blacks into the middle class.[17] Indeed, Cornel West identifies the "black nationalist moment" of the post-1965 civil rights era as "principally the activity of black petit bourgeois self-congratulation and self-justification upon reaching an anxiety-ridden, middle-class status in racist American society."[18] Yet after the dismantling of black radicalism in the late 1970s, the conservative backlash of the Reagan era encouraged the assimilation of many in the black middle class, even as the impoverished black majority receded from the national stage.[19] And by 1993, when Fletcher made his comments, blacks across the socioeconomic spectrum had begun to realize that a number of those who had "made it" in the eyes of mainstream America were completely divorced from the continuing realities of black life.[20]

Fletcher's dire forecast taps into this seeming opposition between mainstream success and racial consciousness—but misses, in the process, what Henry Louis Gates has suggested is a nearly universal fact of black life in the United States: "the truth is that blacks—across the economic and ideological spectrum—often feel astonishingly vulnerable to charges of inauthenticity, of disloyalty to the race."[21] If anything, Fletcher's comments demonstrate that this "near universal" vulnerability to accusations of racial inauthenticity applies with special intensity to the black middle class; after all, what are his predictions of "light-skinned flight" other than covert charges of racial disloyalty on the part of the fair-skinned and/or bourgeois?

This question of black racial loyalty, which plays a central role in Morrison's novel, seems a quintessentially intraracial question, one concerned with the complex internal politics of African American identity. Surprisingly, however, *Paradise* has been read by a number of critics as Morrison's commentary on white American exceptionalism and the Puritan roots of the American republic, including the "city on a hill" rhetoric of the nation's founding fathers.[22] Even the work of a scholar like Richard Schur, who situates the novel within critical race theory and takes for granted the notion that Morrison's writing is suffused with the politics of her contemporary moment, overlooks the fact that Morrison's text—while certainly preoccupied with race—seems deliberately to focus on intraracial rather than interracial concerns.[23] The central conflicts of the novel have to do with the perceived boundaries of black identity and community; indeed, it may be fair to describe *Paradise* as a novel about black nationalism and its discontents. Thus in this chapter I want to take seriously, and rather literally, Morrison's depiction of "the one all-black town worth the pain."[24] Rather than interpreting this town, Ruby, as some sort of allegorical version of Euro-American nationalism—a critical move that takes the rather remarkable step of re-centering whiteness while discussing a text from which overt representations of whiteness have deliberately been excluded—I intend to read it as precisely what it seems to be. That is, a deeply flawed model of African American community-building, driven by what is undeniably a black nationalist impulse.

Jeffrey Stout makes an important geographical distinction in his discussion of the term "black nationalism," suggesting that the ideology is concerned specifically with African American culture and community.[25] This distinction is crucial, because while black nationalism (or nationalisms) in the broadest sense might certainly be understood as a "global phenomenon," the nationalism that I believe is taken up by Morrison's novel is quite specific to the United States.[26] Indeed, it has taken on a peculiar and ironic importance among African Americans, given their lack of geographic or political autonomy, situated as they are within the larger national body of the United States.[27] Wahneema Lubiano defines black American nationalism as "black common sense," and suggests that it "has acted both as a bulwark against racism and as disciplinary activity within the group."[28] Further, she describes it as a "sign, an analytic," which describes "a range of historically manifested ideas about black American possibilities that include any or all of the following: racial solidarity, cultural specificity, religious, economic, and political separatism."[29] All of these seem to be at work in Morrison's fictional all-black town of Ruby, Oklahoma.

Furthermore, and perhaps not surprisingly, given what we have already come to understand about the African American subject's fraught relationship to issues of sexuality and domesticity, the issues of black community, racial identity, and nation-building in *Paradise* remain closely linked to the issue of intimacy. Lubiano has suggested that black nationalism "reinscribes the state in particular places within its own narratives of resistance[. . . .] most often [. . .] within black nationalist narratives of the black family."[30] Indeed, as was also evident in the previous chapter of this volume, the idea of a nationalist "family romance" is deeply dependent upon conservative notions of domestic and sexual decorum—particularly on the part of black women—that resonate quite strongly with uplift ideology and historical notions of black respectability.[31] Ultimately, my reading of *Paradise* in this chapter draws a parallel between the strict policing of group borders, which is often necessary in the ideological construction of black nationhood, and the policing of intimate boundaries required by the particular manifestation of uplift ideology that I call the salvific wish. Individual indiscretions must be suppressed in either case, for they pose a literal and figurative threat to fictions of community inviolability held sacred in both political and personal contexts.

"In the Convent were those women": Paradise and the Salvific Wish

I will return specifically to *Paradise* in a moment, but at this juncture it might be useful to offer a few additional details about this concept of the "salvific wish," as I have outlined it in previous chapters. The salvific wish is best understood as an aspiration, most often but not solely middle-class and female, to save or rescue the black community from white racist accusations of sexual or domestic pathology through the embrace of conventional bourgeois propriety. Historically, it has been located in social institutions such as the black church, as well as the black women's club movement, which began in large part as a response to moral defamation of black women in the U.S. public sphere. At the end of the nineteenth century, both black women's church groups and secular women's clubs were grounded in the popular ideology of racial "uplift," which consisted primarily of the conviction that a communal focus on "self-help, racial solidarity, temperance, thrift, chastity, social purity, patriarchal authority, and the accumulation of wealth" would improve the situation of blacks in American society.[32]

The salvific wish is closely related to (and, indeed, springs from) this ideology of "uplift," although unlike uplift in its larger sense, the salvific wish limits its focus to fostering black domestic and sexual respectability. In addition, because the salvific wish has historically placed such a high value on maintaining a protective illusion of black sexual and familial propriety, it has been most interested in observing and policing *female* behavior—precisely because the black female body has so often been characterized by whites as the sole source of black intimate or domestic irregularity. Yet it is also crucial to note that the expression of the salvific wish need not be limited to women—even if its disciplinary emphasis attends mostly (or solely) to women's behavior. In other words, as we saw in chapter 3, the salvific wish is just as easily expressed by men in reference to women as it is expressed by women in reference to themselves.

Given the endurance of pathologizing narratives of black intimacy and domesticity in the U.S. cultural imaginary, the continued presence of the salvific wish in contemporary black culture should not be difficult to perceive, in spite of the virtual disappearance of uplift ideology more generally as a viable political strategy for contemporary blacks. Indeed, I argue that the salvific wish remains culturally relevant in the twentieth century, and continues to shape the ways that blacks publicly express sexual and familial issues. At the very least, the logic of the salvific wish remains subject to interrogation and critique in black women's fiction of the twentieth century. Twentieth century fictional narratives by black women are most likely to challenge the salvific wish's exclusive emphasis on black female behavior and the double standard created when the wish, even as it is expressed by men, remains single-mindedly focused on the disciplining of women.

I would like to return to Morrison's 1997 novel, *Paradise.* Set in the fictional all-black town of Ruby, Oklahoma, the novel opens with a provocative and oft-remarked-upon first sentence: "They shoot the white girl first."[33] The "white girl" in question is one of five women living in an abandoned mansion and former Indian girls' school seventeen miles outside of Ruby, ironically called "The Convent" by Ruby residents (presumably because the defunct school was once run by Catholic nuns). The Convent, and the women who inhabit it, are perceived by several of Ruby's male leaders to be a serious threat to Ruby's stability:

> Outrages that had been accumulating all along took shape as evidence. A mother was knocked down the stairs by her cold-eyed daughter. Four damaged infants were born in one family. Daughters refused to get out of bed. Brides disappeared on their honeymoons. Two brothers shot each other on New Year's Day. Trips to Demby for VD shots

common[. . . .T]he one thing that connected all these catastrophes was
in the Convent. And in the Convent were those women. (11)

Upon reading this passage, narrated from the perspective of the men
who seek to eliminate the Convent women, it should be immediately apparent that an interrogation of the salvific wish is at work in
Morrison's narrative. This is evident not simply in the men's single-
minded focus on scapegoating and disciplining the Convent women
as women, but also in the actual examples of social calamity for which
these women have been blamed. Each piece of "evidence" given (in-
solent daughters, warring brothers, vanishing brides) has at its center
a concern with black intimate disruption, the very social ill that the
salvific wish hopes to guard against. And in light of the salvific wish's
nearly exclusive focus on women's behavior, the fact that the cure for
this disruption is the policing of a group of women seen to embody
sexual and domestic *im*propriety is hardly surprising.

Still, I would like to suggest that this scapegoating of Convent
women is only one way in which Morrison's narrative interrogates the
salvific wish—and a superficial one, at that. It would be all too easy to
use a rather simplistic binary opposition between the town of Ruby and
the space of the Convent (which Morrison's own narrative structures
initially seem to encourage) to interpret the novel as a straightforward
critique of the patriarchal tyranny of Ruby's (male) leaders and an un-
complicated defense of libertine community "outsiders" represented by
the Convent women. The fact that Ruby is an all-black town and the
Convent is all-female, racially integrated by at least one "white girl," further supports this binary, and suggests that *Paradise* intentionally overlaps interrogation of (black) patriarchy with interrogation of a racially
exclusive black nationalist agenda.[34] While there is certainly accuracy
in and value to this reading, I believe that there is more to be said, and
with more complexity, about the ways in which Morrison's narrative is
both interrogative and critical of the salvific wish—and the source of
this alternative reading lies not simply in the opposition between Ruby
and the Convent, but also within the confines of Ruby itself.

Some additional information about the town of Ruby might be useful here. Ruby was established in 1949 from the remnants of another,

once-thriving Oklahoma town called Haven, founded by nine black families in 1890. Disillusioned with the way they were being treated in the post-Reconstruction South, these families had traveled west from Mississippi and Louisiana to Oklahoma, "unwelcome on each grain of soil from Yazoo to Fort Smith" (13). Not only were the families turned or chased away by "rich Choctaw and poor whites," they were rejected by other blacks, "too poor, too bedraggled-looking to enter, let alone reside in, the communities that were soliciting Negro homesteaders" (14). Yet each of these rejections dims in comparison to the final rebuff, the one that gives the town its ultimate shape—Haven comes into existence only after the nine families are denied entry to yet another black town, aptly named "Fairly, Oklahoma."

This town, Fairly, is peopled by light-skinned, middle-class blacks. Fairly's leaders reject the nine families on the basis of those families' "8-rock" skin color, which as the text suggests, is almost supernaturally dark: "8-R. An abbreviation for eight-rock, a deep deep level in the coal mines. Blue black people, tall and graceful" (193). This rejection, called "The Disallowing" by Haven families and their offspring, forms the basis of Haven's, and later Ruby's, sense of community, giving them a historical incident around which to unify themselves: "Afterwards the people were no longer nine families and some more. They became a tight band of wayfarers bound by the enormity of what had happened to them" (189). As the text makes clear, Fairly's rejection of the 8-rock families is one of numerous refusals that the group experiences on its way to Oklahoma, but this rejection alone has the power to define the town and its descendants: "Everything anybody wanted to know about the citizens of Haven or Ruby lay in the ramifications of that one rebuff out of many" (189). As I will discuss further in a moment, part of the community's subsequent bond was based in their adherence to a retaliatory "blood rule," which demanded that 8-rocks marry only other 8-rocks rather than introduce any white or part-white genes into their families.

In this history of Haven, Morrison highlights how intraracial class and color discrimination resonates with white racism—a point that several of the novel's critics have already made. Schur, for example, argues "this border between light- and dark-skinned black constituted an internalization of the system of racial hierarchy established by whites."[35] Morrison's narrative certainly seems to critique the "blue-eyed, gray-eyed yellowmen in good suits" (195) who simultaneously value black community (in the form of their own all-black settlement) and "disallow" blacks of a certain caste and color from that community (in the form of the dark-skinned and impoverished families they turn away). Yet this story of Haven's founding is also a reminder of contradictions inherent to what might be understood as the black nationalist impulse, from that idea's earliest inception. As Wilson Moses has suggested in his study of black nationalism at the turn of the twentieth century, early black nationalist figures often covertly (or overtly) embraced aspects of white culture, espousing "assimilationist attitudes" which ultimately evidenced contempt for the very blackness they worked to preserve.[36]

The response of Haven's leaders to this contradiction is to create one of their own, for the founding families of Haven, and later Ruby, enact another intraracial hierarchy—which as Magali Michael suggests, "simply reverse[s] the racism they themselves suffered by excluding all who are not so dark as themselves."[37] As I have already mentioned, Haven and Ruby residents' adherence to the "blood rule," the demand that 8-rock blood be kept "pure" and unadulterated by whiteness in any form, is a disciplinary condition of the bond they share. Individuals who violate the rule, while not actually banished from the community, are subject to multiple forms of correction, including but not limited to the figurative expulsion of their families from the community's narrative of origins (this narrative is represented in the text by a holiday play in which children from the community reenact the Disallowing in a format similar to the Christian nativity).

In this chapter, I agree with other critics who suggest that Morrison's depiction of the 8-rocks' blood rule can be read allegorically. But rather than the common contention that the blood rule serves as an inverted metaphor for white racism, I argue that it stands in for specifically *black* discourses of cultural authenticity, usually nationalist in origin. In other words, Morrison's 8-rocks corporealize something that usually exists for African Americans as a social ideal—intraracial loyalty. And in critiquing the 8-rocks, Morrison implicitly critiques the very notion of racial authenticity, in the process commenting upon the frequent suppression of the multiracial in authenticity discourse. I will return to this point in more depth later, but I want first to look more closely at how the blood rule operates in Morrison's novel. There are two characters in the text who violate the rule directly—Roger Best and Menus Jury—and a third, Deacon Morgan, who comes very close to it. Both of the first two characters' experiences in the text raise larger questions about black intimacy *and* black nationhood. I will try to outline some of these here before turning to a more detailed reading of Deacon's extramarital affair, which I think is the most provocative (and productive) racialized encounter in the novel, and which will return us to the question not only of the Convent, but of intimacy and the so-called "monoracial" versus "multiracial" black body.

"The dung we leaving behind": Class, Sex, and (Black) Racial Purity

Roger Best is the first founding member of the 8-rock families to violate the "blood rule," marrying a "hazel-eyed girl with light-brown hair" named Delia, "who'd had his child during the war" (201). This child is Pat (Patricia) Best, who as an adult becomes the self-appointed "historian" of Ruby; Morrison's readers learn of Delia's arrival in Haven, as well as her tragic death in Ruby only a few years later, in a section of the text entitled "Patricia." In a combination journal entry and letter to her long-dead parent, Pat writes: "Their jaws must have dropped when [you] arrived, but [. . . . o]nly Steward had the gall to say out loud, 'He's bringing along the dung we leaving behind'" (201). The implication of this comment from Steward (another 8-rock, and a financial and social leader of the town) is clear—in a peculiar reversal of the "one drop rule" historically used to exclude mixed-race blacks from whiteness, Delia's "polluted" racial history makes her unfit for membership in the 8-rocks' *black* community.

Further, although Roger is allowed to bring his wife and their child along with him on the journey from Haven to Ruby, Delia's seemingly unnecessary death in childbirth after her arrival might easily be interpreted as a punishment indirectly exacted for Roger's disobedience to the blood rule:

> The women really tried, Mama. [. . .] You must have believed that deep down they hated you, but not all of them, maybe none of them, because they begged the men to go to the Convent to get help. I heard them. [. . .] Even with their wives begging [the men] came up with excuses because they looked down on you, Mama, I know it, and despised Daddy for marrying a wife with no last name, a wife without people, a wife of sunlight skin, a wife of racial tampering. (197)

Not surprisingly, it is the men of Ruby, its economic, social and political leaders, who overrule the women and allow Delia to die. Just as in Walker's *The Color Purple*, the men of a community take as their prerogative the disciplining of errant female behavior. The men make this decision for the community because Delia's death serves an additional political purpose in the narrative, beyond even that of punishing Best. This woman whose skin color represents only "racial tampering" to the 8-rocks is permitted to die, in part, because she reminds them that the purity they so cherish is maintained in deliberate response to the anguish of the Disallowing. Her presence—and the presence of her surviving, light-skinned child—signifies that from which the 8-rocks have defensively distanced themselves in order to become a cohesive community. As Pat notes, "[Your skin] bothered them. Reminded them of why Haven existed, of why a new town had to take its place" (200).

It is no coincidence, however, that this human emblem of racial pollution, whom the 8-rock men so callously eliminate, might also be understood as an embodiment of *sexual* pollution, and that the racial contamination she threatens comes in the sexualized form of adulterated offspring. After all, Pat is born to Delia out-of-wedlock, and only later becomes Roger's legitimate child. This transgression alone marks Delia as outside of social norms of respectability in Ruby, as Pat's description of herself as "bastard-born" (203) makes clear. More importantly, Delia is described more than once in the text as a woman with "no last name," a woman without "people"—in other words, a woman who may herself be "bastard-born," and who has no established family origins. Delia, with her lack of traceable parentage, with her illegitimate child, is situated outside those markers of sexual and domestic respectability so cherished by the salvific wish; she is as much of an outsider to the wish-driven values of the Ruby community as are the Convent women, but because she is Roger Best's wife, she is a source of intimate pollution living *inside* the community, corrupting it from within.

It is crucial to recall, here, that the history of miscegenation in the United States has been largely a history of illegitimacy, since at least the moment when a statute dictating that offspring of interracial sexual unions should "follow the condition of the mother" was written into law in the seventeenth century.[38] This statute, along with the "one drop" rule of hypodescent that was established later, made the sexual exploitation of enslaved black women by white male slave owners a culturally defensible, economically viable behavior for wealthy white men, and created the wide variety of skin colors and other phenotypic traits which, as Robert Reid-Pharr notes in this chapter's first epigraph, "exist more or less comfortably under the sign of blackness."[39]

The 8-rocks in Morrison's narrative are well aware of this history and its implications about the origin of skin as light as Delia's. This awareness is concretized in the group's horror of the "white man's kitchen," not because of a distaste for domestic labor per se, but because of the proximity to whites and the potential for exploitation and abuse that came along with it:

> They were proud that none of their women had ever worked in a white man's kitchen or nursed a white child. Although field labor was harder and carried no status, they believed the rape of women who worked in white kitchens was if not a certainty a distinct possibility—neither of which they could bear to contemplate. So they exchanged that danger for the relative safety of brutal work. (99)

The irony, of course, is that the possibility these 8-rock men cannot "bear to contemplate" had already achieved the status of certainty on plantations throughout the South—for what was to prevent a slave owner from himself going out to the fields and slave quarters in search of his victims?[40] The 8-rocks may have fantasized that field labor shielded the women they claimed from harm, but centuries of history had already proven otherwise, as Morrison herself, author of a carefully researched, prizewinning novel about slavery, was surely aware.[41] Already it is clear that a willful blindness to the realities of black American history is a part of the 8-rocks' carefully maintained "purity," a point to which I will return later.

Nonetheless, Delia's not-quite-white body provides one conceptual link, in Morrison's narrative, between the regulation of the Convent women's sexual and domestic behavior, driven by the salvific wish, and the disciplining of the (male) 8-rocks racial behavior, driven by a conservative black nationalist impulse. Delia's light skin, her incomplete, "polluted" blackness, is implicitly associated with sexual degeneracy—a connection that is made explicit in later generations. Menus Jury, for example, the second of the 8-rock men to attempt to violate the blood rule, is persuaded not to wed the "pretty sandy-haired girl from Virginia" whom he brings home to marry (195). Interestingly enough, the first time this woman is mentioned in the novel, she is described, with no further explanation, as a prostitute. Musing about the townspeople's reactions to her own unstraightened hair, Anna Flood makes the association in passing: "The subject [Anna's natural hair] summoned more passion, invited more opinions, solicited more anger than that prostitute Menus brought home from Virginia" (119). Any reader who is aware of the complex politics of hair in African American culture will probably notice the irony, here, that a town full of putatively "pure" black people nonetheless expects women to artificially straighten their hair—yet I am ultimately more interested in Anna's uncritical, color-driven classification of Menus's fiancée.[42]

The motivation behind Anna's thinking becomes clear only much later in the text, in sections of the novel narrated from the perspectives of Pat Best and of Lone DuPres, an orphan who was adopted by the DuPres family as the nine 8-rock families journeyed toward Haven in 1890. The town's former midwife, a never-married woman in her 80s,

Lone is enough of an outsider to see Menus's story more objectively—as is Pat, who rather neutrally notes that the 8-rock fathers forced Menus "to give back or return the woman he brought home to marry" (195). Lone's commentary on the subject reveals even more than Pat's, as she acknowledges "the shame [Menus] felt at having let Harper and the others talk him out of marrying that woman he brought home. That pretty redbone girl they told him was not good enough for him; said she was more like a fast woman than a bride" (278). Lone's description of the events surrounding the woman's arrival and departure reveals that Anna's use of the term "prostitute" is probably not based in fact— Menus's fiancée was only "*like* a fast woman." The question of what about her seems so "fast" is answered via further attention to the text.

By the time Menus has brought home a "redbone" woman of his own, nearly twenty years after Delia's death in 1953, the miscegenated body's assumed illegitimacy of *origins* has been transformed into an assumed sexual availability, an embodied *desire* for the illegitimate. In other words, for Ruby's second generation of 8-rocks, no longer does light skin signify merely "racial tampering" and the moral frailty of white men who have repeatedly violated enslaved black women's bodies. Instead, that skin has come to signify a deeper corporeal flaw—Ruby's citizens translate the prior violence of interracial victimization into a symbol of pure, future violability. This eerily reverses the racialized sexual politics of contemporary Western culture, in which darker skin is continually associated with sexual excess.[43] Hence Menus's fiancée is read by Anna, almost in passing, as a prostitute—not coincidentally, in that moment in the narrative her fair skin goes unmentioned, for it is implied in the description of her as a whore.

Similarly, when Patricia Best's daughter, Billie Delia, is first referenced in the novel, she is described as "the fastest girl in town and speeding up by the second" (59), but her "odd, rosy-tan skin and wayward brown hair" (93) are not mentioned until many pages later. As Rob Davidson notes, "Billie Delia is denigrated not for the stated moral reason—an innocent childhood event of dropping her britches in public when she was three years old (150–51), [. . .] but for the unstated reason: she is light-skinned."[44] In fact, despite the town's belief that she is the "wild one" (151), Billie Delia is actually a virgin, while her 8-rock best friend Arnette has sex at fourteen and becomes pregnant out of wedlock. Yet because "skin color trumps morality every time in Ruby"[45]—indeed, because skin color *concretizes* morality in the town—Billie Delia's sexual depravity is assumed.

This certainly explains Pat's realization that "ever since Billie Delia was an infant, she [Pat] thought of her as a liability somehow. Vulnerable to the possibility of not being quite as much of a lady as [Pat] would like" (203). This reference, not only to being a "lady" but to the complex, racialized vulnerability that ladylike behavior is meant to hide, resonates openly with the ideology of the salvific wish. Indeed, in what clearly seems a capitulation to the wish's logic of individual and communal recuperation through a rigidly maintained social decorum, Patricia has already worked strenuously to discipline her own behavior:

> She [. . .] had trained herself to reasoning and soft manners and discretion and dignity[.] Educated but self-taught also to make sure that everybody knew that the bastard-born daughter of the woman with sunlight skin and no last name was not only lovely but of great worth and inestimable value. (203)

As such, Billie Delia's skin color, and subsequent reputation, is a liability to Pat—one that Pat cannot overcome as easily as she believes she has overcome the stigma of her own skin color. Like Lutie's violent disciplining of Bub in *The Street*, necessary in order to distance herself symbolically from the moral laxity represented by Lil, Patricia's attempts to control the *ideological* meaning of Billie Delia's body result in a physical confrontation. Grasping a "1950s GE electric iron called Royal Ease," she "missed killing her own daughter by inches" (203); this violence, Pat belatedly realizes, has little to do with the truth of Billie Delia's character: "The Royal Ease in her hand as she ran up the stairs was there to smash the young girl that lived in the minds of the 8-rocks, not the girl her daughter was" (204).

It would seem, then, that Ruby's citizens have created a neat reversal of the Western color hierarchy that privileges whiteness and derides blackness, and ranks those in-between according to how they fall on the phenotypic spectrum. This is perhaps why so many of Morrison's critics read the novel as a comment on (white) American history, for by portraying what appears to be a mirror image of white racism and Eurocentric obsessions with physical and ideological purity, *Paradise* does speak to the limitations and social consequences of interracial bias. A more nuanced reading of the text is not only possible, however, but necessary, for the reverse color hierarchy that exists in Morrison's all-black town of Ruby is neither an exact equivalent to white racism nor a consistently applied arbiter of light skin—in fact, at key points in the text, light skin, and the racial commingling that creates it, is admired, even idealized. To understand this is to begin to understand the intricate relationship between race/nation and intimacy that Morrison's novel outlines.

One necessary point to make, in distinguishing Ruby's intraracial color hierarchy from its seeming polar opposite, is that Morrison's 8-rocks are painfully aware of their precarious position within the (white) American body politic:

> Ten generations had known what lay Out There: space, once beckoning and free, became unmonitored and seething; became a void where random and organized evil erupted when and where it chose—behind any standing tree, behind the door of any house, humble or grand. Out There where your children were sport, your women quarry, and where your very person could be annulled; where congregations carried arms to church and ropes coiled in every saddle. Out There where every cluster of whitemen looked like a posse, being alone was being dead. (16)

"Out There" is, of course, the American countryside, historically full of physical and ideological danger for a black person of any color. Morrison's language speaks to both individual ("random") acts of bigotry and systematic, state-sanctioned ("organized") racial oppression, as well as to the ways that white racist violence crosses boundaries of class and encompasses both public and private spaces ("behind any standing tree, behind the door of any house, humble or grand"). Her narration recalls, as well, the way that organized religion, particularly Christianity, has been used in the service of white supremacist ideology.

Yet the rurality suggested by "space, beckoning and free" is not the only place "Out There" resides, and is not America's only danger—which is precisely why Soane believes her sons are safer in Vietnam than in any city in the United States: "Safer in the army than in Chicago [. . .] Safer than Birmingham, than Montgomery, Selma, than Watts. Safer than Money, Mississippi, in 1955 and Jackson, Mississippi, in 1963. Safer than Newark, Detroit, Washington, D.C. She had thought war was safer than any city in the United States" (100-101). The mention of Money, Mississippi, in 1955, the year and location of fifteen-year-old Emmett Till's kidnapping and lynching, and Jackson, Mississippi, in 1963, the place and time that Medgar Evers was murdered, lend specificity to a list of cities recognizable for their large black populations and for either their roles in the civil rights movement (Birmingham, Montgomery, Selma), or their function as backdrop to major black rebellions, such as the Watts riots of 1965. The idea that Vietnam seemed less dangerous to Soane than any of these cities indicates the manner in which America's urban spaces have functioned, for African Americans, as sites of open warfare in their own right.

Recalling these very physical dangers faced by all black people *outside* of Ruby—dangers upon which the text dwells in enough detail to signal their significance—it becomes more difficult to read the 8-rocks' blood rule as simply a mirror image of white racism, since the 8-rocks have little power outside the confines of their tiny black hamlet. Even the deaths of a white family in a blizzard more than fifteen miles outside of Ruby lead to apprehension in the town about the possible involvement of white lawmen: "The problem was whether to notify the law or not. Not, it was decided. Even to bury them would be admitting to something they had no hand in" (273). In fact, what Ruby's black supremacists fear most is that which white supremacy has historically been able to count as its greatest ally—the involvement of the state.

Perhaps more intriguing than this difference, however, is the inconsistency within the narrative on the issue of light skin. For while "cracker-looking" (196) Delia and her progeny signify moral negligence to the 8-rocks, one of the novel's central images of black *respectability* has at its core another, far more idealized vision of light-colored skin. The "nineteen Negro ladies" (109) of two 8-rocks' recollection provide this startling counterpoint in Morrison's text, and as I will argue below, their image proves definitively that the 8-rocks' racialized disdain for light skin is far more contingent and complex than white racism's disdain for dark.

Identical twins Deacon and Steward Morgan are the undisputed leaders of Ruby, the two men who lead the assault on the Convent in 1976. As young boys, however, they accompany their father, uncle, and older brother on the "Second Grand Tour" of other all-black towns in the area—this second tour, in 1932, is a follow-up to a tour of four towns that Deacon and Steward's father, uncle, and brother had taken in 1910, before the twins were born. A number of the towns visited on the first tour no longer existed by the time of the second one; still others were "sad," or "looked like slave quarters, picked up and moved" (109). Yet a few others, like Haven, were thriving, and it is in one of these that Deacon and Steward witness the event that is to stay with them for the rest of their lives. I quote the passage at some length, below:

> In one of the prosperous [towns] he [Deacon] and Steward watched nineteen Negro ladies arrange themselves on the steps of the town hall. They wore summer dresses of material the lightness, the delicacy of which neither of them had ever seen[. . . .] Their waists were not much bigger than their necks. Laughing and teasing, they preened for a photographer lifting his head from beneath a black cloth only to hide under it again. Following a successful pose, the ladies broke apart in small groups, bending their tiny waists and rippling with laughter, walking arm in arm[. . . .] Slender feet turned and tipped in thin leather shoes. *Their skin, creamy and luminous in the afternoon sun, took away his breath*[. . . .] Even now the verbena scent was clear; *even now the summer dresses, the creamy, sunlit skin excited him*. If he and Steward had not thrown themselves off the railing they would have burst into tears. So, among the vivid details of that journey [. . .] Deek's image of the nineteen summertime ladies was unlike the photographer's. His remembrance was pastel colored and eternal. (109–10, my emphasis)

Deacon takes an openly sensual pleasure in his memory of these women—hence the suggestion that they "took away his breath" and "excited him." What proves surprising, however, is that this sexualized ideal so clearly includes the eroticization of their fair skin. Although skin of any color might become "luminous" in sunlight, Morrison's repetition of the adjective "creamy" seems to signify that these nineteen Negro ladies have skin far lighter in color than that of the 8-rocks. In fact, the phrase "sunlit skin" resonates not only phonically but visually with the "sunlight skin" (197) of Delia Best, suggesting that the nineteen ladies, like Delia, may even be light enough to pass for white.

Reading the above passage, one wonders, in fact, whether the Second Grand Tour has stopped off in the still-thriving town of Fairly, home of the "blue-eyed, gray-eyed yellowmen" (195) who were the villains of the 1890's Disallowing. Given that these light-skinned men are portrayed later in the text, in Ruby's annual holiday pageant, using "yellow and white mask[s] featuring gleaming eyes and snarling lips, red as a fresh wound," (208) we as readers might invest a level of certainty in the fact that such pale skin is simply reviled in Ruby. Yet a group of women who seem to be these men's female counterparts represent an idealized, "pastel colored and eternal" vision of black womanhood, one that sets the standard for other women in the text. Indeed, a part of Steward's justification for attacking the Convent is that the women there "were for him a flaunting parody of the nineteen Negro ladies of his and his brother's youthful memory and perfect understanding. They [the Convent women] were the degradation of that moment they'd shared of sunlit skin and verbena" (279).

This narrative contradiction at first borders on astonishing; how is it that "sunlight skin" constitutes the "dung" of a miscegenated America that the 8-rocks are all too eager to abandon, while cream-colored, "sunlit skin" amounts to a pedestalized fantasy of "Negro" womanhood? This question becomes much easier to answer, however, if we recall the context surrounding Delia's "sunlight" skin and compare it to that surrounding the nineteen Negro ladies. Delia, as I have already noted, was a woman of "no last name," a woman "without people" (197).

And while these descriptive phrases do suggest the sexually illicit, they also imply poverty, a lack of access to the sort of family legitimacy traditionally distributed via patriarchal inheritance.[46] In contrast, the nineteen Negro ladies bear the markers of wealth that cement their status as members of a social aristocracy (hence they are described as ladies, not women), and that clearly mark them as the property of wealthy men. They wear dresses made from light, delicate materials, the kinds of materials that would have been quite expensive in 1932, at the height of the Depression. Their shoes are cut from "thin leather," and are likely high-heeled, as suggested by the word "tipped"—these are shoes made for style, not for practicality, a luxury of women who have been spared the necessity of hard labor. These nineteen Negro ladies are clearly legitimate members of a patriarchal order; they are the wives, mothers, and daughters of men who provide for them a life of relative leisure.

Marita Golden writes, in her new book about the "color complex" in African American culture, that "the unmistakable color preference of the men of this 'Talented Tenth' class[. . . .] has a lot more to do with power and privilege and economic status than with concepts of beauty."[47] Although Golden refers to upper-middle class blacks at the turn of the twenty-first century, her words correlate surprisingly well with the color politics Morrison narrates, color politics that are driven by class standing. It is no coincidence that the story of the Second Grand Tour comes on the heels of an adult Deacon's acknowledgment that other blacks were awestruck by "the magical way he (and his twin) accumulated money" (107). Deacon and Steward, for whom this memory looms large, are not only the town of Ruby's civic leaders, but its financial leaders as well—their family has owned the town's only bank for generations. In *Paradise*, the twins represent a kind of black entrepreneurial spirit that is simultaneously driven by individual advancement and dependent upon community exploitation, disguised as participation. Hence Steward's suspicion of Ruby's new minister, Richard Misner, who forms a small, nonprofit credit union for the town after he arrives, is couched in financial terms: "A man like that, willing to throw money away, could give customers ideas. Make them think there was a choice about interest rates" (56). Deacon and Steward respect wealth, and as boys they recognize the nineteen Negro ladies as the trappings of wealth—the gleaming trophies of propertied men whose presence in this unnamed town is no less definite for its lack of explicit mention.

Thus for two of the most prominent of Ruby's 8-rocks, the ideological meaning of skin color is dependent upon the social class status attached to it; Delia may have passed a poverty-derived infamy on to her daughter and granddaughter, but the nineteen Negro ladies hold the power to "excite" desire, or to inspire awe and admiration, because of their conspicuous (and conspicuously male-controlled) wealth. In this chapter's opening epigraph, Robert Reid-Pharr suggests that the corporeal manifestation ("eyes, skin, hair") of putatively "black" people in the United States reveals a history of "contact and conquest [. . .] slavery and rebellion" that includes but is by no means limited to the African. Morrison's 8-rocks certainly read a history of often violent African/European racial intermingling into a figure like Delia Best. Yet the nineteen "Negro ladies," equally marked by the European, manage to escape this interpretation, presumably because their wealth and their presence in a black patriarchal order protects them, literally erases the "mocking presence" of the exploitative white father who always, historically, reserves the right to refuse paternity.[48]

This perhaps explains why the women of the Convent inspire such distaste in the men of Ruby—they are women unprotected, socially or financially, by men. One of these women, however, provides a final clue to the related politics of intimacy and black identity in Morrison's novel—and despite the interest of *Paradise*'s critics, she is not the infamous "white girl."[49] Indeed, while the white woman's presence in the Convent—and the text's refusal to distinguish her from the others—does allow for an analysis of the Convent community's "racial ambiguity," it would be a mistake to forget that at least one of the women in the Convent, arguably the one with the greatest connection to Ruby, *is* racially marked.[50] I am speaking, of course, of Consolata, whose peculiarly multiracial "blackness" provides an important counterpoint to the 8-rocks' so-called purity.

Facing the Vulnerability of Blackness

Even within the confines of an all-black town such as Ruby, there are other forms of interracial contact, apart from European and African, which might be written on the putatively "black" body. The "Old Fathers' refrain," repeated by Deacon and Steward, reveals as much: "Oklahoma is Indians, Negroes and God mixed. All the rest is fodder" (56). While whites and certain miscegenated blacks qualify as "fodder," the founding fathers of Ruby seem to find nothing disturbing in the mixture of Indian and Negro. As such, at least one of the 8-rock families—all of whom pride themselves on their "midnight skin" and its associated racial purity—has a surname ("Blackhorse") that suggests Native American ancestry, along with "that Blackhorse feature of stick-straight hair" (198). Clearly, then, even an 8-rock body can contain within itself—and can reveal on its surface—varied "traditions of racial commingling." Morrison's narration here reminds her readers of purity's literal *impossibility* in the Americas, given the reach and complexity of cross-racial contact in the earliest years of the New World.

I use the word "Americas," plural, advisedly, for the "contact and conquest, slavery and rebellion" that characterized the African encounter with the European and the Indian/indigenous was certainly not unique to the geographical area that we now call the United States. *Paradise,* a text that is truly herculean in its breadth, does not let us forget this, as one of the central characters of the novel, Consolata, was adopted by a Catholic nun as a child of nine, snatched from the "shit-strewn paths" of a city in Brazil.[51] This nun brings the orphan with her to her next assignment, the school for Indian girls in Oklahoma that will later become known as the Convent. There, Consolata outstays even her rescuer, who eventually dies on the Convent's premises. As such, Consolata is the longest-standing inhabitant of the Convent at the time of Ruby's assault on it, having lived there for over fifty years.

Written in Consolata's "green eyes," "tea-colored hair," and "smoky, sundown skin" is the same complex history worn by other "black" bodies in the New World. Yet for Deacon Morgan, who begins an extramarital affair with Consolata (then thirty-nine years old) after he sees her buying supplies in Ruby, her face and body are a mystery to be solved: "I've traveled. All over. I've never seen anything like you. How could anything be put together like you?" (231). For Consolata, by contrast, Deacon and his fellow 8-rocks represent something inarticulately familiar. Her first glimpse of Deacon comes as the town is celebrating the first paved street in Ruby with an impromptu horse race:

> As Consolata watched that reckless joy, she heard a faint but insistent Sha sha sha. Sha sha sha. Then a memory of just such skin and just such men, dancing with women in the streets to music beating like an infuriated heart, torsos still, hips making small circles above legs moving so rapidly it was fruitless to decipher how such ease was possible. These men here were not dancing, however; they were laughing, running, calling to each other and to women doubled over in glee. And although they were living here in a hamlet, not in a loud city full of glittering black people, Consolata knew she knew them. (226)

The "sha sha sha" that Consolata hears suggests a samba rhythm, but also something more nebulous. "Sha sha sha," reminiscent of the sound of the ocean, the music of the wind, perhaps even a gesture toward the language that she had long ago begun to lose: "Every now and then [Consolata] found herself speaking and thinking in that in-between place, the valley between the regulations of the first language and the vocabulary of the second" (242). The sound as it is written seems meant to suggest the currents of memory that Consolata navigates, a kind of amorphous but insistent internal chorus that leads her directly into Deacon's arms.

Consolata and Deacon's affair begins passionately nearly two months after they first see each other. Morrison's narration makes it clear that their connection is deeply physical, erotic, based in an inexplicable and nearly inarticulable sexual attraction: "On the way back they were speechless [. . .] What had been uttered during their lovemaking leaned toward language, gestured its affiliation, but in fact was un-memorable, -controllable or -translatable" (229). This notion, of a passion beyond the revisionary power of memory, beyond external control and linguistic translation, suggests a level of emotional and physical pleasure that supersedes social regulation. Yet such passion does not, in this text that is so concerned with such regulation, seem meant to last. Their involvement ends when Consolata accidentally bites Deacon's lip, then "hum[s] over the blood she lick[s] from it"; he, believing that she is "bent on eating him like a meal," recoils in disgust (239).

In spite of the fact that Consolata's behavior in this instance is motivated only by her overwhelming feeling of kinship with Deacon ("Dear Lord, I didn't want to eat him. I just wanted to go home" [240]), the relationship cannot survive his horror of her actions. And the significance of Deacon's revulsion is not difficult to read; he literally fears being *devoured*—physically, emotionally—by Consolata's unregulated pleasure-seeking, consumed by what Samuel Delany has described as "the red, Edenic forces of desire that could only topple society, destroy all responsibility, and produce a nation without families, without soldiers, without workers[.]"[52] This is the imagined danger of intimacy, that its pleasures will expand beyond social constraint, beyond social responsibility. Delany's specific reference to a "nation" bereft of workers, soldiers, and families seems particularly fitting: given that the 8-rock characters in *Paradise* can be read as devotees of a kind of black nationalist ideology, it is no wonder Deacon is unwilling to risk the town of Ruby's security on his continued involvement with Consolata. As Deacon's wife Soane says to the other woman while the two are still "sharing" him, "Listen to me. He can't fail at what he is doing. None of us can. We are making something" (240). Of course, what the 8-rock familes are making is a paradise founded upon isolation and exclusion, and Consolata's response is telling: "What do I care about your raggedy little town?" (240).

Perhaps it would be worthwhile to consider, for a moment, this tension between Consolata's disdain for the exclusionary "nation-building" that Ruby's residents are attempting, and her palpable, if inarticulate, feeling of connection to Deacon and to the other 8-rocks, her childhood memory of "just such skin and just such men." After all, whatever the literal translation of "Sha sha sha," its true meaning for Consolata is clear enough once the affair has ended: "Sha sha sha. Sha sha sha, she wanted to say, meaning, he and I are the same" (241). If Consolata accepts their sameness—a sameness rooted in the 8-rocks deeply black skin color and the memories of Afro-Brazilian culture that it elicits— then why is she unmoved by the town itself, and the ideological work that the 8-rocks have undertaken? The answer to this question lies precisely in the rigid boundaries of the 8-rocks' community, bound- aries that exclude a figure like Consolata because her body does not read as adequately "pure." The irony of this exclusion is emphasized by Consolata's clear self-identification with blackness in the text. Yet be- cause of their preoccupation with biological purity, Morrison's 8-rocks seem simply unable to fit her identification into their racial schema.[53]

Via the interaction of these characters, Morrison's novel thus cri- tiques the black nationalist desire for a "pure," and purely "authentic," form of African American identity. Yet it is crucial to recall that such debates within the African American community have rarely, in the twentieth century, taken biological purity as their focus. Indeed, as I have already pointed out, in her depiction of the 8-rocks obsession with black bloodlines, Morrison literalizes in biology what usually ex- ists for African Americans as a *cultural* ideal. Lubiano suggests that "cultural production and its consumption" are what "stand in" for the state in black nationalism, indeed, that "cultural imperialism becomes the black nationalist cultural equivalent to actual imperialism (land seizure) because, lacking a homeland and a sovereignty, culture is all [U.S. blacks] can 'own.'"[54] As such, within black nationalism, "claims of authenticity or criticism of its lack are the last defenses against cul- tural imperialism."[55]

Given this substitution of culture for biology in black national- ist discourses of racial authenticity (read: purity), it becomes easier to understand why such a panoply of phenotypes "exist more or less comfortably" under the rubric of American blackness. This is a conse- quence of the one-drop rule, yes, but also of an understanding of racial belonging that—contrary both to historical conceptions of whiteness and to Morrison's exaggerated 8-rock allegory—is far more dependent upon *behavior* than biology. Most African American people have, out of necessity, adopted an understanding of "race" that inherently ac- knowledges its contingent and conditional nature—or, as a comrade of mine often insists, "Black folks have always known race is a social construction."[56] This knowledge does not mean that black people in the United States have been exempt from narrow and exclusionary conceptions of "blackness," only that the grounds upon which these conceptions are founded have rarely been linked *directly* to a biological imperative.[57]

I emphasize "directly," above, because the biological has not been completely erased from black conceptions of racial authenticity, as Arthur Fletcher's statements indirectly reveal. Even though his accusations of "light-skinned" abandonment clearly suggest a conflation of skin color and class privilege, they also remind us that so-called loyalty to the race often requires one to overlook the true multiraciality of putatively "black" bodies. After all, as Patricia Williams notes, "In the United States, being 'black' virtually always means some mixture of African, Native American, and European ancestry."[58] Yet race in the United States has rarely been allowed to function with the same fluidity as it does in Latin America and the Spanish-speaking Caribbean— places where this mixture is readily and openly acknowledged. Instead, the rigid *social* meaning of blackness has been applied to individuals with appearances that vary wildly, a phenomenon largely unique to the United States.[59] In fact, the very range of skin colors, facial features, and hair textures that exists "under the sign of blackness" speaks to the fact of that sign's inherent complexity, a complexity that must be suppressed in the United States—by both blacks and whites—in order to conceptualize "blackness" as a monolithic and fixed identity.

What is often forgotten in contemporary discussions of miscegenation and its history, particularly in the United States, is that so-called "black" people can be just as uncomfortable with hybridity as can "white" people—even if this black discomfort is most often expressed through the language of culture. As Reid-Pharr notes, "The rejection in the United States of racial ambiguity [. . .] was not simply a social phenomenon that happened to the Black American community but instead one in which it participated actively."[60] *Paradise* narrativizes this phenomenon in its representation of Ruby and the 8-rocks, yet in the character of Consolata, the text offers an alternative conceptualization of black identity, one that is more capable of accommodating the physical and cultural aspects of this so-called "racial ambiguity."

Indeed, I want to suggest that Consolata's character simultaneously represents the concepts of African diaspora and of a specifically "black" multiraciality in this text. This may explain why her character is figured as so powerful, and her involvement with Deacon as so threatening—witness, for example, the depth of Steward's horror at "the memory of how close his brother came to breaking up his marriage to Soane[. . . .] Steward seethed at the thought of that barely averted betrayal of all they owed and promised to the Old Fathers" (279). In the essay from which this chapter's second epigraph is drawn, Stuart Hall writes that "the diaspora is a place where traditions operate but are not closed, where the black experience is historically and culturally distinctive but is not the same as it was before."[61] Diaspora, in other words, is dependent upon cultural transformation, what Richard Schur calls the "path of negotiation and hybridity."[62] Yet embracing the transformative, syncretic power of diaspora necessitates a certain risk—as the final line of the epigraph makes clear. "Taking in a bit of the other" is no small thing when that Other is whiteness, historically a source of aversion and dread for the black subject, as the 8-rocks' fear-driven avoidance of the world "Out There" makes clear. Even "being what [you, yourself] are" can present an ideological challenge, particularly in the case of the unacknowledged multiraciality of the "black" body. Such acknowledgment will always be difficult for those who have been obsessed with the idea of racial purity—and as *Paradise* reveals, white Americans hold no monopoly on such an obsession.

Deacon and the other 8-rocks, in their preoccupation with purity, cannot see that they, too, are a part of a wider, African-descended community. Soane Morgan, for example, is offended by the "ugly names" that the young people wanted to call themselves: "Like not American. Like African" (104). Soane "had the same level of interest in Africans as they had in her: none. But [the young people] talked about them like they were neighbors or, worse, family" (104). Pat Best, too, after dismissing the rest of the world as "foreign Negroes," tells Richard Misner that "Slavery *is* our past. Nothing can change that, certainly not Africa" (210). Yet while the 8-rocks prefer to believe that their history begins and ends with American slavery, theirs is a slavery that has somehow avoided the "bloody history of miscegenation" associated with the institution in every part of the New World.[63] Refusing to be African, but refusing also—in spite of tangible evidence to the contrary in certain of their own bodies—to be anything other than a rigidly "pure" type of black American, the 8-rocks depend upon a kind of historical, genealogical transparency that is impossible without total segregation from the world "Out There." Yet such total segregration is also impossible. Richard Misner's response to Patricia is telling: "We live in the world, Pat. The whole world[. . . .] Isolation kills generations. It has no future" (210).

It is no wonder that the men of Ruby are so bent upon destroying the women of the Convent, *and* on regulating the sexual and domestic behavior of Ruby from within. In order to remain "pure," the people of Ruby must believe that 8-rock blood is "unadulterated and unadulteried," which requires a level of knowledge about one's own and others' bodies that is literally unattainable—particularly for the multifaceted subjects of diaspora. Deacon's involvement with Consolata raises not only the danger of the Other/lover who is unknowable, the mystery of the lover's body, but also the danger of the (miscegenated) Self. This is why, in the moment before Steward shoots her in the head during their assault on the Convent, Deacon "looks at Consolata and sees in her eyes what has been drained from them and *from himself as well*" (289, my emphasis). Literally, the "mint-green" color of her eyes has faded over the years (she is 60 years old in this scene), but what this color signifies is a vividly drawn racial hybridity, one which Deacon shares despite his insistence that his body is 8-rock "pure."

Indeed, when they first meet, Deacon looks into Consolata's face and sees something he believes he has never seen before—but the hybridity that is so foreign to him is a function of his angle of vision, rather than her unfamiliarity. After all, he is for her a memory of home, not because she recognizes their "essential" African commonality across the boundaries of geography and ethnicity, but because she sees in him yet another iteration of the cultural creolization that is African diaspora. She is willing to recognize what he is not—that the very "Americanness" he and his community insist upon (an Americanness set up in deliberate contradistinction to Africanness) marks him as a product of the New World. The fear and hatred of the miscegenated "black" person in Ruby is due to the inscrutability of all so-called "black" bodies—"black" by choice and by culture, "black" according to the illogical laws of hypodescent, yet containing visible *and* invisible traces of historical violence, family secrets, unsolved mysteries, and unanswerable questions about who African Americans really are. And while Consolata's body might wear this mystery more perceptibly, Deacon's is by no means exempt from it.

I have spoken, at earlier points in this volume, of the doubled vulnerability of black intimacy, the notion that the African American subject is vulnerable on the basis of race and on the basis of human connection. This is the vulnerability that underlies the salvific wish, and its gestures toward a self-protective, intimate discipline. Yet perhaps the word "doubling" is misleading; perhaps the racialized vulnerability of blackness holds *within itself* the notion of human relationship, interracial contact, sexual and domestic overlap and confusion. As Patricia Williams writes, "Almost all African Americans are to some degree the taboo-saddled descendants of Great White Slaveholders—very, very few of us do not have [. . .] some complex, messy relation to a famous white progenitor."[64] The "black" body *is* an impure body, although not in the sense that white racism has always needed to accuse, of blackness as ultimate corporeal pollutant. Rather, the "black" American is impure because on her own she is never ideologically black enough, never that ultimate, pure black thing that can exclude, once and for all, the feared and despised "white" (biological *or* cultural) ancestor. This is why Fletcher's assumptions are all wrong, and why, as Morrison's *Paradise* seems to suggest, the idealized borders of black intimacy continually overlap the idealized borders of the black national or political "body"—or, in Reid-Pharr's words, why black Americans "have not allowed the demise of the black family, the site [which is . . .] *the* central location in the production of American racial difference."[65] The very terror of "blackness"—the fact that it always already contains, is inhabited by, the Other—is also the thing that forces us perpetually to seek and reseek it, to write and rewrite its limits.

In the last chapter of *Private Lives, Proper Relations,* I turn again to this concept of doubled vulnerability, the black subject made susceptible to exposure and violation by the simultaneous operation of racial scrutiny and human intimacy. While in the present chapter I have looked most closely at the vulnerability of "blackness," in the next chapter I revisit the human vulnerability of intimacy, through a reading of Gayl Jones's 1976 novel *Eva's Man.* Rather than address Jones's novel merely as a product of its period—as one of a number of black women's texts from the late 1970s to take up questions of domestic abuse and other forms of sexual oppression suffered by black women at the hands of black men—this final chapter, itself chronologically "out of order" in the book, considers Jones's novel as somewhat of a temporal and thematic anomaly, a chaotic text with much to tell readers about the related chaos of human desire.

Chapter 5

Doing Violence to Desire

In a way, sex as such is *pathological.*
—Slavoj Zizek, "Love Thy Neighbor?
No Thanks!"

James Baldwin's 1961 essay "Alas, Poor Richard" has the following to say about the sexualized violence evident in much of Richard
Wright's work:

> In most of the novels written by Negroes until today . . . there is a
> great space where sex ought to be; and what usually fills this space is
> violence. . . . The violence is gratuitous and compulsive because the
> root of the violence is never examined. The root is rage. It is the rage,
> almost literally the howl, of a man who is being castrated.[1]

According to Baldwin, the failure of Wright's short story "The Man
Who Killed a Shadow" is located in its lack of sexual energy, in the
sense that "[t]he entire story seems to be occurring . . . beneath cot-
ton."[2] The energy that Baldwin expects from the sexual relationships
in Wright's work exists instead in the violent assault that the story
represents, and for this reason, according to Baldwin, the piece fails
adequately to address "the specifically sexual horror" suffered by black
people, particularly men.

This chapter, which focuses on Gayl Jones's 1976 novel *Eva's Man,*
begins with Baldwin's words for a reason; I find his suggestion that

there is a void in black literature "where sex ought to be" provocative when juxtaposed with the concept of the salvific wish addressed throughout this project. Baldwin's words are particularly striking when considered in relation to that aspect of the salvific wish that has guided black women's attempts, historically, to avoid racist accusation and assault through a self-imposed silence on matters of sexuality.[3] Of course Baldwin is not writing about the salvific wish; indeed, he is not even writing about black women, since what he understands to be the "root" of this sexual void, this empty space filled with violence, is *masculine* rage, specifically the rage of black men suffering the pain of emasculation. This rage exists, Baldwin argues, due to a great "body of sexual myths . . . which have proliferated around the figure of the American Negro," myths that constitute a "cage" from which the black man desperately seeks escape.[4] Baldwin suggests that as a result of this collection of myths, which make the very subject of black sexual expression an impossible one for Wright to address, violence in Wright's work occupies a distinct space in the narrative frame "where sex ought to be," replacing a fuller examination of black erotic character. In other words, violence and sex oppose rather than overlap, displace rather than mutually produce one another in Wright's fiction.

This relationship of mutual production, however, is precisely the situation of violence and sex in Gayl Jones's novel *Eva's Man*; there, violence and sexual expression are forced to occupy the same narrative space, to bleed into and to merge with one another. Rather than a brutal act of murder replacing the sex act, for instance, as Baldwin suggests is the case in Wright's work, Jones's text might align intercourse and brutality, or might just as easily depict murder and mutilation as erotic exchange. Perhaps not surprisingly, this narrative overlap of sex and violence dovetails in Jones's novel with rigidly gendered expectations of sexual behavior; such expectations give men the power to express desire violently while directing women to submit to these expressions passively or even silently. On the one hand, then, the phenomenon that one might call "vicious desire" in Jones's text is one based in conventional structures of gender, which "shap[e] men's sexuality so it expresses the theme of domination."[5]

Following Baldwin, however, I would also suggest that this perverse and overlapping relation between sex and violence has a racial component. Like the opposition of violence and sex that Baldwin identifies in Wright's work, the fusion of violence and sex in Jones's novel is related to a "body of sexual myths" surrounding black people, in this case the same myths of black sexual pathology that have typically provoked the operation of the salvific wish in African American culture. In other words, in Jones's narrative universe, black desire itself is potentially vicious because it is situated within a racialized narrative of intimate deviance that makes black subjects hyperaware of and hypersensitive to the vulnerability that desire engenders. Jones's black characters express desire violently precisely because to combine desire with violence is to lessen the sense of physical and psychic exposure that occurs as a result of desire's expression.

The irony of shielding desire within silence, or within a mask of protective propriety, is that the very nature of desire is to destroy such pretenses: consider Leo Bersani's claim that sexual excitement "disintegrates the constructed self."[6] The salvific wish, which attempts to create a space for black sexual vulnerability through rigidly denying the full spectrum of possibilities for that vulnerability, thus does violence to the very logic of sexual desire. I use the above phrasing advisedly, for there is a relationship, here, between *doing violence to* the logic of desire and *inserting violence into* the logic of desire, which is one way of characterizing Jones's representation of desire in *Eva's Man*. In fact, it might be more accurate to suggest that there is a synonymity, an equivalence, to these two concepts. To do violence to a thing—to attack, to assault, to violate it—is, in effect, to insert violence into it, to introduce the idea of violence where, presumably, it was not before.

There is just such an equivalence between the disciplinary work of the salvific wish and the vicious desire present in Jones's novel. The salvific wish, itself a kind of violent attack upon black intimacy, is perversely reflected in the pages of *Eva's Man*, where intimacy among black subjects always brings with it the specter of violent physical and emotional assault. Indeed, representations of desire in Jones's text, which at first glance appear to be merely forms of *gendered* sexual interaction, are better understood as interpretations of *cultural* desire. This is be-cause desire imbricated with violence can be read as another means, albeit an extreme one, of denying black sexual vulnerability through sexual silencing, thereby reasserting the possibility of and space for that vulnerability. On an only slightly altered axis, then, Jones's "vi-cious desire" functions as exactly the same sort of simultaneous denial and reassertion of desire attempted by the salvific wish.

This parallel is not difficult to comprehend if one acknowledges the similar, and similarly irresolvable, contradictions between exposure and protection evidenced in both the salvific wish and Jones's represen-tations of desire. To express sexual desire violently is to inflict pain on another human being, to engage in a kind of perversely empowering exercise of agency that renders one *in*vulnerable (in the way that power always suggests a kind of invulnerability). Elaine Scarry argues, for example, that a torturer "convert[s] the other person's pain into his own power," thereby "experienc[ing] the entire occurrence exclusively from the *nonvulnerable* end of the weapon."[7] At the same time, be-cause even the most violent moments in Jones's text are overlaid with the experience, the expression, of eroticism, then these moments are fraught with personal exposure for the individuals involved. This is because to experience desire—either in the narrow sense of longing for another or in the wider sense of a more visceral and embodied occurrence of libido or appetite—is to be reminded of one's own sus-ceptibility to human need, one's participation in "the peculiar logic (of ecstasy) by which we must cultivate, rather than destroy, other people in order to recover from the disintegrating excitement into which they plunge us."[8]

In Jones's text, however, these two sides of vicious desire work to mitigate, even to neutralize one another, such that the characters who express such desire are both able to limit their psychic and physical vulnerability *and* able to acknowledge or express that vulnerability—to experience the benefits of desire without any of its risks. And the fact that these two aspects of vicious desire seem incompatible, even ir-reconcilable, is culturally fitting, since the two-sided approach of the salvific wish contains what seems just as great of an impossibility—an attempt to preserve sexual expressivity while foreclosing the possibility

of erotic exposure, to create an alternative space for sexual vulnerability *through* the increasingly rigid denial of a vulnerable sexual desire.
Thus Jones's text implies that vicious desire, and the salvific wish that
it parallels—both attempts to produce simultaneous vulnerability and
impermeability in the context of black sexual behavior—result finally
in chaos, in uncontrolled and uncontrollable madness that itself produces only more violence.

I am reminded of another comment from Baldwin, in his essay
"Freaks and the American Ideal of Manhood."[9] There, he criticizes
"those relentlessly hetero (sexual?) keepers of the keys and seals, those
who know what the world needs in the way of order and who are ready
and willing to supply that order," concluding that "this rage for order
can result in chaos, and in this country, chaos connects with color."[10]
The parenthetical inclusion of "sexual?" here again calls attention to
the impossibility of aligning erotic expression and "order," the rigid
invulnerability sought by the salvific wish. That this order, according to Baldwin, is the very source of the racial chaos that it is bent
on subduing is hardly a surprise. For while Eva's violent and violently
sexualized acts throughout *Eva's Man* are both belated participation in
and deliberate retaliation for a gendered structure of vicious desire that
disproportionately victimizes women, they are also, and much more
importantly, reminders of her racialized madness, a madness which,
at its source, is driven by the impossible goal of concurrently denying
and displaying black sexual vulnerability. In other words, the "chaos"
of Eva Canada's madness grows out of a cultural propensity for order at
the expense of the riskier aspects of intimate involvement. Jones's text
exposes such risks as inevitable; indeed, in this chapter I ultimately
argue that the vicious desire narrated in *Eva's Man* speaks to the haz-
ardous qualities of human intimacy more broadly, qualities that make
the fundamental futility of the salvific wish glaringly clear.

Vicious Desire Part I: Gender Structures and Sexualized Violence

As I explain above, Jones's novel suggests that black desire itself is potentially vicious as a result of the community's vulnerability to narratives

of black pathology. The particularly "black" aspects of this viciousness are not immediately evident in the text, however, and are instead displaced by an opposition between active and idle, aggressive and passive expressions of such desire. Perhaps not surprisingly, men most commonly embody the first set of behaviors in the narrative, women the second. Eva's own parents, for instance, provide a particularly vivid example of the gendered behavior that can take place within an incident of sexualized violence. The couple enacts a terrifyingly brutal scene of lovemaking once Eva's father discovers her mother's lover sitting in the family's kitchen. Eva recalls her experience of the exchange:

> [Daddy] said, "Close that door, will you, honey." He said it just like that, real soft, real gentle.
>
> I got up and closed the door that separated the living room from their bedroom.
>
> Then it was like I could hear her clothes ripping. I don't know if the gentleness had been for me, or if it had been the kind of hurt gentleness one gets before they let go. But now he was tearing that blouse off and those underthings. I didn't hear nothing from her the whole time. I didn't hear a thing from her.
>
> "Act like a whore, I'm gonna fuck you like a whore. You act like a whore, I'm gonna fuck you like a whore."
>
> He kept saying that over and over. I was so scared. I kept feeling that after he tore all her clothes off, and there wasn't any more to tear, he'd start tearing her flesh.[11]

The reference to "hurt gentleness" in the first part of the passage is a vivid reminder of Eva's father's vulnerability in this moment, a vulnerability that is soon combined with destructive rage. In effect, the exchange allows him to maintain the vulnerability of his desire for Eva's mother while simultaneously protecting himself with the armor of sadistic violence. Eva's mother's profound silence throughout the encounter suggests that she is expected to (and does) accept this sexualized punishment without resistance—demonstrating an extreme sexual passivity, almost a masochism, which seems to counter her husband's extreme sexual aggression.

Indeed, the striking contrast between each parent's use of voice in this scene—Eva cannot "hear a thing" from her mother, but her father speaks constantly, repeating the words that define and justify his sexual violence—is part of a larger parallel between speaking and individual expression in Jones's text. As Zizek has noted, following Derrida, "'hearing oneself speak' [s'entendre parler] . . . is the very kernel, the fundamental matrix, of experiencing oneself as a living being[.]"[12] Human beings can be said to speak themselves into existence, to use language to mark a space for their own symbolic survival. As such, speaking might be understood as an affirmation of self, one means by which the subject asserts its presence in the world. And if desire does, indeed, "threaten constantly to outmanoeuvre [sic] and outclass our verbal resources, the principal means at our disposal for ordering and making sense of our lives," then locating a means of speaking desire, of "fixing" it in place linguistically, becomes even more important, a crucial means by which to articulate the self.[13]

Thus Eva's father's repetitive, violently erotic speech may serve as a means by which to reemphasize his (sexual) identity—particularly since his status as husband has been threatened by another man's presence. That his speech is accompanied by sexual aggression is no coincidence; violence, like speech, here serves as a means of self-affirmation, similar to Laura Tanner's notion of the empowered violator: "[T]he forceful imposition of the assaulter's form on the victim may serve as a means of empowerment for the violator[. . . .] For the violator, violence may come to serve as a temporary affirmation of an unstable self[.]"[14] This affirmation certainly seems to apply to Eva's father in the passage. For Eva's mother, however, violence operates as a self-effacement of sorts, because she is its victim rather than its perpetrator, reconfirming the gendered divide that exists in the vicious desire evident throughout Jones's narrative.

This gendered expression of violent desire is replayed in the narrative when Eva recounts her own husband's reaction to her perceived infidelity. Her husband, James Hunn, comes home to find her sitting in the living room with one of her college classmates. Although Eva's narration has already suggested that she was not sexually involved with this young man, the parallel to her parents' relationship begins here, because in the earlier scene, her father walks in on the lovers while they are talking, not actually engaging in sexual activity. James's assumption that Eva is committing adultery is based on an equally slim amount of evidence—simply the presence of another man in the home. Hunn, whose mysterious past includes the murder of his former wife's lover, reacts to what he perceives as Eva's indiscretion with a physical assault:

> [H]e just reached over and grabbed my shoulder, got up and started slapping me.
> "You think you a whore, I'll treat you like a whore. You think you a whore, I'll treat you like a whore."
> Naw he didn't slap me, he pulled my dress up and got between my legs.
> "Think I can't do nothing. Fuck you like a damn whore."
> Naw, I'm not lying. He said, "Act like a whore, I'll fuck you like a whore." *Naw, I'm not lying.* (163, author's emphasis)

While Madhu Dubey reads Eva's insistence that she is not lying to be evidence of her insanity, since Eva eventually attributes to James the same words that she hears her father say to her mother, I would suggest that Eva's commentary earlier in the passage quite sanely highlights the similarities between the two incidents.[15] Eva's first description of Hunn's reaction, that he slaps her and calls her a whore, is followed immediately by the claim that instead of slapping her, he forces himself on her, enacting a scene of violent sex remarkably similar to that which her father committed with her mother. While it might be true that Eva's memory is unreliable, what this juxtaposition accomplishes in the text is the alignment of presumably nonsexual assault (slapping) with the image of the sex-act-as-punishment. While the representation of this sex act—or of the specific words that accompany it—may relate to Eva's mental instability, their inclusion does reiterate the notion that in this novel, sex and violence are interchangeable. Eva's insistence that she is not lying may thus be based more on her recognition that the two events are equivalent, rather than simply on her madness.

This gendered divide in the expression of violence-inflected desire also plays out in the novel in the relationship between Eva's cousin Alfonso and his wife, Jean. Together Alfonso and Jean enact a rigidly predictable, yet inexplicable, pattern of abuse: he always beats her in the same way, in front of the same hotel, seemingly without provocation. It is, Eva reports, "like a spell or something that come over him" (39). Otis, the relative who makes it his "mission in life" to break up the beatings, is confounded by Jean's passive acquiescence to Alfonso's abuse, but one day discovers not only the motivation behind Alfonso's violence, but the fact that Jean seems deliberately to provoke it:

> "It ain't Alfonso, it's Jean," Otis said[. . . .]
>
> "We had to pass this hotel, and then she said—said it real quiet, I almost didn't hear it. 'I had to think he was you before I could do anything,' she said. I just looked at her, you know.
>
> "'Then why the hell did you let him fuck you then? I don't wont nobody fuckin you.'
>
> "'I didn't let him fuck me.'
>
> "'I said I don't wont nobody fuckin you.'
>
> [. . . .]
>
> "Then there wasn't no words, just him hitting her[. . . .] She starts it, Marie. Not him. She starts it and he finishes it. She's the one wonts it, though, Marie. I'm living in a crazy house." (92)

Otis's description of the exchange suggests that the abuse is a sort of sexualized ritual for the couple. Jean recalls Alfonso's control over and sexual possession of her body when she claims that imagining Alfonso allowed her to connect sexually with another man. Her invocation of this other man, however, like Eva's mother's infidelity, recalls Alfonso's vulnerability by presenting a direct threat to this sexual possession, as Alfonso's desperately repeated "I don't wont nobody fuckin you" demonstrates. Thus Jean's murmured commentary demands the reassertion of Alfonso's dominance, which takes place through the violence of physical assault. Like the sex act wielded as punishment in other instances in the text, Alfonso's abuse constitutes a fusion of intimacy and brutality, because it violently reasserts the couple's union, literally "marking" Jean's body as Alfonso's sexual and social property.

This process of violence-as-sexual-marking is reminiscent of a scene in Zora Neale Hurston's 1937 classic, *Their Eyes Were Watching God*, in which the idealized romantic bond between Tea Cake and Janie is solidified through battery. In this case, as well, the violence is inflicted against a wife by a husband, and is instigated by the presence of a threat to the male spouse; a meddling neighbor introduces Janie to the neighbor's eligible brother in hopes of matching up the two, and Tea Cake's response is to "whip" Janie:

> [I]t relieved that awful fear inside him. Being able to whip her re-assured him in possession[. . . .] Everybody talked about it next day in the fields. It aroused a sort of envy in both men and women. The way he petted and pampered her as if those two or three face slaps had nearly killed her made the women see visions and the helpless way she hung on him made men dream dreams.[16]

Just as Alfonso's beating of Jean, accompanied by the words, "I don't wont nobody fuckin you," reaffirms his masculine dominance, Tea Cake's effort to "sla[p] Janie around a bit to show he was boss" reassures every-one, and especially Tea Cake himself, that Janie is "helpless" in the face of his power. In this instance as well, violence reaffirms a gendered and eroticized hierarchy of man over woman; Tea Cake follows a logic of male dominance that suggests that "to love a woman is to have power over her and to treat her violently if need be."[17]

While Hurston's text suggests that the community surrounding Janie and Tea Cake perceives this incident favorably, however, Jones's narrative is far more ambiguous. Otis's remark about Alfonso and Jean, that "It was like I didn't wont to cut in, you know. Like I wanted to just keep watching. Like they were working all that blues out of them, or something" suggests a fascination that could in some ways be similar to the "envy" of the community in Hurston's novel (92, 93). It is no coincidence that he explains this fascination by making refer-ence to the "blues," an African American expressive art form, for this sexualized violence does seem to have a specifically racial component in Jones's narrative—a point I will return to shortly. But Otis's deci-sion to interfere ultimately marks his fascination as inappropriate: "I knew I couldn't just stand by watching like that" (93). In other words, the community in *Their Eyes* seems reassured by Tea Cake and Janie's altercation, particularly since Tea Cake's aggression is mitigated, in the text, by his post-beating tenderness toward and indulgence of Janie. In contrast, Alfonso and Jean's reenactment of a sexualized ritual of violence is far more disturbing to outsiders, perhaps because it does not seem to be followed by a similar episode of tenderness. Indeed, what may be most disturbing about Alfonso and Jean's ritual interaction is that the violence seems to *contain* the tenderness—rather than a palliative to remedy a momentary lapse in affection, Jones's text deliberately situates depictions of erotic and even emotional connection within episodes of male-to-female brutality.

This evidence of desire's gendered viciousness in the novel may explain why Jean repeatedly provokes her husband; she seems to need and seek out Alfonso's violence the way that one might seek the security of a lover's embrace. Jean herself expresses that need to Eva's mother; she recounts her reaction after she tried to leave Alfonso but was brought back home: "'You want to know something? When he came and got me, I was ready to go back'" (56). Her narrative indicates that women in the novel are as enmeshed in conventional patterns of sexualized brutality as men are, that, indeed, women's sexual subjectivities in this text are as implicated in and dependent upon violence as men's. Mae Henderson argues in another context that "the sexual fantasies and practices of women have been conditioned by an ideology of female submission, thereby perpetuating patriarchal violence and domination."[18] Jean and Alfonso's story recalls the ways that women might voluntarily participate in figures of vicious desire, willingly offering their bodies up for violent consumption by men. Otis finds Jean's behavior "crazy," and the fact that Jean herself prompts violence from Alfonso is indeed symptomatic of a kind of insanity. The abuse itself, however, does fit an oppositional approach to gender that positions men as violators and women as victims.

Except for Eva, whose singular relationship to sexual violence is the subject of a later portion of this chapter, even women characters who succeed in inflicting pain against men in Jones's text seem to do so involuntarily, rather than in retaliation for this conventionally gendered hierarchy. A central figure in the novel, for instance, is the "queen bee," a woman who is believed to be poisonous to the men she takes as lovers, since they all die shortly after becoming involved with her. Ironically enough, this does not deter men from pursuing her. As Miss Billie, a friend of Eva's mother, claims, "[T]hey think won't nothing touch them. They think they caint be hurt" (17). This masculine conviction of invincibility likely arises from the gendered divide in the very under-standing of desire in *Eva's Man*; men in Jones's text assume that the queen bee is harmless to them precisely because of the gendering of "vicious" desire that takes place in the narrative. Women are expected to be passive recipients of male desire/violence; the possibility that a woman could inflict her own violent desire on a man thus verges on the conceptually incredible. The character of the queen bee, supposedly the embodiment of dangerous female desire, ultimately succumbs to this logic as well, surrendering her own life rather than risk the life of a man she actually loves.

Vicious Desire, Part II: Violence in Cultural Context

As may be evident from the aforementioned examples, in *Eva's Man* women are largely expected to be the passive recipients of men's sexu-alized violence, and not vice versa. The reason for this juxtaposition of eroticism and violence in Jones's text is more than simply the ad-herence to a conventionally gendered divide in expressions of desire, however; instead, this juxtaposition has a cultural logic that allows for its alignment with the racialized suppressions of the salvific wish. As I have already noted, the African American community has a fraught relationship to the vulnerability of desire because of that communi-ty's prior vulnerability to racist accusations of sexual and familial pa-thology. It is no coincidence that each example of vicious desire so far cited from *Eva's Man* is related to a disrupted domestic scene, for the black domestic milieu is overlaid with a history of white assumptions about blacks' inability to create or maintain a "normal" environment of familial intimacy.

As such, the violence that surrounds erotic disruptions of the con-ventional domestic sphere in Jones's novel can be understood as both a wish-driven reaction to the endangering of black community sanctity represented by these disruptions as well as a means of mitigating the doubled vulnerability—to accusations of deviance and to desire itself— that might emerge from such disruptions. In other words, on the one hand violence is a means of expressing frustration with a domestic scene that is "out of order," such as the marital couplings, cited above, that have been disturbed by perceived or actual instances of extramarital sex. On the other hand, however, the manner in which violence can shield against physical and psychic vulnerability through the empow- erment of its perpetrator may provide a way of protecting the already vulnerable black subject, open to accusations of black sexual pathology, from further vulnerability—by foreclosing the corporeal and psychic vulnerability of desire. In both cases, the violence of Jones's characters might be read as a specific cultural response to narratives of pathology that circulate only around black sexual subjects, narratives which, like Baldwin's "cage" of sexual mythology, burden black domesticity in par- ticular with the weight of maintaining an always necessary propriety.

Evidence of the burden carried by black domesticity in Jones's text can be found in both Eva's secrecy around her own marriage and her reaction to Davis's revelation that he himself is married. Eva, who claims that she "married [James Hunn] out of tenderness," refuses to talk about that relationship to any of the people interested in her life. This unwillingness to talk about her own marriage lies in stark con- trast, in the text, to her general eagerness to tell and retell aspects of her story: "I tell them so much I don't even get it straight anymore. I tell them things that don't even have to do with what I did, but they say they want to hear that too" (5).[19] Of her husband, however, Eva remarks: "I didn't talk about my husband. He was the part of my life I didn't talk about" (102). One way to read Eva's unwillingness to discuss Hunn is to posit that for her he represents the sphere of con- ventional domesticity, the "private" space held to be inviolable by the salvific wish. Hence when Davis asks "'Were you ever married, Eva?'" she replies "'No,'" adding, "I wouldn't tell him that" (101). By refusing to reveal this particular aspect of herself, Eva maintains a sense of her own participation in a scene of domestic sanctity, a protected "series of tendernesses" that recalls the sacred space of vulnerability that the salvific wish hopes to make possible through the suppression of extra-marital indiscretion.

Eva is at first unaware, however, that through her involvement with Davis she is herself a participant in such extramarital indiscretion, placed inadvertently in the position of an interloper to the black domestic scene. While at the start of the narrative, Eva says "[t]here were people saying I did it because I found out about his wife . . . that was the easiest answer they could get" (4), implying that those who make such an assumption are in error, Eva's behavior at the moment of the revelation seems to indicate that the fact of Davis's marriage af-fects her a great deal. This is particularly true since Eva's murder and castration of Davis takes place shortly after she is made aware of his marital status. Ironically enough, in the scene in which Davis reveals that he is married, Eva initially makes the mistake of suggesting that she and Davis together constitute a kind of domestic coupling, another version of the domestic "tenderness" and vulnerability Eva experiences with James Hunn. Her miscalculation is made evident by Davis's harsh response: "'It's like you were a husband,' I said. He looked at me hard. He was frowning." (95). The reason for Davis's frown is exposed only a few moments later, when he admits that he is already married, that it would be impossible for him to function "like . . . a husband" to Eva.

It is worth noting, here, that Davis's secrecy about his marriage, as well as his "hard" look and frown when Eva attempts to usurp his wife's place, so to speak, may indicate that he holds his marriage as sacred as Eva holds her own, and that his motivation for this desired sanctity is similar to hers. In other words, Davis, too, may hope to maintain a "private" space of inviolable domesticity for himself and his wife, identical to that which Eva seems to require for herself and James Hunn. Nonetheless, Eva does not recognize the similarity in their po-sitions; her reaction to Davis's revelation reveals her uneasiness with what she reads as his deception:

"You didn't tell me you were married."
"I thought I told you."
"No, you didn't tell me."

> Big rusty nails sticking out of my palms. But I let him fuck
> me again. (95)

The suggestion of nails in Eva's palms seems to be a clear reference
to the Christian image of Jesus nailed to the cross. That Davis's revelation thus "crucifies" Eva indicates her sense that Davis has betrayed
her, indeed, that she is made a kind of martyr in the face of his betrayal, particularly since she allows him to have intercourse with her
again postrevelation. This martyrdom may have everything to do with
the complicated relationship to domesticity shared by black people, in
which the domestic space is understood as sacred and inviolate precisely because, as Rhonda Williams has noted, African Americans "live
without the benefit of an assumed familial and sexual wellness[.]"[20]

At a later point in the text, Davis questions Eva's continued silence,
which proves again to be related to his former omission:

> "Eva, why won't you talk?"
>   I turned with a smile and handed him his plate. "You meant to tell
> me, didn't you?" I asked.
>   "Yes, I meant to tell you. . . .
>   "I thought you were the kind of woman who'd understand."
>   "I understand."
>   "I thought I could turn to you for something I needed. Not
> romance," he said.
>   I closed my eyes. I said nothing. (116)

The section break that comes after the above scene begins with the
following words, in reference to yet another man Eva encounters: "He
asked me if I'd been hurt in life. He said I looked like a woman who'd
been hurt in life" (117). The juxtaposition of these two scenes suggests
that Eva's "hurt" is partly a function of her relationship to Davis. And
if Eva has been hurt by Davis, it is because in neglecting to admit his
marital status to her, he has forced her participation in a scene of disrupted family intimacy that places her in the role of domestic intruder.
Davis's use of Eva's body in the service of effecting his own domestic
disruption, his willingness to foreclose the possibility of a shared space
of protected intimacy or "romance" with Eva in favor of a culturally
unacceptable sexual coupling, is one source of Eva's sexualized pain in

the narrative—and this pain might be understood as a partial motivation for her violence. When linked to the gendered silencing that Eva experiences throughout the text, it is thus possible to understand Eva's brutality toward Davis as a retaliation for the manner in which his secrecy has exposed their relationship to familiar accusations of sexual pathology.

Gaze and Voice: Silencing (Female) Desire

Here I want to return for a few moments to the gendered divide in expressions of vicious desire that I outlined early on in the chapter, in order to explore the ramifications of that divide for Eva; I would suggest that the gendered division within vicious desire, and particularly the feminine silencing that comes along with that division, also provides a partial explanation for Eva's expressions of sexualized violence. One way of understanding this connection is to examine more closely the way Jones's text deals with the gendered gaze, which itself has a relationship to both desire and violence. In the previously cited "'I Hear You with My Eyes,'" Slavoj Zizek writes that "[v]oice and gaze relate to each other as life and death: voice vivifies, whereas gaze mortifies."[21] While a superficial reading of Zizek's comment attends merely to the figurative link between gaze and physical mortality, it is just as possible that gaze's relationship to "mortification" simultaneously refers to another kind of death entirely, the "little death" that has historically functioned as a euphemism for orgasm.

Certainly in the text of *Eva's Man*, a symbolic parallel seems to exist between gaze (particularly male) and sexual touch, as well as between sexual touch and death; consistent with the gendering of vicious desire noted above, these links are frequently accompanied by a diminished, absent, or actively silenced female voice. As Madhu Dubey writes, "The acts of looking and interpretation are invariably acts of masculine power in *Eva's Man*; the novel offers no possibility of a looking, a reading that can respect the integrity of the feminine object."[22] In other words, female characters are figuratively violated when they are looked at by male characters in the novel; gaze as a signifier for desire is another means by which men assert a kind of gendered sexual violence against women in the text.

For example, Eva's mother's lover, Tyrone, after once placing Eva's hand on his penis, continually stares at her although she is careful to avoid his eyes: "I didn't even like his eyes on me. Like when I was writing my math problems or reading, I could feel his eyes on me. I didn't dare look up at him" (34). Tyrone's eyes replace his hands in this instance—that Eva describes them as something she can "feel" on her body gives gaze a tangible quality that heightens her sense of violation. It is no coincidence that this violative gaze appears when Eva is doing "math problems" or "reading," both signifiers of Eva's potential empowerment as an educated, thinking female subject. Tyrone's gaze *dis*empowers Eva, in effect neutralizing her potential intellect and reducing her, once again, to merely a violable body.

The consequences for Eva of potentially meeting eyes with Tyrone are unclear in the above scene; perhaps Eva's returned gaze would indicate a reciprocal offering of desire, or consent to his behavior. Instead, with her eyes down she remains merely a victim of his assault, and is compelled continually to reimagine the actual moment of the molestation: "I could still feel my hand down there. Sometimes when I would think about it, I would go and wash my hand" (31). Eva's compulsive handwashing is designed to wash away the uninvited intrusion of Tyrone's sexual appetite; no amount of washing will "sanitize" her, however, because the memory of the touch, like Tyrone's insistent gaze, recreates that appetite in Eva's psyche, inaccessible to the cleaning power of mere soap and water.

This sense of a masculine gaze intruding on the female psyche is made explicit elsewhere in the text; the prison psychiatrist (who as Francoise Lionnet points out, himself functions as an amalgam of various men in the text—"his name is David Smoot, recalling young Freddy Smoot as well as Davis Carter")[23] questions Eva about her castration of Davis in a manner fraught with erotic overtones:

> He leaned toward me. He said he didn't just want to know about the killing, he said he wanted to know about what happened after the killing. Did it come in my mind when I saw him lying there dead or had

> I planned it all along. His voice was soft. It was like cotton candy. He
> said he wanted to know how it felt, what I did, how did it make me
> feel. I didn't want him looking at me. (76)

Here the psychiatrist's gaze, along with his invasive questioning, constitute an unwelcome intrusion into Eva's memory. It is important to
note, however, that this description of the session is from Eva's perspective; the text offers no "objective" narration with which to verify
the truth of Eva's claims. Still, it may be enough that she *perceives* the
psychiatrist's attention as violative, for this perception suggests that
Eva experiences the attention of most or even of all men as a kind of
psychic assault. In this way, Eva enters (or is co-opted by) a masculine
economy of vision in which she is a silenced object of men's observation
and desire.

This interpretation is incomplete, however, in that it fails to account
for Eva's own gaze, which itself functions at several points as a kind
of inadvertent resistance to the expression of masculine power over
her. Indeed, even at moments like the above encounter with Tyrone,
when it seems that Eva is being victimized by a violative masculine
regard, Eva returns the male gaze with an apparently violative gaze of
her own. Frequently, however, she seems unaware of (or incapable of
acknowledging) the content of her gaze, and the (mis?)reading of her
eyes that men are likely to undertake when she looks at them. In the
moments before Tyrone places her hand on his groin, for example, her
eyes seem unintentionally to suggest her own erotic interest:

> I don't know what made me look where I was looking. When I first
> started looking there, I didn't realize that's where I was looking, and
> then when I realized, I kept watching down between his legs. I don't
> know how long he saw me watching there but all of a sudden he took
> my hand and put it on him. I was scared to look up at him. (30)

Of course, what "makes" the adolescent Eva look at Tyrone's groin is
curiosity, soon transposed as desire. That Eva realizes she is staring,
but does not cease the activity, implies a deliberateness to her gaze that
the language of the text obscures, almost as if this language is being
reshaped in the service of propriety. Use of phrases like "I didn't real-

ize" and "I don't know" (as well as "all of a sudden" and "I was scared") in Eva's first-person narration seem to confirm her innocence or vulnerability rather than her potential interest in Tyrone's body.

In fact, however, the two coexist in Eva—while she is fearful, she is also curious enough to maintain her unbroken staring at the place "between his legs." This textual cloaking of potential female desire as expressed through the gaze differentiates feminine looking from the more directly violative gaze that men like the psychiatrist and Tyrone enact against Eva. Indeed, such cloaking suggests the same pattern of "dissemblance" around black female sexuality identified by Darlene Clark Hine: "The dynamics of dissemblance involved creating the appearance of disclosure, or openness about themselves and their feelings, while actually remaining an enigma."[24] According to Hine, it was through the enforcing of sexual secrecy that black women hoped to "accrue the psychic space" necessary for survival.

The sense that Eva is unaware of her own desirous potential, or that she is (consciously or unconsciously) hiding that potential in the service of her own psychic safety, surfaces even earlier in the text, when a pre-adolescent Eva is dragged under the stairs by her adolescent neighbor, Freddy Smoot. Consistent with the feminine silencing that frequently accompanies scenes of sexualized violence in the novel, Freddy is allowed the only dialogue in the scene, saying "'I'ma put it in you like Mama's men put it in her.'" Rather than responding, Eva remains quiet, watching him: "He held my arm and unzipped his pants and took his thing out. Then he kept looking from my eyes to his thing. And then all of a sudden he pushed me away from him, and turned and zipped his pants back up, and went upstairs. I didn't know what he'd seen in my eyes, because I didn't know what was there" (120). The "mortifying" potential of the gaze is at its most literal here: Freddy, prepared to rape Eva, instead runs from her in fear because of the threat that her eyes inadvertently convey. This threat is figuratively "veiled" by Eva's lack of awareness of her own potential for the expression of violent desire; again the text reinforces a gendered divide through the language of innocence (or ignorance).

While Freddy is here able to interpret the vicious character of Eva's regard, the novel is also filled with contrasting moments in which men misread, or read incompletely, the potentially vicious desire in the female gaze, also relying on conventional structures of gender difference both to invoke female desire and to dismiss any possibility of that desire's danger. In *Eva's Man,* men make enigmatic statements about the female gaze: "He said when he first saw those eyes of mine, he knew I could love a man" (163), or "'There was something in your eyes that let me know I could talk to you'" (46). Interestingly, only the first of these comments is directed at Eva; the other is said by Tyrone to Eva's mother, suggesting that Eva and her mother share this mysterious quality to their gaze that persuades men of their interest. The narrative seems to imply that this intergenerational connection also has something to do with the influence of a gypsy on Eva's great-grandmother: "The gypsy Medina, sitting in my great-grandmama's kitchen, said, 'There's something in my eyes that looks at men and makes them think I want them'" (46). Again, the text cloaks female sexual agency; the gypsy euphemistically frames her visible desire as an unnamed "something," and speaks of this aspect of her character as if it were disconnected from her own motives and desires, an alien presence controlling her from within.

Indeed, however, this alien presence may be nothing more than the displacement of *masculine* desire in the direction of women's bodies; for example, Davis's explanation to Eva of why he comes to her table in the restaurant where they meet suggests that he is projecting his own desire on to her:

> He looked at me. "I don't expect you to say nothing. I can read your eyes."
> "Can you?"
> "Yeah, that's why I came over."
> "You couldn't see my eyes then."
> He nodded. "Yes I could." (8)

In other words, even if when he first sees Eva he is too far away actually to see her eyes, he believes that he can "read" them because she fits into gendered parameters of desire that are already fixed. These parameters require his aggression and her silence, which explains why he "don't expect [her] to say nothing." Davis effectively misreads Eva's body, assuming that her gaze contains only a passive desire when instead it too has the capacity to violate. Since Jones's text aligns gaze, desire, and death, Davis's narrow reading of Eva's gaze as passively desirous reveals a potentially fatal ignorance on his part that is dependent upon conventionally gendered patterns of vicious desire.

Eva's conscription into such patterns of male control and female silencing is clearly a source of rage and frustration for her in the narrative. This rage recalls the rage of emasculation that Baldwin claims is the root of sexualized violence in Wright's work. In the case of Jones's protagonist, I would suggest that it is the gendered divide between vicious desire and passive acceptance that, at least in part, replaces emasculation as the source of black female rage in Jones's novel. Eva Canada does seem to be driven by rage, but rather than the rage of a man being castrated, hers is the rage of a woman silenced by the normative sexual order. In fact, Eva's repeated silencing, her passive acceptance of violative male desires, may in part be what leads her to commit the final act of murder and mutilation that so radically counters feminine passivity, since with Davis in particular, Eva seems unable to give voice to her thoughts and emotions, even purposely suppresses them.

Nowhere is this suppression of Eva's voice more evident than in a scene in which the two eat together in Davis's tiny room:

> "You eat food as if you're making love to it," he said.
>
> "I'm sorry."
>
> "No, I like it. I like to watch."
>
> I found it hard to go on eating, hard to find my mouth. I looked up, but he wasn't watching me any longer. I went on eating, my shoulders bent.
>
> "What are you thinking? You're not talking."
>
> "Nothing."
>
> "Why aren't you speaking?"
>
> "I don't have anything to say right now."
>
> [. . . .]
>
> He looked at me hard. He got up and came over and walked behind me and put his hand on my shoulders. He belched, said excuse me. I

> could feel my muscles tighten, my skin withdraw, but he didn't act like
> he could feel it. I held my own belch in, till it made me feel sick. All
> that gas inside. I said nothing. (126)

This scene recalls, again, the relationship between violative desire and
gaze, in Davis's attention to Eva's style of eating. While it is less than
remarkable to link eating and sexual pleasure, as Jones does in this
scene, what is curious here is the way that Davis's observation seems to
thwart Eva's enjoyment.[25]

Once she is aware that Davis "likes to watch" her, Eva is unable
to go on eating; the intervention of his masculine gaze, a stand-in for
his desire, forces her to sacrifice the expression of her own sexual and
gustatory pleasure. Only when she verifies that Davis is no longer observing her can she return to her food, this time with her body in
a tensely self-protective posture ("my shoulders bent"). Eva's physical
discomfort is made evident in the scene through the representation of
her physical response to Davis's touch, including her inability to release
gas. She becomes tense and withdraws from his hands on her shoulders
but is unable actually to voice this tension; while he is comfortable
enough to belch, she holds her own belch inside her body, suppressing it as she suppresses her voice. It is interesting that gas stands in
for voice, here, because it suggests explosiveness, the possibility that
when Eva does release this built-up substance, it will exit her body in a
violent eruption. And Eva does erupt, murdering and castrating Davis
shortly after this incident.

Interestingly enough, at the moment of Davis's death Eva releases
the gas that she had been withholding: "Then he gripped my waist. I
had my back to him and didn't watch. But he gripped my waist hard
enough to break my ribs. 'Bitch.' I belched" (127). This belch, which
only a page before was stifled, indicates that the murder restores Eva's
voice, her ability to articulate herself as subject, precisely because
Davis's death allows her to release her repressed emotion. But while I
have already suggested that Eva's conscription in a pattern of gendered
silencing is the source of her rage, and that rage one reason behind
her murder and mutilation of Davis, I want to reconsider, as well, the

possibility that part of what is silenced in Eva throughout the text is pain, the pain of an exploited vulnerability. This vulnerability recalls that violated black domesticity that marks vicious desire as a particularly black phenomenon throughout Jones's text, and is a way of understanding Eva's violence as driven by more than simply feminine rage.

"I filled in the feelings": Eva's Sexualized Violence

Eva's extreme violence in murdering Davis is presaged elsewhere in the text, through the figurative alignment of Eva and another "violent" female character, the aforementioned queen bee. The queen bee functions as a double for Eva in the narrative. Not only is this connection made explicitly, when Eva's roommate in juvenile detention tells her "You're a queen bee" (153), but the text draws parallels between adult Eva and the character of the queen bee through repetitive language that switches seamlessly between the two figures. For instance, in the text, the statement "The queen bee. Men had to die for loving her" is followed immediately by "James said he was dying to kiss me. He said he was dying to kiss me" (131). Such language suggests that like the queen bee, Eva's sexual affection is potentially toxic, even dangerous.

In a similar instance, a chapter consisting of these two sentences: "'Let's play,' he asks. The sweet milk in the queen bee's breasts has turned to blood" (132), is followed only a few pages later by Eva's first-person narration: "My breasts are rocks that turn to bread and then to milk. Blood is inside my breasts. What would you do if you broke bread and blood came out?" (138). The imagery of milk turning to blood again recalls the brutal possibilities within desire; in this instance, the nourishment of the lover that is suggested by breasts as bread, or as a source of "sweet milk," is transformed, seemingly without warning, into a more sinister image, of breasts as containers for blood.

Such an image in fact recalls Alice Walker's short story "The Child Who Favored Daughter," in which a man consumed by incestuous desire for his dead sister cuts off the breasts of his daughter, who resembles that sister.[26] In Walker's text, the association of breasts and blood is deliberate, however, a form of punishment meted out by the father for the girl's alleged promiscuity, while in Jones's text the association seems to come as an unwelcome surprise. This sense in Jones's narrative that the transformation is both unexpected and unpleasant is implicit in the question that Eva poses; what, she asks, would you do if you made a gesture designed to bring pleasure (here, the breaking of bread, because of the prior association between breasts and bread, takes on an erotic meaning in addition to its suggestion of consumption or nourishment and the attendant satiation) and were greeted instead by violence, brutality?

The actual character of the queen bee responds to this circumstance by opting for self-destruction. Eva's response, in contrast, is to turn this destructiveness outward, against the very group of people who throughout her life have conflated desire for her with violence against her—men. A less obvious aspect of Eva's reaction, however, is grief; while it is certainly true that Eva's murder and castration of Davis are a function of her rage over masculine violence and sexual control, there is evidence in the text that such rage grows out of an initial vulnerability to pain. In the following lines from a fantasy sequence, for instance, the imagery of the queen bee and of violent mutilation is juxtaposed with an impassioned confession about emotional wounding:

> The man says, Loneliness, you feel loneliness when there's no one you can go to, for anything—no one woman you can go to—I couldn't find one woman.
>
> He's naked on the church steps. The woman takes her clothes off too and holds her hand out to him[. . . .]
>
> He has no thumb on one hand, and the other hand is slashed red. It drips between his legs.
>
> Your breasts are loaves of bread, he tells her. You look like a woman who's been hurt by love.
>
> Yes, I was hurt by love. My soul was broken. My soul was broken. (143)

The man in this passage has injuries that suggest he is another amalgamation of men, all of whom have participated in real-time attempts to control and possess Eva sexually; his thumb is missing like a man who tries to pick her up while she sits with her cousin Alfonso in a bar, and his other hand is "slashed red" like the hand of Moses Tripp, whom a teenaged Eva stabs after he tries to assault her outside the same bar. In addition, the blood dripping between his legs suggests Davis's castrated form. The woman in the passage can be read as Eva in her role as textual double for the queen bee, because of the repetition of the breasts/bread imagery that has linked these two figures earlier in the narrative.

It is thus possible to read the repeated statement "my soul was broken" as Eva's, to interpret as hers the claim that intimate relationships have harmed her emotionally and spiritually. It is important to note that both woman and man are naked in this scene, which might suggest a laying bare of the body, a willing physical and emotional vulnerability. This is confirmed by both man's and woman's willingness to acknowledge weakness: the man confesses to an extreme "loneliness" while the woman, Eva, admits that she was "hurt by love." This vulnerability is exploited later in the scene, however, when the woman is once more alone:

> She stands naked on the street. She asks each man she sees to pay her debt. But they say they owe her nothing.
> The owl is perched on the stairs.
> "I've come to protect this woman," he says.
> But he turns into a cock, and descends. A lemon between his legs. She has made the juice run. (144)

The source of the woman's "debt" is unclear; perhaps it refers to a racialized loss, the debt of black vulnerability to a racist sexual mythology, which according to the logic of the salvific wish, can only be "paid" through the re-establishment of an inviolate domesticity. The men in the passage are unwilling to help in solving this conundrum, however, ignoring the naked vulnerability with which she approaches them. Even the image of the owl, at first a recuperative one, disintegrates into a figure of violation. The owl refers to an equally ambiguous moment earlier in the text, where Mr. Logan "hoots" from the top of the stairs to protect an adolescent Eva from Tyrone, who intends to pull her under the stairs and molest her (35, 36). Mr. Logan's value as rescuer is diminished, however, by Miss Billie's claim that Logan himself molested her when she was a child: "'Don't let that old man mess with you, now, cause he ain't nothing but a shit.'" (12) Thus in the passage above, the hooting owl, perched above Eva on the stairs like an angel, soon transforms himself into a man like any other in the novel, a walking "cock" that steps down from its pedestal in order to approach Eva sexually. The "juice" that she releases might be read as both semen and blood, fitting symbols of simultaneous pleasure and pain, which again recall the motif of vicious desire.

This dream-like passage implies that Eva has been wounded by intimacy, and that her violence is at least in part a result of this wounding. Eva admits as much directly, in another exchange with the psychiatrist; he asks, "What do you think is the matter with you?" and she replies, "Loneliness. I filled in the spaces. I filled in the spaces and feelings." To his question "Why did you kill him?" Eva repeats again, "I filled in the feelings" (169). The word "loneliness" recalls the earlier sequence, in which the man and the woman face one another naked; here in this scene the word seems to suggest a similarly painful moment of vulnerability. The question of what is the matter with Eva is an important one, for it gestures toward a justification of her madness. This justification comes not from anger, but from pain, exposure— "loneliness" is the problem. That the murder "fill[s] in the spaces and feelings" suggests one of two things: either Eva herself is empty, devoid of feeling, or she perceives Davis himself as a site of emptiness due to his unwillingness to extend himself to her emotionally. The second interpretation is certainly reminiscent of Davis's insistence that he seeks only sexual gratification from Eva, "not romance"; like the male passersby in the dream sequence, Davis insists that in spite of Eva's obvious vulnerability, he "owe[s] her nothing." In either case, Eva seems to use the murder to regain access to emotion, to "fill in the feelings" that her own emptiness, or Davis's emptiness, have denied her. I am reminded again of Baldwin's words, his notion that a "great space" exists in black literature where sex should be. Eva is the embodiment of this idea, using murder and castration to fill in what she explicitly says are "the spaces and feelings" in her life.

Thus on the one hand, I do want to suggest that Davis's murder is Eva's retaliative reaction against the man who has come to embody the entirety of male desire for and violence against her. As the psychiatrist later speculates: "I think he came to represent all the men you'd known in your life" (81). On the other hand, however, I also want to consider the possibility that this violence is a means of simultaneously denying and reasserting the vulnerability of desire, for a woman whose relationship to desire is complicated by racialized narratives of pathology. Eva's brutal behavior may be both a reaction to her own victimization by masculine desire, and an opportunity to express her own vulnerability to desire from the relatively *in*vulnerable position of empowered violator, rather than as the doubly vulnerable black and female body so often assumed to be the source of black domestic deviance.

The climactic scene of the castration, which I quote at length below, offers the most powerful example in the text of how desire and violence are enmeshed throughout the text and in Eva's actions in particular. Eva approaches Davis's dead body with the gentleness of a lover, but ends up committing a grotesque act of mutilation:

> I put my hand on his hand. I kissed his hand, his neck. I put my fingers in the space above his eyes but didn't close them [. . .] He was warm. The glass had spilled from his hand. I put my tongue between his parted lips. I kissed his teeth.
>
> *"That kiss was full of teeth," James said. He stood back and laughed and then kissed me again.*
>
> I opened his trousers and played with his penis. My mouth, my teeth, my tongue went inside his trousers. I raised blood, slime from cabbage, blood sausage. Blood from an apple. I slid my hands around his back and dug my fingers up his ass, then I knelt down on the wooden floor, bruising my knees. I got back on the bed and squeezed his dick in my teeth. I bit down hard. My teeth in an apple. A swollen plum in my mouth. *How did it feel?*
>
> [. . . .] Blood on my hands and his trousers. Blood in my teeth. *A woman like you. What do you do to yourself?*

> I [. . .] kissed his cheeks, his lips, his neck. I got naked and sat on
> the bed again. I spread my legs across his thighs and put his hand on
> my crotch, stuffed his fingers up in me. I put my whole body over him.
> I farted[. . . .]
>   "Bastard."
> I reached in his pants, got my comb, took the key he'd promised,
> washed my hands, finished my brandy, wiped his mouth, and left. (128,
> 129, author's emphasis)

The italicized sentences in this scene are all words voiced by various
men in the text. Their repetition here intially reinforces the notion that
Davis's body represents the focal point of all Eva's aggression and desire for men. The narrative's structure suggests that Eva hears each of
these voices as she mutilates Davis, in a sort of internal dialogue with
the male body in front of her, a body that exists both in physical space
and in the psychic space of her mind. In recalling the voices of every
man who has played a significant role in her life, she invests Davis's
body with an excess of meaning, symbolically freeing herself from the
sway of that hugely powerful body by desecrating it. The invocation
of James Hunn, however, reminds readers that Davis also represents
Eva's co-optation by a violated domestic sphere, rather than simply her
silencing in the service of masculine dominance. Thus her violation of
Davis's body is related to that prior domestic violation; here Davis is
punished for the manner in which his actions have made Eva herself
vulnerable.

Throughout the depiction of this process, images of pleasure and
supreme tenderness are juxtaposed with moments of grotesque violence. Eva kisses Davis's lips, hands, cheeks, but also raises blood and
"slime" from his body by biting his penis, farts on him while attempting to penetrate herself with his lifeless fingers. These juxtapositions
of tenderness and viciousness suggest that in mutilating Davis, Eva
is able to "safely" express her desire for him without the risk of making herself vulnerable to either his masculine power over her (which
is the typical operation of vicious desire in the text) or to the intense
exposure of desire plus an assumed pathology. While the pathology
is always present, conscripting Eva's body into a narrative of black

intimate vulnerability simply by virtue of that body's blackness, the vulnerability of desire itself is at least mitigated by the presence of an empowering violence. As Eva notes afterwards, "[The doctors] think I was trying to fuck him when he couldn't fuck back[. . . .] I think I was trying to *get* fucked" (159, 160, author's emphasis). In both cases, Davis's incapacity to "fuck back" suggests the removal of his ability to make Eva vulnerable by dominating her or by giving her pleasure. Her sexualized violation of his body is thus more than a rage-filled declaration of her power; it is also a means by which she can partially express her own vulnerability without being made doubly vulnerable to emotional and racialized assault.

The final moments of the scene, however, are decisive in their anger—"'Bastard'" expresses Eva's last sentiment toward Davis and what he has come to represent. That it is voiced aloud rather than in a mental dialogue only strengthens its emphasis. The gestures of closure Eva makes also are fraught with psychic significance in the text. Removing her comb from Davis's pocket reasserts her own power over her appearance, a power that he had taken from her. Likewise, taking the key to the room signifies a reclamation of Eva's right to come and go as she pleases, rather than being Davis's captive. Even washing her hands recalls the compulsive handwashing that Eva goes through after touching Tyrone's groin; in this case, however, it suggests a final cleansing gesture, in which Eva washes her hands of all the acts of violation that have peppered her history. The scene of the castration thus serves as a sort of profane ritual that frees Eva from the violent grip of not only Davis, but all the men in her past. In a reversal of the power differential that has made her the victim of violence all her life, Eva becomes the empowered violator, writing her own identity on a supine male body.

In this way, Eva's behavior here recalls Vanessa Freidman's assertions about the meaning of female murder: "She may speak her rage through her murderous act. She uses her body, and his body, as tools— his body, his blood fertilizes the (re)creation of her identity . . . [T]he content of her act of murder is about using his body to speak, to make a

final statement, to make herself understood and visible at last[.]"[27] Part
of what Eva "speaks" through her murder of Davis is her own sexual
vulnerability, however, rather than simply her rage over her previous
victimization. In part, this two-pronged message marks Eva's insanity
in the text, although this insanity is not simply a result of her attempts
both to maintain and to mask the vulnerability of desire through violence. In fact, Jones's narrative ultimately suggests that Eva's vicious
desire is a marker of her insanity because Eva's extreme actions ruth-
lessly expose the unpleasant "truth" of desire in the novel.

Reading the Insanities of Vicious Desire

Evidence of Eva's madness in Jones's novel can be found in several different locations in the narrative. Exchanges between other characters
often affirm her insanity; for instance, a detective in the police sta-
tion after her arrest says to another police officer, "Look at those eyes.
A woman got to be crazy to do something like that" (65). In other
places in the narrative, italicized phrases indicate that Eva is remembering another person's comments about her: *"I submit the insanity of
Eva Medina Canada, a woman who loved a man who did not return that
love. Crumbled sheets and blood and whiskey and spit. You born fucking
and you. Your honor the court recommends that . . ."* (150). Of course the
two sentence fragments imbedded in the legal language here exemplify
another means by which Eva's mental instability is communicated in
the text—she is unable to recall others' words reliably. Instead, she
continually intersperses them with her own thoughts, or with profane details from dreams and fantasies. In part, this jumbled narration
seems designed to confound the process of textual analysis, since it
seriously undermines the novel's readability. One critic goes so far
as to suggest that Eva's insanity, unbalanced in the text by an alternative, "sane" narration, "diminish[es] the text's power to illuminate
the reader's world."[28] I would argue, however, that Eva's insanity has
everything to do with the recurrence of vicious desire throughout the
text, and that her chaotic narration might serve as a reminder of the

impossibility, for Eva or anyone, of "sanely" participating in this kind of brutal vulnerability.

This is particularly true given the way that Eva's most chaotic statements all seem to invoke the gendered and racialized imagery of vicious desire. In the above instance, for example, "crumbled sheets" and "fucking," phrases that invoke sexual interaction, are juxtaposed with the more vicious images of "blood" and "spit." A few pages later, the text returns to the phrase "born fucking" in another of Eva's jumbled tirades, this time more clearly associated with hostility and violence: "I bet you were born fucking and will die fucking, you fucking bastard. That bitch stuck me" (153). The notion of one being "born fucking" recalls narratives of pathology that insist that black bodies are "naturally" predisposed to sexual excess. In still another example of desire's association with pain in the text, in a later scene Eva lies in her jail cell and begins to imagine that Davis is in the room with her. There, a potent sexual fantasy soon becomes a moment of eroticized violence:

> He was there. He wasn't laughing. He just watched me. Then he got on my back. He hung onto my back. We were naked. . . . We were fucking. "What am I doing to you?" "You fucking me." Both his hands fingered my clit. He made me. "Oh, Jesus. It's your pussy, Davis. It's your pussy." After I came he kept touching my clit and it hurt. "Please don't."
> He parted my hair with a comb, scratching my scalp till it bled. (156)

The juxtaposition of intense desire with first the discomfort of sexual touch post-orgasm and then the painful image of a scalp being scratched open certainly demonstrates a preoccupation with desire's viciousness, the hurtful and even grotesque aspects of intimacy. Jones's text makes such juxtapositions repeatedly, as Eva's disjointed narration returns again and again to sexual pleasures suffused with blood, wounding, and pain. That these juxtapositions happen most frequently in the context of Eva's mental instability suggests that vicious desire itself is a form of insanity, that the doubled movement it contains, of reaching toward vulnerability through desire while pulling away from that vulnerability through the infliction of pain, is an unreasonable project. In that the two are parallels to one another, it is thus also possible to read the doubled movement of the salvific wish as a form of insanity, for the hope of protecting black sexual vulnerability through denying its existence is nothing if not an exercise in futility.

I contend, however, that the juxtaposition of the intimate and the abhorrent in Jones's novel is repeatedly associated with Eva's madness for another reason—namely, that Eva's behavior is the most extreme example of a larger cultural insanity that is evident throughout the novel, in violent couplings such as that of Alfonso and Jean, or of Eva's own parents. In effect, Eva's madness is not simply that she expresses desire viciously, but that she takes such expressions to their fullest extreme. Eva's vicious desire, in that it habitually links the sexual and the grotesque, recalls Zizek's claim in the essay from which this chapter's epigraph is drawn, that sexual pleasure (in his words, "jouissance," which he defines as "libido, or drive") is "by definition . . . ugly; it is always 'too close.'"[29] In other words, the viciousness of erotic expression does not depend on violence; it can be found in the closeness of another human being. Intimacy itself is a kind of horror because it forces one to accept the painful reality of another individual, and to gain pleasure from that acceptance. Indeed, according to Zizek, the capacity to clothe that experience of another being's painful reality in the veil of the sublime is the "true enigma" of human desire.[30] As such, the reason that Eva's madness is repeatedly associated with her desire, and that desire is repeatedly associated with violence, may not be simply that the harshness of violence can efface the vulnerability of sexual pleasure. Instead, this harshness also *mirrors* the experience of sexual pleasure, the sense, in Zizek's words, that another person has come "too close." Vulnerability itself does a kind of violence to the subject, by opening him or her to this painful intimacy.

Eva's insanity in the eyes of other characters may thus grow out of her admission of this repulsiveness, her embrace of the possibility that sex itself contains a kind of ugliness because it brings one close to the physical body of another. Other characters' behavior hints at this "truth" about desire, but by remaining locked into gendered patterns of erotic expression, their actions mask the possibility that intimacy itself might contain a viciousness that transcends gender and even racial difference. Eva, however, who expresses an active version of vicious desire, who both affirms her own vulnerability and forces the vulnerability of her male partners, places this universalized viciousness at the center of her sexual expression. As such, Eva's vicious desire is not a symptom of insanity for what that desire tries to accomplish (the simultaneous repudiation and embrace of vulnerability) but for what it refuses to resist. And the salvific wish is therefore an exercise in futility not just because it is impossible to create a safe space for black sexual vulnerability by foreclosing that vulnerability, but because the truth of all sexual vulnerability is that it can never be made safe. To enter the realm of the sexual, the erotic, is to take a risk, and no amount of silencing, no amount of propriety will erase that risk—even for those already-at-risk black bodies that have the most to gain from trying.

Thus I return again to the words of James Baldwin, who in his critique of those who fear and loathe homosexuality on the grounds that it is "inhuman" or "unnatural" makes the following observation: "What we really seem to be saying when we speak of the inhuman is that we cannot bear to be confronted with that fathomless baseness shared by all humanity[.]"[31] Baldwin's words make it clear that the human condition is in many ways a condition fraught with vulgarity, that human beings share a kind of messy reality that confounds every effort at denial. Or, as Zizek puts it, "'ugliness' ultimately stands for existence itself."[32] Therefore the project of the salvific wish, to sanitize and purify black sexual (and familial) character, is a project that finally works to erase black humanity. Not because black humanity is defined by depravity, which the salvific wish hopes to mask, but because all humanity contains a kernel of "ugliness" which the salvific wish fearfully denies.

Perhaps the greatest tragedy of this denial is that it is committed by black people as a reaction to, and therefore in the service of, a racist culture that has already done everything in its power to deny black humanity, to restrict African Americans' access to the fullest reaches of human experience. That one attempt to counter that denial and restriction involves a self-imposed dehumanization through the embrace of rigid standards of propriety reminds us not only of the incredible conscriptive effects of power, what Michel Foucault calls "the micro-relations of power," but also the incredible necessity of resisting these conscriptive effects.[33] Indeed, such circumstances demand recognition of the fact that the way to move past a history that has pathologized and dehumanized black people is *not* by embracing the very discourses used to effect this pathologization. After all, these discourses have also worked to dehumanize their creators, since they use black bodies as the symbolic (and sometimes the literal) receptacles of all pathology, so that white people, and especially white women, could occupy a space of "purity" that was defined in opposition to a mythic black "depravity."

For African Americans to embrace discourses of propriety derived from white bourgeois models is thus for us to embrace the madness of a Western culture that insists upon denying human ugliness, disease, weakness, pain, by projecting it onto the dark body of a distant (or, in the case of the United States, an all-too-near) Other. As such, the power of Eva Canada's madness is that it explodes the possibility of such projection, and recalls the inescapable fact that we are all in some way marked by pain, by violence, by ugliness—all vulnerable, and in that vulnerability, all human.

Epilogue

"Baldwin's a good writer but depressing as hell.
I don't ever want to love like that."
"Maybe that was the point," I said.
"What?"
"To take risks for love, not to be afraid of it."
—SHAY YOUNGBLOOD, *BLACK GIRL IN PARIS*

On August 22, 2004, the cover story of the *New York Times Magazine* was the article "Raising Kevion," about the challenges that young black men in the inner city face when attempting to live as gainfully employed, committed fathers to their children.[1] The article follows a young man named Ken, an ex-con and former pimp and drug dealer who now works as a pizza deliveryman and shares a household with his girlfriend Jewell, their two-year-old son, Kevion, and Jewell's two teenaged sons from previous relationships. While Ken and Jewell are committed to one another, Ken refuses marriage, in part because he is unwilling to accept the sort of wedding that the couple's financial circumstances might necessitate: "'I ain't having a City Hall wedding[.]'" Instead, Ken wants to marry "on a tropical beach, like the eponymous star of the sitcom 'Martin,' who tied the knot . . . amid exotic flowers, crashing waves and a cellist in black tie."[2] That sort of fantasy wedding is, unfortunately, well out of Ken and Jewell's economic reach. What's more, Ken, like many of the other young, poor black people the author interviews, wildly idealizes marriage itself, viewing it as a kind of "relationship perfection" that therefore goes hand in hand with "intimidating risks," including the risk of a partner's infidelity.[3]

Ken and Jewell's story intrigues me for a number of reasons. I place it here, in the concluding pages of *Private Lives, Proper Relations,* because it returns us to the matter of the real-world contexts for and consequences of the narrative representations of black intimacy that I have outlined in this volume. Throughout this book, I have considered the politics of intimacy in black *literary* production, the ways that particular authors from the latter half of the twentieth century have highlighted the black intimate subject's doubled vulnerability in their fiction, frequently through an interrogation of discursive practices designed to make intimacy "safe." Yet Ken and Jewell speak more directly to the lived intimate experiences of black subjects, particularly the working-class subjects who, as I argued at the end of chapter 1, are so often erased by critical naturalization of the bourgeois sensibilities underlying disciplinary responses to black intimacy. Indeed, my emphasis on "literary" in the sentence above is deliberate, as intratextual examination of the sociocultural discourses that surround intimacy seems particular to literary rather than popular black fiction—a division that has clear class implications. The work of commercial authors is usually far less invested in sustained attention to bourgeois codes of sexual and domestic respectability, which reminds us that such codes are always already marked by material aspiration or privilege.

Black gay writer E. Lynn Harris, whose neo-romance novels, beginning with 1991's *Invisible Life,* have almost single-handedly created a mass market for popular black "relationship" and "urban" fiction, is one useful example of this phenomenon.[4] Harris's work handles sexuality very differently than the texts I examine throughout *Private Lives, Proper Relations,* and not only because his writing frequently takes black bisexual men as its focus. Indeed, his early novels' frank and sometimes graphic sexual content has been repeated in other commercially successful black novels that are clearly heterosexual in their approach, including work by popular authors like Eric Jerome Dickey, Omar Tyree, and Zane. Although a full discussion of black popular fiction is beyond the scope of *Private Lives, Proper Relations,* it may be worth recalling here that the contemporary publishing divide between black literary and popular fiction reflects a real material divide within African American culture—one that highlights the class politics of the restrictive ideologies surrounding discourses of black intimacy, and that points up the ways such ideologies apply differently to the lived experiences of blacks from different socioeconomic backgrounds.

I will say more about this question of class shortly. First, however, to return to Ken and Jewell, I certainly agree with journalist Jason DeParle's assessment of the couple that "Wanting to marry only when you can do it on a tropical beach is [. . .] not to want it in any meaningful sense."[5] Indeed, the fact that Ken's vision of marriage is actually drawn from a television sitcom indicates that marriage is, to him, patently unreal, the fictional product of an imaginary world. I also wonder, however, whether Ken's literally *fantastic* vision of his own hypothetical wedding, and of marriage more broadly, might signal something larger—something related to the hegemony of heterosexual practice in American culture, what Lauren Berlant and Michael Warner call "national heterosexuality."[6] I wonder, in fact, whether the restrictive gestures of the salvific wish, along with the black doubled vulnerability that these gestures seek to mask, are not in many ways dependent upon that hegemony for coherence. Is there something about the way African American subjects relate to the larger culture's codification of heterosexuality as normative that creates, or at least enforces, the black intimate problematic I have identified throughout this book? If so, might a movement toward dismantling heteronormativity be one way of circumventing this seemingly irresolvable tension between the vulnerability of black intimacy and ultimately violent efforts to remedy that vulnerability?

Before answering these questions, I want to clarify what I mean when I say that the salvific wish, along with efforts to alleviate black doubled vulnerability, is dependent upon the hegemony of heterosexual practice for coherence. The idea that human intimacy can be made safe—actually an impossible notion, as the final chapter of *Private Lives, Proper Relations* makes clear—is to my mind exceedingly heterosexual in character. After all, the understood apotheosis of the heterosexual intimate relation is the married couple. This couple, and the familial and generational relations that it produces, function in American culture as the privileged, state-sanctioned repository of all things *legitimately* intimate and private. Importantly, however, the marriage coupling also operates as a founding organizational paradigm of *public* culture, not just individual but civic belonging; witness the definition of "national heterosexuality" as "the mechanism by which a core national culture can be imagined as a sanitized space of sentimental feeling and immaculate behavior, a space of pure citizenship."[7] In other words, heterosexual marriage is repeatedly fantasized, in American cultural parlance, as the sacred space that can take human beings, unpredictable social subjects with potentially errant personal *and* political desires, and make them "safe" both privately and publicly.

The salvific wish, an intraracial desire to rescue the black community from accusations of pathology through the embrace of bourgeois propriety, taps into this fantasy of the marriage relation as intimate hallowed and hallowing ground. But the problem of applying "the most fundamental geometry of social reproduction" to the African American subject is that black bodies have never been allowed to play the same role in majority American fantasy as everyone else.[8] The stigma of blackness is always a corrupting strike against the "pure citizenship" that marriage supposedly makes possible. Referring to queer sexuality, Michael Warner makes several pertinent observations about this concept of stigma:

> Stigma, like its etymological kin *stigmata*, refers to a mark on the body, like a brand or a tattoo or a severed ear, identifying a person permanently with his disgrace[. . . .] It marked the person, not the deed, as tainted. This is what the modern metaphor of stigma singles out. It is a kind of "spoiled identity[.]"[9]

Warner's commentary is instructive here because black people, and particularly black intimate behaviors, have certainly been so stigmatized in the United States, from slavery onward. The "mark on the body" that stigmatizes African Americans is their very skin color, the metonymic stand-in for a whole host of cultural assumptions about the alleged deviance of African Americans as sexualized subjects. These assumptions about black intimate character make up a large part of the racialized vulnerability that black people experience on a regular basis in American society.

The imagined power of heterosexual marriage to purify and discipline human desire thus has an altered resonance in the case of the black subject. And what I want to suggest here, in the concluding pages of *Private Lives, Proper Relations,* is that the very existence of the salvific wish as a phenomenon within African American culture suggests that some black people's response to this altered resonance has been to invest heterosexuality in general, and the heterosexual marriage relation in particular, with an even greater power than does the majority culture. Would not the institution of marriage—or our fantasies of it—need to be *hyper*powerful in order to counter a level of stigma that can exclude black people as a body from the realm of so-called normalcy? How might such fantasies reify heteronormativity in African American culture in ways that are problematic, even ultimately unhealthy? Here I am thinking, for example, of the early head-in-the-sand response of the black church to the AIDS epidemic, as well as the sensationalized phenomenon of black men "on the down low"—putatively straight men, often married, who secretly sleep with other men.[10] Very few of the alarmist stories about this phenomenon that have appeared in national media have taken seriously the idea that men might choose such behavior because the possibility of a *public* life narrative that deviates from the heterosexual norm is often simply unavailable to black people in black communities.[11]

What would be the alternative possibilities for black subjectivity if the heterosexual marriage coupling were abandoned as a guiding trope of "normal" intimate life? Here I am not advocating that black people refuse to marry (although Ken and Jewell's story seems to indicate that this is already happening on some level, as fantasies of marriage make the living institution somewhat more difficult to inhabit), but rather that we stop venerating marriage as *the* normative intimate relation for human beings. In other words, I am interested in what Berlant and Warner call "the changed possibilities of identity, intelligibility, publics, culture, and sex that appear when the heterosexual couple is no longer the referent or the privileged example of sexual culture."[12] These changed possibilities are a consequence, for Berlant and Warner, of a particularly "queer" perspective on the world, and this is exactly the perspective that I would suggest African American communities consider embracing.

I do want to distinguish, here, between actual gay, lesbian, bisexual, and transgender (GLBT) subjects or practices, and the notion of "queerness" more broadly and theoretically defined.[13] The two cannot be completely separated, of course; as Cathy Cohen notes, it would be not just impossible, but also disingenuous, "to seek to erase the historical relation between the stigma of 'queer' and the sexual activity of gay men, lesbians, bisexual, and transgendered individuals."[14] Yet I believe it is possible to consider "queerness" as not merely sexual practice, but also as a particular—and particularly open and radical—sociopolitical outlook and point of view. The editors of the new anthology *Black Like Us* note, for instance, that "the term 'queer' [. . .] signifies identity and ideological nonconformity—not a particular sexual orientation."[15] It is this ideological nonconformity that I suggest become the chosen approach to intimacy in African American culture. There is certainly some historical precedent for "tolerance" of GLBT subjects within black communities; Marlon Ross has noted, for example, that particularly before 1960, such communities refused to shun black gay men because of a widespread belief that "the need for racial solidarity was much more important than the impulse to ostracize individuals whose sexuality seemed to vary from the norm."[16] Yet I wonder what it would mean for a *public* narrative of black community to move beyond mere tolerance, beyond a kind of "we won't ask, you don't tell" willingness to overlook individual behavior, and to adopt queerness *as an ideology* of black sexual culture.

I realize that what I am arguing for here may read to some like pure fantasy, the kind of wildly impractical goal whose achievement can only be pushed perpetually into an unimaginable future. Yet given the ways that black communities have always already functioned, in the United States, as "outsider" spaces, this sort of shift actually seems to me to be particularly possible, a matter of embracing rather than defending against the intimate vulnerability that African American subjects face daily. And after all, the recurrent project of defending African American people from white America's accusations of pathology gives those accusations greater power than they have ever truly merited, and forces a kind of deliberate blindness to the complexities of lived black experience. Maurice Stevens suggests that black "narratives of self and community," because they work so desperately against the dehumanizing power of majority American culture, have often required "the conscious or unconscious excising of images suggesting the devaluation, social infirmity, and inhumanity assigned to African Americans as people and 'blackness' as a signifier."[17] Such narratives are, for Stevens, rigidly homogenizing in their quest for cultural "vindication."[18]

As alluded to previously, the black middle class today remains the bearer of such vindicating narratives—which another recent real-life racial saga makes clear. On May 17, 2004, comedian Bill Cosby gave a speech at Washington, D.C.'s Constitution Hall, during an NAACP–sponsored gala commemorating the fiftieth anniversary of the *Brown vs. Board of Education* desegregation ruling. During his speech, Cosby railed against the black poor for "not holding up their end" of the post–civil rights bargain, citing purely anecdotal evidence of poor blacks' lack of personal responsibility for problems such as high-school dropout rates, unwed pregnancies, and high rates of imprisonment for young black men.[19] During the year following this first incident, Cosby repeated portions of his incendiary remarks at other public speeches and events, and pointedly defended himself in interviews. Lauded by many blacks for "telling the truth," Cosby's vitriolic comments have also been soundly criticized for their implicit elitism by figures such as Michael Eric Dyson, whose book *Is Bill Cosby Right?* appeared in 2005.[20]

Cosby's remarks included several comments about poor blacks' alleged sexual pathology; in the first few lines of the speech, for example, he states "No longer is a person embarrassed because they're *[sic]* pregnant without a husband. No longer is a boy considered an embarrassment if he tries to run away from being the father of the unmarried child."[21] During a particularly notable passage later in the speech, Cosby goes on to suggest that the suppressive practices of the "old days" in regard to adolescent sexuality were better examples of black parenting: "In the old days, a girl getting pregnant had to go down South, and then her mother would go down to get her. But the mother had the baby. I said the mother had the baby. The girl didn't have a baby. The mother had the baby in two weeks. We are not parenting."[22] In other words, Cosby prefers the shame and silence that surrounded unwed pregnancy in the earlier decades of the twentieth century, including outright misrepresentation of the event by the family of the young woman in question. His words suggest that such silence would be a more reasonable response to the "improper" spectacle of unmarried sexuality, particularly among adolescents, than the frankness of current practice.

The kind of social cover-up that Cosby advocates here is precisely the sort of intimate secret-keeping demanded by the salvific wish. Thus Cosby's contemporary remarks remind us, again, of the class origins of the wish and its restrictive ideology. It seems that in the twenty-first century, rather than disappearing with the years' advancement, the salvific wish is becoming more and more the sole purview of the black elite, the group that Dyson calls the "Afristocracy."[23] What once had political resonance, however problematic, for all or most African Americans, now has become a kind of intraracial weapon that black elites such as Cosby can wield against the black poor—in much the same way that whites historically have wielded accusations of black sexual pathology against all blacks, across intraracial categories of class. The salvific wish, originally one of the "narratives of self and community" designed to protect blacks as a whole from discourses of racial pathology, is revealed implicitly in Cosby's comments and explicitly in the texts examined throughout this study as a kind of sociocultural violence, one that demands the disciplining or even the expulsion of "improper" blacks in pursuit of an elusive intimate safety for the remainder of the community.

Ironically, neither such protective narratives, nor the surplus that they excise, can free black subjects of any class from the centuries-old racial history within which all Americans are enmeshed. Instead, the salvific wish's *über*-conventional black hetero(sexual) couplings and the notion of the *über*-deviant, animalistic black (hetero)sexual promiscuity that such behaviors are meant to guard against, ultimately seem to be two sides of the same coin, immersed in the same narrow ideologies of racialized intimacy. On the one hand, we have the protected, hyper-private space of the bourgeois marriage coupling, and on the other, the spectacular, often consumable bodies of contemporary black social icons, the performers, athletes, and other household names who are so frequently the visible repositories of black intimate excess, the aberrant "outside" to the "inside" of black middle-class conventionality.[24] What would it mean for African American culture publicly to turn away from this intimate Catch-22? Queer sexual culture is not a perfect alternative by any means, and it, too, has been constructed within social narratives shaped by hierarchies of race, class, and gender.[25] Yet there does seem to be a kind of political strength in what Cathy Cohen calls *"theoretical conceptualizations* of queerness," a remarkable energy in the associated "acknowledgment that through our existence and everyday survival we embody sustained and multisited resistance to systems (based on dominant constructions of race and gender) that seek to normalize our sexuality, exploit our labor, and constrain our visibility."[26] Perhaps moving away from heteronormativity and toward queerness, even if primarily on the level of ideology, has the potential to grant black intimacy true subversive power—rather than merely the power to imitate, or titillate, the dominant subject.

Would such a move alleviate the "intimidating risks" that mark the marriage relation for a working-class African American couple such as Ken and Jewell? Perhaps not, but perhaps it would help us to reconsider the very significance of marriage in certain social contexts. After all, nowhere in his article on Ken and Jewell does DeParle articulate precisely *why* the two need marry at all. Ken works a legitimate (if low-paying) job, and so does Jewell; the two are monogamous, and Ken has taken on Jewell's two older sons as his own. In many ways, they epitomize stable, "respectable" family life. Yet the article clearly insinuates that they are falling short as a couple, and a family, because they are not legally married. Cohen has noted that welfare mothers, particularly black welfare mothers, "may fit into the category of heterosexual, but [. . . their] sexual choices are not perceived as normal, moral, or worthy of state support[.]"[27] Similarly, Ken and Jewell seem to be "queered" in the eyes of mainstream society despite their clear commitment to heterosexuality; their story suggests that the "intimidating risks" of marriage may have mostly to do with that institution's ideological link to a larger culture that already marginalizes subjects like the two of them on the basis of race, class, and gender. Would marriage erase those prior risks, or merely highlight them? It is worth remembering that Ken and Jewell will never, in the end, be the privileged "white, middle-class, heterosexual" subjects that marriage presumably is designed to make socially and politically *in*vulnerable.[28]

But then, perhaps avoiding risk, and vulnerability, misses the point. The epigraph that opens these final pages, drawn from black lesbian writer Shay Youngblood's second novel, *Black Girl in Paris*, seems to suggest as much. The novel tells the story of Eden, a 26-year-old black woman who travels to Paris in the 1980s to become a writer. It follows Eden through a series of odd jobs, adventures, and tortured love affairs, as well as near-miss encounters with her literary idol, James Baldwin, whom she actually meets, briefly, at the end of the text. The epigraph depicts a conversation between Eden and another young black woman, Luce (Lucienne), born in Barbados to a black father and French mother, and raised "on the streets of London" after her parents' marriage fell apart and her mother abandoned her and her sister.[29] While Luce suppresses the pain she still feels about her mother with a "soldier in her voice, cold and hard," Eden seems to find value in the pain that genuine intimacy sometimes elicits. It is no coincidence that the discussion between Eden and Luce centers on Baldwin, whom I identified in the early pages of this volume as one of the few black male authors in the twentieth century to represent intimacy— both hetero- and homosexual, and mediated *through* the complexities of U.S. racial politics—explicitly in his fiction.

It seems important to consider, for a moment, what it might mean that James Baldwin (or, more accurately, the characters he creates) is willing to "love like that," in Luce's words. Eden's cryptic response to Luce, her refusal to disavow the notion that Baldwin's narratives are "depressing as hell," suggests not only that the rewards of love make the risks worth taking, but also, more unpredictably, that risk, vulnerability, embrace of and expansion beyond fear, might be the most important outcomes of the intimate encounter. "Maybe that was the point"; Eden's "that," at first indeterminate, is revealed in the following lines as a referent for "to take risks," "not to be afraid[.]" In other words, whether the love affair ends well or badly, whether it proves, in the end, uplifting or "depressing," opening oneself to the vulnerability of intimacy produces its own kind of liberation—from unnecessary fear, from the uncomfortable lie of "safety." How ironic, then, that Eden avoids acting on her desire for Luce, who sweetly attempts to seduce her during a visit to the Turkish baths, because Eden fears the intensity of their connection: "I could see that loving [Lucienne] could consume me" (213). Afraid that sex would "jeopardize [the] friendship," Eden refuses Luce's advances with the words "Don't break my heart too" (213). Perhaps Eden's inability to risk a broken heart is a reminder of the human contradiction contained within intimacy, a contradiction that the African American subject may already know all too well—the risk of connection itself can save us, but that risk always verges on impossible to take.

Acknowledgments

This book would not have been possible without the encouragement and support of a truly diverse group of people and institutions. A Career Enhancement Fellowship from the Woodrow Wilson National Fellowship Foundation allowed me to take a year's leave from teaching in order to complete the manuscript. I would like to thank Richard Hope, Sylvia Sheridan, and Bill Mitchell at Woodrow Wilson, as well as Lydia English at the Mellon Foundation, for their support of that program and of the larger project of diversifying the academy—recent assaults on that project only clarify its importance. Thanks go, as well, to the Research Foundation of the City University of New York; a 2004 PSC-CUNY grant helped to make this book a reality.

My interests in gender, class, and sexuality as they intersect with race were sparked many years ago, while I was an undergraduate at Spelman College. The faculty of the English department there were the first to open my eyes to literary studies as a discipline, and to the possibilities of academia as a profession. I thank, especially, Judy Gebre-Hiwet and Gloria Wade Gayles for showing me not only the meaning of good teaching but the long-term value of critical thinking.

Many thanks, as well, to "Sister President" Johnnetta Cole, for her personal and professional guidance over the years.

Like many first books, this one began its life as a dissertation. A DeWitt Wallace Fellowship from Duke University, as well as research grants from the Mellon Foundation and the Social Science Research Council, provided financial support for the dissertation writing process. I owe a great many thanks to my fellow graduate students, who helped me through that writing process in both large and small ways. I am grateful to Mikki Brunner, Kevin Haynes, Amardeep Singh, Nicole Waligora-Davis, and Rebecca Wanzo for being patient and charitable colleagues, and to Ifeoma Nwankwo, in particular, for so gracefully walking this path just a few steps ahead of the rest of us. Special thanks go to Evie Shockley, for continuing after all these years to be an outstanding partner-in-crime, and to Mendi Lewis Obadike (and Keith Obadike, who deserves the credit for shifting my thinking about this project in the direction of racial vulnerability), for being great spiritual and intellectual company since the beginning.

The group of faculty that guided me during my years at Duke merit singular appreciation; I am grateful to Tom Ferraro for his wit and insight, and to Wahneema Lubiano for her compassion and her always perceptive and rigorous reading. Maurice Wallace has been both a role model and a friend for many years, and I thank him for his faith in me and for the high standard he continues to set. My deepest thanks go to my dissertation director, Karla F. C. Holloway, who has been a mentor in the truest sense of the word—her wisdom, kindness, and generosity of spirit have helped me to grow exponentially, as a scholar and as a person. I am so grateful to her for continually challenging me to move forward.

My years as an assistant professor at Hunter College have brought with them a group of exceptionally warm and supportive colleagues. Many thanks, in particular, to Richard Barickman, Cristina Alfar, Barbara Webb, Lynne Greenberg, and Sarah Chinn—as well as to Juan Flores, for giving me some much-needed perspective from outside my department. Nora Eisenberg and the CUNY Faculty Fellowship Publication Program came into my life at a crucial moment in the crystallization of the book's ideas. Thanks especially to Kenneth Speirs and Elizabeth Garcia for their attentive reading and for sharing their own marvelous ideas. I would like also to thank Robert Reid-Pharr for his unstinting mentorship and his sense of humor, and Shelly Eversley for her always-timely words of wisdom. I am grateful to Kiini Ibura Salaam for her support of and commiseration with me as a writer, across boundaries of genre and subject matter.

Monica Miller and Stefanie Dunning have both read large sections of this book and offered questions and suggestions that made it far stronger than it otherwise would have been. I thank them for their friendship and their unending encouragement throughout this process. I also thank the anonymous reviewers chosen by the University of Minnesota Press, whose scrupulous reading and thoughtful recommendations demonstrated such faith in the book's possibilities. My editor, Richard Morrison, has been a delightful advisor and critic from early on, and I thank him and the entire staff at the University of Minnesota Press for their hard work in bringing this project to fruition.

Finally, there are those who, in their unconditional love and support of me as a person, make this "life of the mind" so much easier to inhabit. The constancy of old friends Jalyn Spencer-Harris, Libya Doman, Brian Gaffney, and Doug McLachlan keeps me grounded, and I am deeply grateful for their continued presence in my life. I also would like to thank my family, especially my mother, Betty D. Jenkins, for her unshakable belief in me. She remains my earliest and greatest champion, and I am so lucky to be her daughter. Last and most of all, I am grateful to my wonderful husband and partner, Kamau, for saving me from myself on so many occasions. Thank you for making this vulnerable space of intimacy such a truly remarkable place to be.

Notes

Introduction

1. Quoted in Lillian Faderman, *To Believe in Women: What Lesbians Have Done for America—A History* (Boston and New York: Houghton Mifflin, 1999), 181.

2. Faderman, 182.

3. In addition to noting the extent of the silence on this matter at my alma mater, I also emphasize "possibility" here in order to acknowledge that Faderman's claims cannot be fully verified. Even if a great deal of circumstantial evidence points to Packard and Giles's lesbianism, there is no way to know anything for certain so many years later. This relative uncertainty, however, does not change the fact that on Spelman's campus, "lesbian" is a word usually left unsaid, even or perhaps especially in reference to the founders.

4. Sheila Alexander-Reid, "Voice of Reason: Spelman's Dirty Secret." *Women in the Life* (online) 12.5 (May 21, 2001): 2.

5. Alexander-Reid, 2.

6. Gail Bederman, *Manliness and Civilization: A Cultural History of Gender and Race in the United States, 1880–1917* (Chicago and London: University of Chicago Press, 1995), 25. Bederman goes on to argue, in a point salient to this book's larger argument, that this "dominant" discourse of civilization

also had powerful gender implications, which were closely linked with race: "[T]he pronounced sexual differences celebrated in the middle class's doctrine of separate spheres were assumed to be absent in savagery, but to be an intrinsic and necessary aspect of higher [white] civilization" (25).

7. The African slave trade and its domestic counterpart in the United States are only two examples of such violations; treating African people as chattel was made possible, in part, by the assumption (or the assertion) that blacks were less-than-human because their societies did not bear marks of Western "civilization" such as devotion to Christianity or an extensive written language.

8. I am aware that since Packard and Giles were white women, their potential lesbianism is not exactly an example of black sexual behavior. Still, as founders of a black women's college, the sexual practices of these particular white women have everything to do with how the black female bodies associated with that institution might subsequently be pathologized—particularly if it is assumed that Spelman students choose the school because of its history. Hence the silence about Packard and Giles' relationship both within Spelman's gates and among her alumnae.

9. Lauren Berlant, *The Queen of America Goes to Washington City* (Durham: Duke University Press, 1997), 19.

10. Toi Derricotte, *The Black Notebooks* (New York: Norton, 1997), 184, 185.

11. Derricotte, 185.

12. Elizabeth Alexander, "Can You Be BLACK and Look at This?: Reading the Rodney King Video(s)," in *Black Male: Representations of Masculinity in Contemporary Art*, ed. Thelma Golden (New York: Whitney Museum of American Art, 1994), 95.

13. The phrase "double jeopardy," coined by Frances Beale in 1970, was originally used to describe the position of black women in a racist and sexist society. See Frances Beale, "Double Jeopardy: To Be Black and Female" in *Words of Fire*, ed. Beverly Guy-Sheftall (New York: The New Press, 1995), 146–55. Though subsequent work in black feminist theory has expanded upon and moved beyond Beale's original model (see, for example, Deborah King's "Multiple Jeopardy, Multiple Consciousness: The Context of a Black Feminist Ideology," in Guy-Sheftall, 294–317), I invoke the phrase here not as a return to its original and most specific usage but simply to suggest the notion of a doubly vulnerable subject.

14. Michael Grossberg, *Governing the Hearth: Law and the Family in Nineteenth Century America* (Chapel Hill: University of North Carolina Press, 1985), 10.

15. See especially Lora Romero, *Home Fronts: Domesticity and Its Critics in the Antebellum United States* (Durham: Duke University Press, 1997). I discuss problems with and challenges to the separate spheres model in more detail in the next chapter.

16. For more on how the nuclear family was perceived as the foundation of a stable U.S. republic, see Mark E. Kann, *A Republic of Men: The American Founders, Gendered Language, and Patriarchal Politics* (New York: New York University Press, 1998), especially 79–104.

17. Grossberg, 9.

18. For a sociological analysis of African family retentions, see Niara Sudarkasa, "Interpreting the African Heritage in Afro-American Family Organization," in *Families in the US: Kinship and Domestic Politics*, ed. Karen V. Hansen and Anita Ilta Garey (Philadelphia: Temple University Press, 1998), 91–104.

19. Hortense Spillers, "Mama's Baby, Papa's Maybe: An American Grammar Book," in *Within the Circle: An Anthology of African American Literary Criticism from the Harlem Renaissance to the Present*, ed. Angelyn Mitchell (Durham: Duke University Press, 1994), 470, author's emphasis.

20. Barbara Welter, "The Cult of True Womanhood: 1820–1860," originally published in *American Quarterly* 18.2 (Summer 1966); reprinted in *Locating American Studies: The Evolution of a Discipline*, ed. Lucy Maddox (Baltimore: Johns Hopkins University Press, 1999), 44.

21. Welter, 46.

22. Jacobs's narrative of her enslavement and eventual escape from bondage, *Incidents in the Life of a Slave Girl*, was published in 1861 under the pseudonym "Linda Brent." In her narrative, she recounts her own efforts to protect her chastity in the face of her owner's constant pursuit. Forbidden by him to marry the free black man whom she loves, Jacobs ultimately chooses to accept the advances of another white man, the eventual father of her two children, in order to maintain control over her own sexuality. She responds to this man, in part, because he is unmarried and therefore less morally debased, in her view, than her adulterous owner. Jacobs's narrative thus demonstrates that enslaved women were neither ignorant of conventional morality nor passively available to sexual exploitation, even if circumstances and racism excluded them from the protections that white women were afforded.

23. Hazel Carby, *Reconstructing Womanhood: The Emergence of the Afro-American Woman Novelist* (New York and London: Oxford University Press, 1987), 30.

24. Bederman, 11.

25. Martin Summers, *Manliness and Its Discontents: The Black Middle Class and the Transformation of Masculinity, 1900–1930* (Chapel Hill and London: University of North Carolina Press, 2004), 1.

26. Sander Gilman, "Black Bodies, White Bodies: Toward an Iconography of Female Sexuality in Late Nineteenth-Century Art, Medicine, and Literature," in *"Race," Writing, and Difference,* ed. Henry Louis Gates Jr. (Chicago and London: University of Chicago Press, 1986), 250.

27. Nell Irvin Painter, "Hill, Thomas, and the Use of Racial Stereotype," in *Race-ing Justice, En-Gendering Power: Essays on Anita Hill, Clarence Thomas, and the Construction of Social Reality,* ed. Toni Morrison (New York: Pantheon, 1992), 443. Historian Deborah Gray White notes that "in every way Jezebel was the counterimage of the mid-nineteenth century ideal of the Victorian lady. She did not lead men and children to God; piety was foreign to her. She saw no advantage in prudery, indeed domesticity paled in importance before matters of the flesh." Deborah Gray White, *Ar'n't I a Woman?: Female Slaves in the Plantation South* (New York: Norton, 1985), 29.

28. Gilman, 231.

29. Paula Giddings, "The Last Taboo," in *Race-ing Justice, En-Gendering Power,* ed. Toni Morrison (New York: Pantheon, 1992), 209.

30. Summers, 8. Summers's text goes on to historicize the ways that intraracial definitions of black manhood also began to change in the early twentieth century, paralleling the shift of dominant definitions of manhood away from Victorian strictures.

31. Daylanne K. English, *Unnatural Selections: Eugenics in American Modernism and the Harlem Renaissance* (Chapel Hill and London: University of North Carolina Press, 2004), 4. See Charles Darwin, *The Origin of Species by Means of Natural Selection; or, The Preservation of Favoured Races in the Struggle for Life,* ed. J. W. Burrow. [1859]. (London: Penguin, 1985); or Francis Galton, *Hereditary Genius: An Inquiry into Its Laws and Consequences* [1869] (New York: D. Appleton, 1870). For additional historical analysis of the eugenics movement, see, for example, Stephen Jay Gould, *The Mismeasure of Man* (New York: Norton, 1981); Wendy Kline, *Building a Better Race: Gender, Sexuality, and Eugenics from the Turn of the Century to the Baby Boom* (Berkeley: University of California Press, 2001); or Steven Selden, *Inheriting Shame: The Story of Eugenics and Racism in America* (New York: Teachers College Press, 1999), among many others.

32. Daylanne English usefully points out that this term is in some ways a misnomer, as the phrase "survival of the fittest," often attributed to Darwin, was actually coined by English philosopher Herbert Spencer (4). In any case, while the notion of intellectual, social, and cultural evolution implied by the phrase "social Darwinism" was not necessarily limited to the advancement of racial and ethnic hierarchies, social Darwinist theory was certainly embraced by many proponents of eugenics in this period.

33. Michele Mitchell, *Righteous Propagation: African Americans and the Politics of Racial Destiny after Reconstruction* (Chapel Hill and London: University of North Carolina Press, 2004), 80. Mitchell's work points out the ways that black activists in the early years of the twentieth century nevertheless used eugenic concepts for their own purposes, drawing on eugenic theory's suggestion that "individuals possessed the potential to improve their offspring through strategic mating" (80) to advocate specific sexual and social practices with the goal of racial advancement. See also Daylanne English, 35–64, on W. E. B. DuBois's selective embrace of eugenics.

34. English, 8.

35. English, 177.

36. Daniel Patrick Moynihan, *The Negro Family: The Case for National Action* (Washington, D.C.: U.S. Department of Labor, 1965). I address more fully the work of both Moynihan and his predecessor, E. Franklin Frazier, in chapters 1 and 2 of this volume.

37. E. Franklin Frazier, *The Negro Family in the United States* (Chicago: University of Chicago Press, 1939), especially 47–49 and 102–13.

38. Frazier, 102.

39. Rhonda M. Williams, "Living at the Crossroads: Explorations in Race, Nationality, Sexuality, and Gender," in *The House that Race Built,* ed. Wahneema Lubiano (New York: Pantheon, 1997), 140.

40. Williams, 147.

41. Painter, 210.

42. Ashraf Rushdy, *Remembering Generations: Race and Family in Contemporary African American Fiction* (Chapel Hill and London: University of North Carolina Press, 2001), 2; Avery Gordon, *Ghostly Matters: Haunting and the Sociological Imagination* (Minneapolis: University of Minnesota Press, 1997), 195. More recently, Arlene R. Keizer has echoed these scholars' words, writing at the start of her monograph on neo-slave narratives, "Slavery haunts contemporary African American and Afro-Caribbean literature." Keizer, *Black*

Subjects: Identity Formation in the Contemporary Narrative of Slavery (Ithaca and London: Cornell University Press, 2004), 1.

43. Wahneema Lubiano, "Black Ladies, Welfare Queens, and State Minstrels: Ideological War by Narrative Means," in *Race-ing Justice, En-Gendering Power,* ed. Toni Morrison (New York: Pantheon, 1992), 339.

44. For more on racially motivated interventions to black reproduction in the United States, see Dorothy Roberts, *Killing the Black Body: Race, Reproduction, and the Meaning of Liberty* (New York: Pantheon, 1997).

45. Personal Responsibility and Work Opportunity Reconciliation Act of 1996. Public Law 104–193. 104th Cong., 2d sess. (22 Aug. 1996.) Stat 110.2105.

46. Carby, *Reconstructing Womanhood,* 116. See also Carby, "Policing the Black Woman's Body in an Urban Context," *Critical Inquiry* 18 (Summer 1992): 738–55.

47. For more on the history of uplift movements in the religious sector, see Evelyn Brooks Higginbotham, *Righteous Discontent: The Women's Movement in the Black Baptist Church, 1880–1920* (Cambridge, Mass.: Harvard University Press, 1993). Mitchell's *Righteous Propagation* historicizes both religious and secular uplift movements in light of the post-Reconstruction concept of "racial destiny" (7).

48. Paula Giddings suggests, for instance, that "Neither [black nor white women's clubs] questioned the superiority of middle-class values or way of life. . . . Black and White women saw the family as a microcosm and cornerstone of society." Giddings, *When and Where I Enter: The Impact of Black Women on Race and Sex in America* (New York: Bantam, 1985), 94.

49. Giddings, "The Last Taboo," 454.

50. Giddings, "The Last Taboo," 454.

51. Evelynn Hammonds, "Toward a Genealogy of Black Female Sexuality," in *Feminist Genealogies, Colonial Legacies, Democratic Futures,* ed. M. Jaqui Alexander and Chandra Talpade Mohanty (New York: Routledge, 1997), 174.

52. In my doctoral dissertation, the salvific wish is my sole focus; see Candice M. Jenkins, "Cultural Infidels: Intimate Betrayal and the Bonds of Race," *Dissertation Abstracts International, Section A: The Humanities and Social Sciences,* 63.6 (December 2002), 2242.

53. Williams, 142.

54. As Kevin Gaines writes: "Through uplift ideology, elite and less-privileged African Americans were striving for bourgeois respectability in the absence of rights or freedom." Kevin Kelly Gaines, *Uplifting the Race: Black*

Leadership, Politics, and Culture in the Twentieth Century (Chapel Hill and London: University of North Carolina Press, 1996), 16.

55. Mitchell, 10.

56. Darlene Clark Hine, "Rape and the Inner Lives of Black Women in the Middle West: Preliminary Thoughts on the Culture of Dissemblance," in *Words of Fire*, ed. Beverly Guy-Sheftall (New York: The New Press, 1995), 380.

57. Hammonds, 175.

58. In her essay, "Black Nationalism and Black Common Sense: Policing Ourselves and Others," Lubiano calls black nationalism "black American common sense," defining it as "ideology lived and articulated in everyday understandings of the world and one's place in it" (Wahneema Lubiano, in *The House That Race Built*, ed. Lubiano [New York: Pantheon, 1997] 232). In a claim related to this project, Lubiano goes on to note that "even as [black nationalism] functions as resistance to the state on one hand, it reinscribes the state in particular places within its own narratives of resistance. That reinscription most often occurs within black nationalist narratives of the black family" (Lubiano, 236).

59. W. E. B. DuBois, *The Souls of Black Folk* [1903]. Introd. Randall Kenan. (New York: Penguin, 1995), 45.

60. Lauren Berlant, "Intimacy: A Special Issue," in *Intimacy* (Chicago and London: University of Chicago Press, 2000), 1.

61. Keith Harvey and Celia Shalom, eds., *Language and Desire: Encoding Sex, Romance and Intimacy* (New York: Routledge, 1997), 3, authors' emphasis.

62. Berlant, "Intimacy," 2.

63. Leo Bersani, *A Future for Asytyanax* (New York: Columbia University Press, 1984), 296.

64. Berlant, "Intimacy," 2. Of course, the alleged "safety" of the domestic sphere is gendered in particular ways; as I discuss further in chapter 3, part of the notion of this arena's safety is dependent upon patriarchal conceptions of male dominance both within and beyond the home.

65. Michael Hanchard, "Jody," in *Intimacy*, ed. Lauren Berlant (Chicago and London: University of Chicago Press, 2000), 199, author's emphasis.

66. Lee Quinby, *Anti-Apocalypse: Exercises in Genealogical Criticism* (Minneapolis: University of Minnesota Press, 1994), 135, 140.

67. For more on relationships among enslaved blacks or between the enslaved and whites, see Eugene D. Genovese, *Roll, Jordan, Roll: The World the Slaves Made* (New York: Pantheon, 1974); Herbert G. Gutman, *The Black*

Family in Slavery and Freedom, 1750–1925 (New York: Vintage Books, 1976); or Kenneth M. Stampp, *The Peculiar Institution: Slavery in the Ante-bellum South* [1956] (New York: Vintage Books, 1989). See also Spillers, "Mama's Baby, Papa's Maybe."

68. bell hooks, "Selling Hot Pussy," in *Black Looks: Race and Representation* (Boston: South End Press, 1992), 77.

69. Alexander, 92.

70. Ed Guerrero, "The Black Man on Our Screens and the Empty Space in Representation," in *Black Male: Representations of Masculinity in Contemporary Art*, ed. Thelma Golden (New York: Whitney Museum of American Art, 1994), 184.

71. Deborah Gray White reminds us that even after slavery's demise, "[b]lack women continued to be perceived by white America as individuals who desired promiscuous relationships, and this perception left them vulnerable to sexual crimes" (164).

72. See Jacqueline Goldsby, "The High and Low Tech of It: The Meaning of Lynching and the Death of Emmett Till," *The Yale Journal of Criticism* 9.2 (1996): 245–82, for an insightful discussion of Thomas's use of this phrase and the notion of lynching as "rhetorical trope" (247).

73. Alexander, 105. It is certainly worth noting that accusations of sexual impropriety, and in some cases criminal charges, have been leveled at so many prominent black men in recent years (most recently, at the time of this writing, performer Michael Jackson, popular comedian Bill Cosby, and another NBA star, Kobe Bryant), that it would be impossible for me to address them all in detail. It seems safe to suggest, however, that each subsequent accusation or arrest, and the accompanying media frenzy, helps to solidify the notion of black sexual degeneracy in the U.S. imaginary.

74. Quinby, 148.

75. Tricia Rose, *Longing to Tell: Black Women Talk About Sexuality and Intimacy* (New York: Farrar, Straus and Giroux, 2003), 388.

76. Robert Reid-Pharr, *Conjugal Union: The Body, the House, and the Black American* (New York: Oxford University Press, 1999), 31.

77. Mason Stokes, *The Color of Sex: Whiteness, Heterosexuality, and the Fictions of White Supremacy* (Durham and London: Duke University Press, 2001), 3.

78. Claudia Tate, *Domestic Allegories of Political Desire: The Black Heroine's Text at the Turn of the Century* (New York: Oxford University Press, 1992), 5.

79. For other examples, see Ann DuCille's *The Coupling Convention: Sex,*

Text, and Tradition in Black Women's Fiction (New York and London: Oxford University Press, 1993); Hazel Carby's *Reconstructing Womanhood*, or Robert Reid-Pharr's *Conjugal Union*, some of which are cited elsewhere in this writing. For a study that addresses the Victorian obsession with racial and domestic purity through British literature, see Jennifer DeVere Brody's *Impossible Purities: Blackness, Femininity, and Victorian Culture* (Durham and London: Duke University Press, 1998).

80. Tate, 15, 18.

81. Madhu Dubey, *Signs and Cities: Black Literary Postmodernism* (Chicago and London: University of Chicago Press, 2003), 10.

82. Mark Currie, *Postmodern Narrative Theory* (New York: St. Martins, 1998), 32. Currie makes this point as part of an analysis of Laura Mulvey's early feminist work in film studies, pointing out the ways that Mulvey's writing is both an outgrowth of and a move beyond Althusser's influential concept, interpellation. See Mulvey, "Visual Pleasure and Narrative Cinema" Screen 16.3 (Autumn 1975): 6-18, and Louis Althusser, "Ideology and Ideological State Apparatuses: Notes Towards an Investigation" in *Lenin and Philosophy*, trans. B. Brewster (London: New Left Books, 1971), 127–86.

83. Keizer, 12. Keizer's suggestion that "imaginative writers [. . . are] weather vanes for the cultures they inhabit—they tell us which way (and how hard) the social and cultural winds are blowing" (15) is similarly persuasive.

84. The quoted definition is from Bederman, 24. See also Michel Foucault, *The History of Sexuality, vol. 1*, trans. Robert Hurley [1978] (New York: Vintage, 1990), especially 100–102.

85. Michel Foucault, *Power/Knowledge: Selected Interviews and Other Writings, 1972–1977*, ed. Colin Gordon (New York: Pantheon, 1980), 119.

86. Foucault, *Power/Knowledge*, 193.

87. Nella Larsen, *Quicksand, and Passing*, edited and with an introduction by Deborah E. McDowell [1986] (New Brunswick, N.J.: Rutgers University Press, 1989). Subsequent references to the 1989 edition will be included parenthetically in the text. Wilson Jeremiah Moses, *The Golden Age of Black Nationalism, 1850–1925* [1978] (New York and Oxford: Oxford University Press, 1988), 254.

88. See Summers, especially 8–10, and Bederman, 232.

89. Carby, *Reconstructing Womanhood*, 164.

90. See W. E. B. DuBois, "The Talented Tenth," in *Writings*, ed. Nathan Huggins (New York: Library of America, 1986), 842–61.

91. Joy James, *Transcending the Talented Tenth: Black Leaders and American Intellectuals* (New York and London: Routledge, 1997), 16. This history is particularly provocative in light of the increasing prominence of eugenic theory in the early years of the twentieth century. As Daylanne English notes, "from about 1900 to 1930, uplift took on a more disturbing quality as the period's notions of racial improvement (for both white and black people) became ever more tightly intertwined with the emerging science of genetics" (36).

92. Moses, 261, 262.

93. Quoted in David Levering Lewis, *When Harlem Was in Vogue* [1979] (New York: Penguin, 1997), 225.

94. Moses, 258.

95. See Summers, *Manliness and Its Discontents*, especially 225–31.

96. Lewis, 231.

97. Deborah McDowell, Introduction to *Quicksand, and Passing* (New Brunswick, N.J.: Rutgers University Press, 1989), xvi.

98. McDowell, xvi.

99. As scholars such as Werner Sollors and Philip Brian Harper have noted, this displacement of sexual excess onto the figure of the mulatta is hardly unique to Larsen; still, a broad examination of the phenomenon is beyond the scope of this writing.

100. J. Martin Favor, *Authentic Blackness: The Folk in the New Negro Renaissance* (Durham and London: Duke University Press, 1999), 96.

101. Gayle Wald, *Crossing the Line: Racial Passing in Twentieth-Century U.S. Literature and Culture* (Durham and London: Duke University Press, 2000), 18.

102. I should clarify, here, that I am not arguing that patriarchy in all of its manifestations is purely the product of white culture, nor that traditional African or African diasporic cultures are free from patriarchal male dominance—rather, I suggest that the loaded concept of "respectability" has particular ties to the Victorian era, as the history of the salvific wish as a concept makes clear.

103. Judith Butler offers a much more detailed psychoanalytic reading of this simultaneous revulsion and attraction in her discussion of Larsen's text. See "Passing, Queering: Nella Larsen's Psychoanalytic Challenge" in *Bodies That Matter: On the Discursive Limits of Sex* (New York: Routledge, 1993), 167–85.

104. The "explanation" for Irene's fair skin is, of course, that white ancestry exists further up on Irene's family tree than it does on Clare's. In chapter 4

of *Private Lives, Proper Relations,* I address the true multiraciality of most putatively monoracial black U.S. subjects in much greater detail. Here, however, I point out this discrepancy merely to make clear that I do not read Irene as a racial mirror of Clare. For a related analysis of *Passing* that focuses much more closely on the intraracial meaning of both Irene's and Clare's bodies in the racially integrated environment of 1920s Harlem, see my essay, "Decoding Essentialism: Cultural Authenticity and the Black Bourgeoisie in Nella Larsen's *Passing,*" *MELUS* 30.3 (Fall 2005): 129–54.

105. See McDowell, ix–xxxv. The most well known of the critics to follow and complicate McDowell's reading is Judith Butler, whose essay "Passing, Queering: Nella Larsen's Psychoanalytic Challenge" I refer to above.

106. See, for example, Carby's *Reconstructing Womanhood,* which ends with an analysis of Larsen's *Quicksand;* see also Ann DuCille's *The Coupling Convention,* which spends considerable time on Larsen's work, and addresses Harlem Renaissance author Dorothy West in its last chapter. Claudia Tate's *Domestic Allegories* also ends with an author typically grouped with artists of the Harlem Renaissance, Angelina Grimké, although Tate focuses on her play *Rachel,* produced in 1916 and published in 1920.

107. DuCille, 147.

108. Black male writer James Baldwin is one of a very few exceptions to this pattern—which should hardly be surprising, given his oeuvre's simultaneous attention to race and sexuality, particularly homosexuality. Interestingly enough, Claudia Tate's later work identifies W. E. B. DuBois as another male author who has challenged this false opposition between the intimate and the political in his writing. In *Psychoanalysis and Black Novels: Desire and the Protocols of Race* (New York and Oxford: Oxford University Press, 1998), Tate argues that "the racial protocol for African American canon formation has marginalized desire as a critical category for black textuality by demanding manifest stories about racial politics" (5), but reads the overt eroticism of DuBois's 1928 novel *Dark Princess* as one example of his "unconscious pattern of consolidating the libidinal economies of desire and freedom" (51). The necessarily "unconscious" nature of this consolidation still confirms, however, that for most black male writers in the twentieth century, perhaps including DuBois, intimacy and desire have been of less than *direct* concern.

109. See, for example, Roderick Ferguson, *Aberrations in Black: Toward a Queer of Color Critique* (Minneapolis: University of Minnesota Press, 2003); E. Patrick Johnson, *Appropriating Blackness: Performance and the Politics of*

Authenticity (Durham and London: Duke University Press, 2003); Dwight McBride, *Why I Hate Abercrombie and Fitch: Essays on Race and Sexuality in America* (New York: New York University Press, 2005), Robert Reid-Pharr, *Black Gay Man: Essays* (New York: New York University Press, 2001), or Siobhan Somerville, *Queering the Color Line: Race and the Invention of Homosexuality in American Culture* (Durham: Duke University Press, 1999).

110. Alexander-Reid, 1.

111. Hortense Spillers, "Interstices: A Small Drama of Words," in *Pleasure and Danger: Exploring Female Sexuality*, ed. Carol S. Vance (Boston: Routledge, 1984), 85.

1. Domestic Oversights

1. *Phylon*, 11.4 (December 1950): 369–90. Women's contributions to the conversation were scarce; indeed, although Gwendolyn Brooks's essay "Poets Who Are Negroes" and Margaret Walker's essay "New Poets" appeared in the same issue of the journal, neither was in the "Symposium" section of the volume.

2. For the opening list of questions, see *The Crisis* 31.4 (February 1926): 165; responses were printed in volumes 31.5 through 33.1 (March to November 1926). The text of DuBois's related NAACP address, "Criteria of Negro Art," appeared in *The Crisis* 32.5 (October 1926): 290–97.

3. Sherwood Anderson writes, for instance, "Naturally I think it is a great mistake for Negroes to become too sensitive[. . . .] Suppose I were to grow indignant every time a white man or woman were badly or cheaply done in the theatre or in books?" *The Crisis* 32.1 (May 1926): 36. Similarly, H. L. Mencken notes, "It seems to me that in objecting to such things as the stories of Mr. Cohen the Negro shows a dreadful lack of humor. They are really very amusing." *The Crisis* 31.5 (March 1926): 219.

4. Sigmund Ro, "Coming of Age: The Modernity of Postwar Black American Writing" in *The Black Columbiad: Defining Moments in African American Literature and Culture*, ed. Werner Sollors and Maria Diedrich (Cambridge and London: Harvard University Press, 1994), 227.

5. Nick Aaron Ford, "A Blueprint for Negro Authors," *Phylon* 11.4 (December 1950): 375; and J. Saunders Redding, "The Negro Writer—Shadow and Substance" *Phylon* 11.4 (December 1950): 373. See also Hugh M. Gloster, "Race and the Negro Writer," *Phylon* 11.4 (December 1950): 369–71.

6. Alain Locke, "Self-Criticism: The Third Dimension in Culture," *Phylon* 11.4 (December 1950): 392.

7. Locke, 391.

8. Ro, 230.

9. Ro, 230.

10. Ralph Ellison, Introduction to *Invisible Man* (New York: Vintage International, 1995), xxii. For a fascinating discussion of the larger sociocultural meaning of Ellison's novel in its moment and beyond, see Kenneth W. Warren, *So Black and Blue: Ralph Ellison and the Occasion of Criticism* (Chicago and London: University of Chicago Press, 2003).

11. Locke, 391.

12. Michele Wallace, *Black Macho and the Myth of the Superwoman* (New York: Warner Books, 1980), 118.

13. See, for example, Gloria T. Hull, Patricia Bell Scott, and Barbara Smith, eds., *All the Women Are White, and All the Blacks Are Men, but Some of Us Are Brave: Black Women's Studies* (Old Westbury, N.Y.: Feminist Press, 1982); and Paula Giddings, *When and Where I Enter: The Impact of Black Women on Race and Sex in America* (New York: William Morrow, 1984), among others.

14. Locke, 393.

15. Locke, 393.

16. Ironically enough, Fauset's work has frequently been criticized for its *exclusive* focus on the world of the black elite—derided as overly conservative and irrelevant to the struggles and concerns of the majority of African Americans. This was true not only during the male-centered decades of criticism following the Harlem Renaissance, but also in the years after 1970, when a revival of interest in black women's writing garnered additional attention for a number of previously neglected authors. In 1980, for example, Mary Helen Washington compared Fauset unfavorably with Nella Larsen, writing that while "Larsen's novels go far beyond the elitism of other novels of the 'Talented Tenth,'" Fauset's novels, by contrast, "never shatter the illusions and pretenses of middle-class respectability; they essentially confirm the necessity for black people to struggle harder to attain it." From "The Mulatta Trap: Nella Larsen's Women of the 1920s" *Ms.* 9 (December 1980), reprinted in Mary Helen Washington, *Invented Lives: Narratives of Black Women 1860–1960* (New York: Anchor Press, 1987), 160. Still, scholars such as Ann DuCille and Deborah McDowell have in later years worked to recuperate Fauset's work as feminist and even progressive for her moment. See Ann DuCille, *The Coupling Convention* (New York: Oxford University Press, 1993), and Deborah McDowell's Introduction to Fauset's novel *Plum Bun* (Boston: Beacon Press, 1990).

17. Scholarship that relies upon and reinforces "separate spheres" ideology includes Ann Douglas's seminal *The Feminization of American Culture* (New York: Knopf, 1977), and Mary Kelley's *Private Woman, Public Stage: Literary Domesticity in Nineteenth Century America* (New York: Oxford University Press, 1984), among many others. A more complicated and critical view of "separate spheres" ideology, which questions the usefulness of such binary conceptualizations of culture, may be found in, for example, Lora Romero's *Home Fronts: Domesticity and Its Critics in the Antebellum United States* (Durham: Duke University Press, 1997), or Cathy Davidson and Jessamyn Hatcher's anthology *No More Separate Spheres!* (Durham and London: Duke University Press, 2002).

18. Robert Reid-Pharr, *Conjugal Union: The Body, The House, and the Black American* (New York: Oxford University Press, 1999), 21.

19. Maurice Wallace, *Constructing the Black Masculine: Identity and Ideality in African American Men's Literature and Culture, 1775–1995* (Durham and London: Duke University Press, 2002), 120.

20. Wallace, 123, my emphasis.

21. Wallace, 123.

22. Locke, 393.

23. Patricia Morton, *Disfigured Images: The Historical Assault on Afro-American Women* (New York: Greenwood Press, 1991), 73.

24. E. Franklin Frazier, *The Negro Family in the United States* (Chicago: University of Chicago Press, 1937), 47, 265, 268.

25. I address Moynihan's work more fully in my next chapter, but it is worth noting, here, how much the scholarship of an earlier era influenced Moynihan's essentially derivative theories.

26. William Chafe suggests that although "millions of women took advantage of the war emergency to improve their economic situation," in fact, "much of that dramatic change disappeared with the war's end." Chafe, "World War II as a Pivotal Experience for American Women," *Women and War: The Changing Status of American Women from the 1930s to the 1950s*, ed. Maria Diedrich and Dorothea Fischer-Hornung (New York: St. Martin's Press, 1990), 23, 21.

27. Susan M. Hartmann, *The Home Front and Beyond: American Women in the 1940s* (Boston: Twayne Publishers, 1982), 11. Of course, the desire in some quarters that women return to the home and the actual sequence of events following the war were not always congruent; as Neil Wynn notes,

"the percentage of women in the labor force was significantly higher after the war than it had been before, and several taboos remained broken." Wynn, *The Afro-American and the Second World War* [1975] (New York: Holmes and Meier, 1993), 17.

28. Chafe, 27.

29. Ruth Feldstein notes, for example, that "discriminatory hiring practices toward black men" led to approximately one-third of married black women working outside the home in 1950, "compared to a quarter of all married women in the population." Feldstein, "'I Wanted the Whole World to See': Race, Gender, and Constructions of Motherhood in the Death of Emmett Till," in *Not June Cleaver: Women and Gender in Postwar America, 1945–1960*, ed. Joanne Meyerowitz (Philadelphia: Temple University Press, 1994), 268–69. See also Jacqueline Jones, *Labor of Love, Labor of Sorrow: Black Women, Work and the Family from Slavery to the Present* (New York: Basic Books, 1985).

30. Farah Jasmine Griffin, *"Who Set You Flowin'?": The African-American Migration Narrative* (New York: Oxford University Press, 1995): 114.

31. Addison Gayle, *The Way of the New World: The Black Novel in America* (Garden City, N.Y.: Doubleday, 1973), 196. See also Robert Bone, *The Negro Novel in America* (New Haven, Conn.: Yale University Press, 1958).

32. See, for example, Gloria Wade-Gayles, *No Crystal Stair: Visions of Race and Gender in Black Women's Fiction, Revised and Updated* (Cleveland: The Pilgrim Press, 1997), 129–38; Mary Helen Washington, *Invented Lives: Narratives of Black Women 1860–1960* (New York: Doubleday, 1987), 297–306; or Calvin Hernton, *The Sexual Mountain and Black Women Writers: Adventures in Sex, Literature, and Real Life* (New York: Doubleday, 1987), 59–88, as well as essays by Bernard Bell and Marjorie Pryse in *Conjuring: Black Women, Fiction, and Literary Tradition*, ed. Marjorie Pryse and Hortense Spillers (Bloomington: Indiana University Press, 1985).

33. M. H. Abrams, *A Glossary of Literary Terms, Sixth Edition* [1957] (New York: Harcourt Brace College Publishers, 1993), 175. Famous examples include Stephen Crane's short story, "Maggie: A Girl of the Streets," and Richard Wright's novel, *Native Son* (1940), to which Petry's work is often compared.

34. Ann Petry, *The Street* [1946] (New York: Houghton Mifflin, 1974), 426. Subsequent references to the novel will be cited parenthetically within this text.

35. Angela Davis, *Women, Race and Class* (New York: Vintage, 1981), 222.

36. Davis, 223.

37. Bernard Bell, *The Afro-American Novel and Its Tradition* (Amherst: University of Massachusetts Press, 1987), 178; Hernton, 67.

38. Gloria Wade-Gayles writes, for example, that "Lutie believes that she and her son, Bub, are better than other blacks in Harlem because she has seen inside the workings of white America and therefore knows how to dream the right dreams" (136). Similarly, Hernton argues, "Lutie's class (and color) biases may be further described as being identified with capitalistic values of the white American middle class[,]" values Lutie acquires while "[w]orking for the rich Chandler family" (81).

39. Paula Giddings, *When and Where I Enter: The Impact of Black Women on Race and Sex in America* (1984; New York: William Morrow, 1996), 101.

40. See Evie Shockley, "Buried Alive: Gothic Homelessness, Black Women's Sexuality, and (Living) Death in Ann Petry's *The Street*," *African American Review* 40.3 (Fall 2006): 439–60.

41. Griselda Pollock, "Feminism/Foucault—Surveillance/Sexuality," in *Visual Culture: Images and Interpretations* (Hanover, Conn.: Wesleyan University Press, 1994), 25.

42. Pollock, 25.

43. Lindon Barrett, *Blackness and Value: Seeing Double* (New York and Cambridge: Cambridge University Press, 1999), 103.

44. Barrett, 103.

45. Barrett, 106, my emphasis.

46. Wade-Gayles, 137.

47. Locke, 394. Though Locke flippantly suggests that such "special racial complexities" are only "interesting variants" on the wider human experience, I would suggest that his seeming unwillingness to acknowledge black women's writing, which as I have already outlined is deeply connected to the racial intimate, betrays the disingenuousness of this dismissal.

48. Ironically, Locke's turn away from black specificity here directly opposes what Robert Reid-Pharr has identified as a central goal of black thinkers in the mid-nineteenth century: "During the antebellum period intellectuals began the arduous, awkward process of establishing the peculiarity of the black body, the distinctiveness that could never be exorcised." Reid-Pharr, *Conjugal Union*, 6. That this *constructed* particularity, the "conjugal union" of "black body and black household" (7) had acquired, almost exactly one century later, a kind of inescapable ideological fixity—for Locke, a literal barrier

to the concept of black experience as "universal"—speaks to the enduring success of that antebellum project.

49. I focus on critics post-1970 because that year marked the beginning of a resurgence of interest in black women's writing in the United States, in which a great number of African American women authors whose work had been neglected (Zora Neale Hurston being perhaps the most notable) were resurrected by black feminist scholars and popular readers.

50. In just one example, Kimberly Drake, author of "Women on the Go: Blues, Conjure, and Other Alternatives to Domesticity in Ann Petry's *The Street* and *The Narrows*," *Arizona Quarterly* 54.1 (Spring 1998): 65–95, makes much of Lutie's "middle-class aspirations" in later portions of the novel, arguing that these aspirations lead Lutie to overlook the super's lover, Min, as a potential ally. While I am less than convinced by Drake's reading of Min as a kind of "blues woman" who ultimately transcends the bourgeois ideologies that ensnare Lutie, what surprises me most in Drake's argument is the fact that she, too, overlooks the character Lil—who although also a "minor" character, may be a better indicator than Min of how Lutie's "middle-class aspirations" lead her astray.

51. Sybil Weir, "*The Narrows*: A Black New England Novel," *Studies in American Fiction* 15.1 (Spring 1987): 86; and Bernard Bell, "Ann Petry's Demythologizing of American Culture and Afro-American Character," in Pryse and Spillers's *Conjuring*, 112. Both scholars seem to read this type of ideology as merely a "white" bourgeois mindset. As I hope my initial discussion of the concept makes clear, I consider the salvific wish to be somewhat more than a mere imitation of whites, born out of what Weir identifies as the desire to "deny [one's] blackness" (86), or an internalized assumption that whiteness is superior. It is, instead, a *strategic* deployment of white, Western values and behaviors, in service of a project of unique benefit to the African American community—personal and communal safety from discursive and material racist violence.

52. As Tricia Rose noted in her presentation at the 2003 American Studies Association annual meeting ("Longing to Tell: Intimacy and Justice in Black Women's Sexual Stories," *Love and Money: Beyond the Recognition/ Redistribution Divide* session, Hartford Civic Center, Hartford, Conn., September 18, 2003), after acknowledging the pervasiveness of those narratives of pathology that surround African American intimacy, black scholars and artists have historically reacted in one of two ways, depending on discipline—in

the technical realm, by contradicting myths of black sexual and domestic degeneracy with evidentiary proof that they are untrue, and in the literary or discursive realm, by creating positive allegorical responses to counter the racist allegory that has cast all black intimate behavior as diseased and perverse. In either case, the complexity of black sexuality and domestic life is lost, as both invidivuals and communities are caught between maintaining (or creating) a façade of black dignity and propriety—the project of the salvific wish—or being ensnared in stereotypes of black sexual excess and degeneracy. Rose rightly suggested that there were simply very few spaces for black women (and I would argue, black people) to have a frank and nonreactionary conversation about the multifaceted experiences that would constitute anything like an "authentic" narrative of black intimacy. See also Tricia Rose, *Longing to Tell: Black Women Talk About Sexuality and Intimacy* (New York: Farrar, Straus and Giroux, 2003), especially 389–400.

2. Pathological Women

1. Though I take up only two such scholars' work in detail here, there are a number of others, most of whom Moynihan actually quotes in order to bolster his argument, including Thomas Pettigrew, Deton Brooks, Dorothy Height, Duncan M. MacIntyre, and Robin M. Williams Jr.

2. Kenneth B. Clark, *Dark Ghetto: Dilemmas of Social Power* [1965] (New York: Harper & Row, 1967), 70, my emphasis.

3. Clark, 70.

4. Whitney M. Young Jr., *To Be Equal* [1964] (New York: McGraw-Hill, 1966), 174.

5. Young, 174.

6. Young, 175.

7. See E. Franklin Frazier's *The Negro Family in the United States* [1939] (Revised and abridged, 1948. Chicago and London: University of Chicago Press, 1969). There Franklin argues, for example, that prior to Emancipation, "[n]either economic necessity nor tradition had instilled in [the black wife and mother] the spirit of subordination to masculine authority. Emancipation only tended to confirm in many cases the spirit of self-sufficiency which slavery had taught" (102).

8. I use "seemed to" here because in fact, Moynihan perceived himself to be doing just the opposite, that is, pointing out the crucial importance of social and economic policies designed to remedy discrimination—by emphasizing the consequences for the black family if such policies were not implemented.

In his words, "Do you see that the object of this report was not to say that jobs don't matter, but rather that jobs matter in the most fundamental way? [. . . W]e can measure our success or failure as a society, not in terms of the gross national product, not in terms of income level, and not in the prettiness and attractiveness or peacefulness of our people, but in the health, and the living, loving reality of the family in our society." Quoted in Lee Rainwater and William L. Yancey, eds., *The Moynihan Report and the Politics of Controversy* (Cambridge, Mass.: M.I.T. Press, 1967), 253.

9. For instance, former Howard University professor Benjamin Payton pointed out "glaring errors" in Moynihan's depiction of the black family, arguing that "these errors have already produced quite damaging political consequences" for blacks. Payton, "New Trends in Civil Rights," quoted in Rainwater and Yancey, 399. *Amsterdam News* columnist James Farmer wrote, "Nowhere does Moynihan suggest that the proper answer to a shattered family is an open job market where this 'frustrated male' Negro can get an honest day's work"—and went on, in the same column, to argue that *The Moynihan Report* "emerges in my mind as the most serious threat to the ultimate freedom of American Negroes to appear in print in recent memory." Farmer, "The Controversial Moynihan Report," quoted in Rainwater and Yancey, 410, 411. Martin Luther King Jr. himself weighed in on the issue in an October 1965 address, countering the conclusions of "a recent study" that, to him, "suggest[ed] that the progress in civil rights can be negated by the dissolving of family structure." Martin Luther King Jr., Address at Abbot House, Westchester County, New York, quoted in Rainwater and Yancey, 403. Instead, King concluded, "At the root of the difficulty in Negro life is pervasive and persistent economic want[. . . .] America owes a debt to justice which it has only begun to pay" (408, 409).

10. Bayard Rustin, "Why Don't Negroes . . ." quoted in Rainwater and Yancey, 418.

11. Rustin, 423.

12. Patricia Morton, *Disfigured Images: The Historical Assault on Afro-American Women* (New York: Greenwood Press, 1991), 3, 4.

13. See also, for example, Paula Giddings, *When and Where I Enter: The Impact of Black Women on Race and Sex in America* (New York: William Morrow, 1984), especially chapter 18, or Angela Davis, *Women, Race and Class* (New York: Vintage, 1983), especially 4, 12–14.

14. Young, "The Real Moynihan Report," quoted in Rainwater and Yancey, 415, my emphasis.

15. Young, 416, my emphasis.

16. Moynihan, 6. Ironically enough, Moynihan's support for this point is E. Franklin Frazier's *Black Bourgeoisie* (New York: Collier Books, 1962).

17. Moynihan, 29.

18. Moynihan, 29, 30.

19. Moynihan, 30.

20. Rhonda Williams, "Living at the Crossroads," in *The House that Race Built*, ed. Wahneema Lubiano (New York: Pantheon, 1997), 140.

21. Moynihan, 30.

22. Frazier, *The Negro Family*, 190.

23. Clark, 56.

24. Young, 221.

25. See essays by Deborah McDowell, Madhu Dubey, Rita A. Bergenholtz, Philip Page, and Phillip Novak, among others. Bergenholtz rather facilely suggests that these oppositions exist to "provoke thought" about black-white racial difference; Bergenholtz, "Toni Morrison's *Sula*: A Satire on Binary Thinking," *African American Review* 30.1 (1996): 99. Novak's work is notable in that he cautions against the deconstructionist sense that "gaps and fissures" created in the text through the destabilizing of such oppositions must always produce narrative meaning. Novak, "'Circles and Circles of Sorrow': In the Wake of Morrison's "*Sula*." *PMLA* 114:2 (1999): 190.

26. Hortense Spillers, "A Hateful Passion, a Lost Love," reprinted in *Modern Critical Interpretations: Toni Morrison's "Sula*," ed. Harold Bloom (Philadelphia: Chelsea House Publishers, 1999), 54.

27. See Kevin Gaines, *Uplifting the Race: Black Leadership, Politics and Culture in the Twentieth Century* (Chapel Hill: University of North Carolina Press, 1996).

28. Toni Morrison, *Sula* (New York: Alfred A. Knopf, 1973; New York: Plume, 1982), 42. Page references to the latter edition will be given parenthetically in the text.

29. Adrienne Rich, *Of Woman Born: Motherhood As Experience and Institution* (New York: Norton, 1986), 243.

30. Moynihan, 16.

31. As Karla Holloway notes in *Codes of Conduct*, her grandmother warned her away from the color red not only because "nice girls do not wear red" but because wearing it "makes [them] look common." The sin of appearing "common" certainly has class connotations, but it also suggests sexual availability—which highlights the complex meaning ascribed to the word

"nice" in her grandmother's warning. Karla F. C. Holloway, *Codes of Conduct: Race, Ethics and the Color of Our Character* (New Brunswick, N.J.: Rutgers University Press, 1995), 16.

32. From *Quicksand*: "Clothes had been one of her difficulties in Naxos. Helga Crane loved clothes, elaborate ones. Nevertheless, she had tried not to offend. But with small success, for, although she had affected the deceptively simple variety, the hawk eyes of dean and matrons had detected the subtle difference from their own irreproachably conventional garments. Too, they felt that the colors were queer; dark purples, royal blues, rich greens, deep reds, in soft, luxurious woolens, or heavy, clinging silks. And the trimmings—when Helga used them at all—seemed to them odd. Old laces, strange embroideries, dim brocades. Her faultless, slim shoes made them uncomfortable and her small plain hats seemed to them positively indecent." Larsen, *Quicksand and Passing* [1928] (New Brunswick, N.J.: Rutgers University Press, 1986), 18.

33. Deborah McDowell notes, for example, that "custard," along with "jelly and pudding," might "function [. . .] as metaphors of sexuality drawn from the classic women's blues lyrics." McDowell, "Boundaries, Or Distant Relations and Close Kin—*Sula*," in *"The Changing Same": Black Women's Literature, Criticism, and Theory* (Bloomington and Indianapolis: Indiana University Press, 1995), 107.

34. Joanne Gabbin, "A Laying on of Hands: Black Women Writers Exploring the Roots of Their Folk and Cultural Tradition," in *Wild Women in the Whirlwind: Afra-American Culture and the Contemporary Literary Renaissance,* ed. Joanne M. Braxton and Andree Nicola McLaughlin (New Brunswick: Rutgers University Press, 1990), 257.

35. Spillers, 74.

36. Spillers, 74.

37. Audre Lorde, "Uses of the Erotic: The Erotic As Power," in *Sister Outsider* (Freedom, Calif.: The Crossing Press, 1984), 53.

38. Lorde, 54.

39. Lorde, 56.

40. See Houston Baker's chapter "On Knowing Our Place" in *Workings of the Spirit: The Poetics of Afro-American Women's Writing* (Chicago and London: University of Chicago Press, 1991), especially 145–49. He writes, "Morrison's own mocking designation of the Phallus, in all of its mystery, as a false harbinger of apocalypse—'Chicken Little'—begins the demystification process that is completed in the little boy's burial by water" (149).

41. See Barbara Smith, "Toward a Black Feminist Criticism," in *All the*

Women Are White, All the Blacks Are Men, but Some of Us Are Brave (Old West-bury, N.Y.: Feminist Press, 1982). For a representative critique of Smith's argument, see Deborah McDowell, "New Directions for Black Feminist Criticism," in *"The Changing Same": Black Women's Literature, Criticism, and Theory* (Bloomington and Indianapolis: Indiana University Press, 1995), 5–23.

42. Eve Kosofsky Sedgwick, *Tendencies* (Durham: Duke University Press, 1993), 8.

43. Bergenholtz, 92.

44. Lorde, 53.

45. Baker, 155.

46. Madhu Dubey, "'No Bottom and No Top': Oppositions in *Sula*," in *Black Women Novelists and the Nationalist Aesthetic* (Bloomington and Indianapolis: Indiana University Press, 1994), 56.

47. Roderick A. Ferguson, "Something Else to Be: *Sula, The Moynihan Report*, and the Negations of Black Lesbian Feminism," in *Aberrations in Black: Toward a Queer of Color Critique* (Minneapolis: University of Minnesota Press, 2004), 132.

48. Novak, 187. See also Baker, 137.

49. In his fascinating discussion of Toni Morrison's *Beloved*, which reads that novel's "apocalyptic" scenes of infanticide against Moynihan's report and its ramifications, James Berger suggests that tension between localized instances of intraracial dysfunction or "self-destruction" and the larger, *macro* context of systemic racism recurs throughout Morrison's oeuvre: "These apocalyptic concerns are, in fact, the twin themes of all of Morrison's work. Racial violence shapes the social and political space of her novels, while in the foreground—in *The Bluest Eye*, in *Sula*, in *Song of Solomon*, in *Jazz*, and in *Beloved*—are forms of individual and collective suicide." Berger, *After the End: Representations of Post-Apocalypse* (Minneapolis: University of Minnesota Press, 1999), 190. The classist hierarchy critiqued in *Sula* is one form of this intraracial "suicide," self-destructive precisely because, as I argue throughout this chapter, it attempts to ignore the broader dangers of systemic racism to black bodies of any class.

50. Robert F. Reid-Pharr, "At Home in America," in *Black Gay Man* (New York and London: New York University Press, 2001), 66.

51. Reid-Pharr, 68.

52. Giddings, 314. While Giddings refers only to the 1960s as the "Masculine Decade," I would extend her description to include the 1970s as well,

which is when the extremely male-centered Black Power movement gained widespread notoriety.

3. Queering Black Patriarchy

1. Deborah McDowell, "Reading Family Matters," in *Changing Our Own Words: Essays on Criticism, Theory, and Writing by Black Women,* ed. Cheryl A. Wall (New Brunswick, N.J.: Rutgers University Press, 1989). Significantly, McDowell herself notes that these hostile critics are not all men. One notable exception, for instance, is Trudier Harris, whose forceful indictment of Walker's novel I quote at length later in this chapter. With this in mind, my subsequent references to a black critical furor over *The Color Purple* will place the qualifier "male" in parentheses.

2. McDowell, 78.

3. McDowell, 85.

4. Here I use the term "queering" as Eve Kosofsky Sedgwick defines it in the introduction to her essay collection *Tendencies* (Durham: Duke University Press, 1993). She asks, "What if . . . there were a practice of valuing the ways in which meanings and institutions can be at loose ends with each other?" (6), and goes on to say, of the "various elements" ascribed to the idea of "the family," that "it's been a ruling intuition for me that the most productive strategy . . . might be, whenever possible, to *dis*articulate them from one another, to *dis*engage them—the bonds of blood, of law, of habitation, of privacy, of companionship and succor—from the lockstep of their unanimity in the system called 'family'" (6, author's emphasis). Alice Walker, I argue, undertakes precisely this queer disarticulation and disengagement when she separates fatherhood and masculinity from patriarchy in her text.

5. See Alice Walker, *The Same River Twice: Honoring the Difficult: A Meditation on Life, Spirit, Art, and the Making of the Film* The Color Purple, *Ten Years Later* (New York: Scribner, 1996), in which she chronicles the making of the film *The Color Purple,* and expresses some surprise at the harsh responses she received from black (male) critics.

6. Michael Awkward, "A Black Man's Place in Black Feminist Criticism," in *Representing Black Men,* ed. Marcellus Blount and George P. Cunningham (New York: Routledge, 1996), 3.

7. Sharon Holland, "Bill T. Jones, Tupac Shakur and the (Queer) Art of Death," *Callaloo* 23.1 (2000): 387.

8. Holland, 387.

9. Ashraf Rushdy, *Remembering Generations: Race and Family in Contemporary African American Fiction* (Chapel Hill and London: University of North Carolina Press, 2001), 109–10.

10. W. E. B. DuBois, *Writings,* ed. Nathan Huggins (New York: The Library of America, 1986), 842. As I noted in this book's introduction, while the phrase "The Talented Tenth" is rightly associated with DuBois based on his 1903 essay of the same title, Joy James points out that the terminology was coined in 1896 by a white liberal missionary society, the American Baptist Home Missionary Society, which founded a number of "Southern black colleges to train Negro elites." James, *Transcending the Talented Tenth: Black Leaders and American Intellectuals* (New York and London: Routledge, 1997), 16.

11. Kevin Kelly Gaines, *Uplifting the Race: Black Leadership, Politics, and Culture in the Twentieth Century* (Chapel Hill and London: University of North Carolina Press, 1996), 12.

12. It may also be true that Walker's own bisexuality, and rumors that circulated about her sexual identity at the time of the book's publication (and later, the film's release) contributed to the virulence of responses to her work from some critics; for the purposes of this chapter, however, I am less interested in how Walker's actual intimate attachments (or perceived desire for such attachments) fueled the controversy surrounding *The Color Purple* than I am in how the operation of the novel itself proved challenging to certain assumptions made by Walker's critics.

13. Walker, *The Color Purple* [1982] (New York: Pocket Books, 1985), 181. Subsequent references to the 1985 edition will be cited parenthetically throughout this chapter.

14. Gaines, 16.

15. Quoted in Lauren Berlant, "The Subject of True Feeling: Pain, Privacy, and Politics," in *Feminist Consequences: Theory for the New Century,* ed. Elisabeth Bronfen and Misha Kavka (New York: Columbia University Press, 2001), 142.

16. Patricia Hill Collins, *Black Feminist Thought: Knowledge, Consciousness, and the Politics of Empowerment* (New York and London: Routledge, 1990), 47.

17. Collins, 47.

18. See Kaja Silverman, *Male Subjectivity at the Margins* (New York: Routledge, 1992), 15–51.

19. David Marriott, *On Black Men* (New York: Columbia University Press, 2000), 103.

20. I understand "bigged" to mean "impregnated" here because throughout the text, "big" is used as a synonym for pregnant.

21. Walker's reference to Bub's grandfather being "the colored uncle of the sheriff" also, of course, highlights the white world's tremendous power over the fate of the black community, a power marked, in this case, by Bub's presumably "illegitimate" family connections to whiteness. Such physical and generational linkages between blacks and whites have frequently been emphasized in African American literature of the twentieth century—from early examples such as Charles Chesnutt's *The Marrow of Tradition* or Pauline Hopkins's *Contending Forces,* to more recent works like Colson Whitehead's *The Intuitionist*—as examples of the overwhelming control exercised upon black bodies by white supremacy. I touch more deeply upon the question of the putatively "black" subject's corporeal connection to whiteness in the next chapter. Yet it is also worth emphasizing, here, that the *salvific wish* is, in fact, one example of how the comprehensive scope of white power can be manifested in black behavior even when whites are not present. In other words, in the twentieth century, white hegemony's *ideological* relation to black bodies has been at least as important as any material relationship.

22. Not coincidentally, the most conventionally feminine articulation of the salvific wish in *The Color Purple*—the Spelman-educated Corrine's misguided efforts to discipline Nettie during their sojourn in Africa—also fails to recuperate black community. Instead, Corrine's obsessive concern with respectability and with maintaining the *appearance* of domestic propriety, especially when she believes that propriety has in actuality been breached by a liaison between her husband and Nettie, effects a kind of intrafamilial and intraracial estrangement in the narrative. Rendered distraught by her suspicions, Corrine isolates herself more and more from her children and from Nettie, her former friend and pupil. Indeed the narrative implies that this estrangement is the real reason for Corrine's untimely death—Nettie writes to Celie that "[Corrine] gets weaker and weaker, and unless she can believe us and start to feel something for her children, I fear we will lose her" (191). Though in her final hour Corrine does realize that her suspicions have been misguided, it is not enough to save her life: "But, Celie, in the middle of the night she woke up, turned to Samuel and said: I believe. And died anyway" (194).

23. Paradoxically, Walker has herself been accused of assuming a kind of tyrannical authority over other women's lives as a result of her activism around the issue of female clitoridectomy (the subject of her 1992 novel, *Possessing*

the Secret of Joy, as well as the book and film she produced with journalist Pratibha Parmar in 1993, *Warrior Marks*). According to some critics, Walker's zeal in condemning the practice (called "female circumcision" in sympathetic quarters, "female genital mutilation" by its most vehement opposition, including Walker) smacks a bit too much of Western condescension and even cultural imperialism. As one scholar writes of the controversy, "Walker seems 'possessed' of the pernicious notion that she can and must rescue those unfortunate women from themselves, from their ignorance, and from their patriarchal traditions." Stanlie M. James, "Shades of Othering: Reflections on Female Circumcision/Genital Mutilation," *Signs* 23 (1998): 1033. Although it is certainly possible (even probable) that the criticism Walker has received around this issue is a defensive response from individuals who do not wish to see the oppressive "dirty laundry" of various African cultures exposed to scrutiny, it also seems likely, ironically enough, that Walker's activism has more in common with the recuperative impulse of uplift ideology than even she realizes.

24. Barbara Ehrenreich "The Decline of Patriarchy," in *Constructing Masculinity,* ed. Maurice Berger, Brian Wallis, and Simon Watson (New York: Routledge, 1995), 284.

25. Karla Holloway, *Moorings and Metaphors: Figures of Culture and Gender in Black Women's Literature* (New Brunswick, N.J.: Rutgers University Press, 1992), 24.

26. Hortense Spillers "'The Permanent Obliquity of an In(pha)llibly Straight': In the Time of the Daughters and the Fathers," in *Changing Our Own Words: Essays on Criticism, Theory, and Writing by Black Women,* ed. Cheryl Wall (New Brunswick, N.J.: Rutgers University Press, 1989), 148.

27. Evelyn Hammonds, "Towards a Genealogy of Black Female Sexuality: The Problematic of Silence," in *Feminist Genealogies, Colonial Legacies, Democratic Futures,* ed. M. Jacqui Alexander and Chandra Talpade Mohanty (New York: Routledge, 1997), 177–78.

28. Paula Giddings, *When and Where I Enter: The Impact of Black Women on Race and Sex in America* [1984] (New York: William Morrow, 1996), 349.

29. Darryl Pinckney, "Black Victims, Black Villains," *The New York Review of Books* (January 1987): 18.

30. Mel Watkins, "Sexism, Racism and Black Women Writers," *The New York Times* (June 1986): 5. Shange's 1977 choreopoem *For Colored Girls Who Have Considered Suicide When the Rainbow Is Enuf,* along with Wallace's 1980

polemic, *Black Macho and the Myth of the Superwoman,* sparked the storm of controversy surrounding black women's writing in the seventies and eighties.

31. Watkins, 4.

32. Pinckney, 17.

33. Gina Dent, ed., and Introduction, *Black Popular Culture: A Project by Michele Wallace* (Seattle: Bay Press, 1992), 3.

34. David Bradley, "Novelist Alice Walker Telling the Black Woman's Story," *New York Times Magazine* (January 1984): 30.

35. Pinckney, 18.

36. Philip Royster, "In Search of Our Father's Arms: Alice Walker's Persona of the Alienated Darling," *Black American Literature Forum* 20.4 (Winter 1986): 360, 359, my emphasis.

37. Watkins, 5.

38. Watkins, 5.

39. Watkins, 6.

40. In her essay, Harris notes that she has become a collector of *The Color Purple*'s reviews, and maintains that she has been largely unable to locate any reviews, from men or women, that criticize the novel: "Though I found and received many reviews, and some hints at criticism, there were no large-scale objections to the novel." Trudier Harris, "On *The Color Purple,* Stereotypes, and Silence," *Black American Literature Forum* 18.4 (Winter 1984): 160. Considering the volume of text devoted to the critique and reproval of the novel only a short while later, it is clear that Harris's essay was published at least a few months before the most virulent of Walker-related reviews began to appear. Since Harris's essay also makes no mention of Stephen Spielberg's film adaptation of the book, it is likely that her piece was written before that motion picture was released (not coincidentally, the time when a great number of negative reviews of both book and film appeared in print).

41. Harris, 157.

42. Harris, 158.

43. Harris, 159.

44. Bradley, 30.

45. Erna Kelly, "A Matter of Focus: Men in the Margins of Alice Walker's Fiction," in *Critical Essays on Alice Walker,* ed. Ikenna Dieke (Westport, Conn.: Greenwood Press, 1999), 178.

46. Martha Albertson Fineman, *The Neutered Mother, the Sexual Family, and Other Twentieth-Century Tragedies* (New York: Routledge, 1995), 205.

47. Ehrenreich, 290.

48. Judith Butler, "The End of Sexual Difference?" in *Feminist Consequences: Theory for the New Century*, ed. Elisabeth Bronfen and Misha Kavka (New York: Columbia University Press, 2001), 421.

49. Paul Gilroy, *Small Acts: Thoughts on the Politics of Black Cultures* (London and New York: Serpent's Tail, 1993), 204, 207.

4. Intimate Borders

1. Executive Office of the President, Office of Management and Budget, "Revisions to the Standards for the Classification of Federal Data on Race and Ethnicity," by Sally Katzen, *Federal Register* 62, no. 210 (October 30, 1997): 58782.

2. Ibid., 58784. For a conservative analysis of the historical context for and social ramifications of the "multiracial" category, see Rainier Spencer, *Spurious Issues* (Boulder, Colo.: Westview Press, 1999); for more on the experiences of multiracial individuals in the United States, see, for example, Maria P. P. Root, ed., *The Multiracial Experience: Racial Borders as the New Frontier* (Thousand Oaks, Calif.: Sage Publications, 1996).

3. *Coalition Statement on Proposed Modification of OMB Directive no. 15*, quoted in Spencer, 148.

4. Testimony of Arthur A. Fletcher before House Subcommittee on Census, Statistics, and Postal Personnel, Committee on Post Office and Civil Service, *Hearings on the Review of Federal Measurements of Race and Ethnicity* 103d Congress, 1st sess. (Nov. 3, 1993), 273.

5. United States Census Bureau. Census 2000 PHC-T-1. Table 4: "Difference in Population by Race and Hispanic or Latino Origin, for the United States: 1990 to 2000. Online at: http://www.census.gov/population/www/cen2000/phc-t1.html.

6. I use parentheses around "blackness" advisedly, as I believe it is important to acknowledge that, in the words of David Lionel Smith, "race is a set of social prescriptions invented by slaveholders and their descendants to exploit and constrain persons classified as black." Smith, "What Is Black Culture?" in *The House That Race Built*, ed. Wahneema Lubiano (New York: Pantheon, 1997), 180. Yet this social fiction called race is not merely fantasy, as it has created and continues to produce real, lived consequences for human beings. As such, I find it counterproductive to insist upon highlighting race as a "fiction" throughout a chapter such as this one; though I will apply quo-

tation marks to racial identifiers at points where I believe they merit special emphasis, the reader should assume that elsewhere they are implied.

7. For more on the one-drop rule, see F. James Davis, *Who Is Black?: One Nation's Definition*, 10th ed. (University Park: Pennsylvania State University Press, 2001).

8. See, for example, Naomi Zack, who writes in *Race and Mixed Race* (Philadelphia: Temple University Press, 1993) that the "class of successful blacks" described by W. E. B. DuBois as the "Talented Tenth" was "in large part, though not entirely, composed of a *mulatto elite*" (95, author's emphasis). See also Joel Williamson, *New People: Miscegenation and Mulattos in the United States* (New York: Free Press, 1980), especially 141–77.

9. For early examples, see texts such as Frances Harper's *Iola Leroy* (1893), Pauline Hopkins' *Contending Forces* (1900), or much of Charles Chesnutt's oeuvre; during the Harlem Renaissance, see works by Jessie Fauset and Nella Larsen, among others. For critical analysis of color and the figure of the "mulatto" in such early texts, see, for example, Claudia Tate's *Domestic Allegories* or Hazel Carby's *Reconstructing Womanhood*. For specific portrayals of dark-skinned, bourgeois characters, see Wallace Thurman's *The Blacker the Berry* (1929), which depicts a middle-class black woman who is very dark skinned and is therefore shunned by those she considers to be her "equals" in class status. Also, Dorothy West's *The Living Is Easy* (1948) portrays a black woman who is born poor, but whose class aspirations are successful in part because of her light-brown skin and green eyes; this character, Cleo Judson, mistakes the wealthy dark-skinned man who will one day become her husband for a servant the first time she sees him, because of his coloring.

10. Kathleen Odell Korgen, *From Black to Biracial: Transforming Racial Identity among Americans* (Westport, Conn.: Praeger, 1998), 105. Korgen's point is anticipated by Kathy Russell et al., in *The Color Complex: The Politics of Skin Color among African Americans* [1992] (New York: Anchor, 1993).

11. See, for example, the anthology of Cedric Herring et al., eds., *Skin Deep: How Race and Complexion Matter in the "Color-Blind" Era* (Chicago: Institute for Research on Race and Public Policy, and University of Illinois Press, 2004), in which a number of studies suggest that skin color continues to influence everything from marital status to job advancement. See also Michael Hughes and Bradley R. Hertel, "The Significance of Color Remains: A Study of Life Chances, Mate Selection, and Ethnic Consciousness among Black Americans." *Social Forces* 68.4 (1990): 1105–20.

12. Here I do not mean to suggest that skin color and "colorism" (the hierarchical approach to skin color that ranks lighter skin as higher in social status than darker), are no longer salient issues within the black community. As the sources I have already cited make clear, these issues are far from being resolved among African Americans, and many blacks, particularly those with very light or very dark skin, still experience painful intra- and interracial reactions to their physical appearance. See, for example, memoirs by Toi Derricotte and Marita Golden, or the work of black philosopher and performance artist Adrian Piper. Yet my point here is that, perhaps because of its continued importance within black culture, skin color often functions as a kind of visual/conceptual shorthand for distinctions in class status among black people, and Fletcher's comments reflect that.

13. Lena Williams, "In a 90s Quest for Black Identity, Intense Doubts and Disagreements," *New York Times*, Nov. 30, 1991, natl. ed.: 1+.

14. Williams, 1.

15. In October 1995, former professional athlete and popular actor and spokesman O. J. Simpson was acquitted of charges of murder related to the stabbing deaths of his ex-wife Nicole Brown Simpson and her friend and alleged lover, Ron Goldman. Across the nation, many whites and blacks had very different reactions to the acquittal, and news media played up the split, televising images of blacks cheering and celebrating after hearing the news. For a number of nuanced and thoughtful analyses of the Simpson case and its aftermath, see Toni Morrison and Claudia Brodsky Lacour, eds., *Birth of a Nation 'Hood: Gaze, Script and Spectacle in the O. J. Simpson Case* (New York: Pantheon, 1997).

16. The Million Man March took place on the National Mall in Washington, D.C., on October 16, 1995, bringing together an estimated 800,000 plus African American men and their supporters for a day of "atonement." A number of photographic and written histories of the event have appeared in subsequent years, most taking an extremely sympathetic approach to the event, despite its leader's notoriety for sexism, homophobia, and anti-Semitism. Two representative examples of such texts are Haki R. Madhubuti and Maulana Karenga, eds., *Million Man March/Day of Absence: A Commemorative Anthology: Speeches, Commentary, Photography, Poetry, Illustrations, Documents* (Chicago: Third World Press, 1996), and Kim Martin Sadler, ed., *Atonement: The Million Man March* (Berea, Ohio: Pilgrim Press, 1996). For a more critical analysis of Louis Farrakhan and the march, see Henry Louis Gates, *Thirteen Ways of Looking at a Black Man* (New York: Vintage, 1997), 122–54.

17. The Civil Rights Act, for instance, which prohibited discrimination on the grounds of "race, color, religion or national origin" was signed into law on July 2, 1964, and was quickly followed by the Voting Rights Act in 1965. As Manning Marable notes, "the Civil Rights era saw broad economic changes, influencing all strata within the black community[. . . .] Most significant was the increase of blacks employed in white collar jobs," which grew from 13 to 24 percent between 1960 and 1970. Marable, *Blackwater: Historical Studies in Race, Class Consciousness, and Revolution* (Niwot, Colo.: University Press of Colorado, 1993), 97.

18. Cornel West, "The Paradox of the African American Rebellion," reprinted in *Is It Nation Time?: Contemporary Essays on Black Power and Black Nationalism*, ed. Eddie S. Glaude Jr. (Chicago and London: University of Chicago Press, 2002), 32.

19. West, 34.

20. One interesting example of this in American popular culture is the 1991 Hollywood film *"Livin' Large,"* about a young black man (dark-skinned actor Terrence "T. C." Carson) who works at his sister's dry cleaning business but dreams of being a news anchorman. As it happens, a fortuitous turn of events—the on-air murder of another black news reporter by an angry sniper—gives him the chance he needs, and he achieves "success" and its attendant risks and contradictions. One of the most interesting, if brief, moments in the movie is the interaction between Carson's character and the murdered reporter, only minutes before that reporter's death. Carson's character Dexter Jackson approaches the reporter, Charles Hempstead, played by fair-skinned actor Joe Washington, only to be rebuffed. Washington's character then asks in disgust, "Why do *these people* always bother me?" It is not at all difficult, in this moment, to recognize that Hempstead's reference to "these people" is not only classed but racially coded—Hempstead believes himself to be above, or even entirely separate from, working-class blacks like Jackson. This is so in spite of Jackson's obvious admiration for and emulation of Hempstead. When Hempstead is shot in the back by a sniper while on the air, it seems clear that he is being punished for his snobbery and racial disloyalty, which is why the murder is played for laughs. *Livin' Large*, dir. Michael Schultz, perf. Terrance "T. C." Carson, Blanche Baker, and Julia Campbell [1991] (DVD, Metro-Goldwyn-Mayer, 2003).

21. Gates, 127.

22. See, for example, Peter Widdowson, "The American Dream Refashioned: History, Politics and Gender in Toni Morrison's *Paradise*," *Journal of American*

Studies 35.2 (2001): 313–35; Widdowson describes *Paradise* as "a fictional intervention in contemporary American historiography" (318). See also Ana Maria Fraile-Marcos, "Hybridizing the 'City upon a Hill' in Toni Morrison's *Paradise*," *MELUS* 28.4 (Winter 2003): 3–33. Fraile-Marcos suggests that "the story works as a mirror to American history as the protagonists both reproduce and invert the cultural codes that have been identified as 'American'" (6); similarly, Katrine Dalsgard writes that Morrison "tak[es] as her starting point the idea that the African American community lives its own version of [American] exceptionalism" (237). Dalsgard, "The One All-Black Town Worth the Pain: (African) American Exceptionalism, Historical Narration, and the Critique of Nationhood in Toni Morrison's *Paradise*," *African American Review* 35.2 (Summer 2001): 233–48. Most recently, Marni Gauthier argues "Morrison creates in *Paradise* a microcosm of America in the utopian all-black community of Ruby, Oklahoma" (396). Gauthier, "The Other Side of Paradise: Toni Morrison's (Un) Making of Mythic History," *African American Review* 39.3 (Fall 2005): 395–414.

23. Critical race theory is an intellectual movement that began among legal scholars in the early 1990s and soon expanded to include, in Schur's words, "scholars from a wide range of disciplines who challenge the way disciplinary formations reinforce the importance of race." Richard Schur, "Locating *Paradise* in the Post-Civil Rights Era: Toni Morrison and Critical Race Theory," *Contemporary Literature* 45.2 (2004): 278, 279.

24. Toni Morrison, *Paradise* [1997] (New York: Plume, 1999), 5.

25. Jeffrey Stout, "Theses on Black Nationalism," in *Is It Nation Time?: Contemporary Essays on Black Power and Black Nationalism*, ed. Eddie S. Glaude Jr. (Chicago: University of Chicago Press, 2002), 235.

26. Stout, 244.

27. This lack of autonomy creates a conceptual conundrum within the concept of black nationalism, since for at least one prominent scholar of nationalism, geographic and political sovereignty is a precondition of nationhood. See Benedict Anderson, *Imagined Communities* (London and New York: Verso, 1991), 6. As Stout writes, "By emphasizing political sovereignty in this way, Anderson's definition of nationalism entails that most varieties of black nationalism that have flourished in the United States would not qualify as species of the basic genus" (244).

28. Wahneema Lubiano, "Black Nationalism and Black Common Sense: Policing Ourselves and Others," in *The House That Race Built* (New York: Pantheon, 1997), 232.

29. Wahneema Lubiano, "Standing in for the State: Black Nationalism and Writing the Black Subject" *Is It Nation Time?: Contemporary Essays on Black Power and Black Nationalism,* ed. Eddie S. Glaude Jr. (Chicago: University of Chicago Press, 2002), 157.

30. Lubiano, "Black Nationalism," 236.

31. The phrase "family romance" is used by Deborah McDowell, following Janet Beizer, to describe the negative reaction of black male critics to black women's fiction in the 1970s and '80s. McDowell, "Reading Family Matters," in *The Changing Same: Black Women's Literature, Criticism, and Theory* (Bloomington and Indianapolis: Indiana University Press, 1995), 121.

32. Gaines, 2.

33. Morrison, 3. Subsequent references to this edition will be made parenthetically in the text.

34. In this, Morrison's *Paradise* aligns itself with a large body of black feminist scholarship that has questioned the masculinist, patriarchal motivations of U.S. black nationalism, including work by Angela Davis, Paula Giddings, Barbara Smith, Michele Wallace, and numerous others.

35. Schur, 288.

36. Moses, *The Golden Age of Black Nationalism, 1850-1925* [1978] (New York: Oxford University Press, 1988), 23.

37. Magali Cornier Michael, "Re-Imagining Agency: Toni Morrison's *Paradise,*" *African American Review* 36.4 (2002): 648.

38. See F. James Davis, *Who Is Black?: One Nation's Definition,* 10th ed. (University Park: Pennsylvania State University Press, 2001), 33, or Joel Williamson, *New People: Miscegenation and Mulattos in the United States* (New York: Free Press, 1980), 8.

39. Robert Reid-Pharr, "At Home in America," in *Black Gay Man: Essays* (New York: New York University Press, 2001), 65.

40. As Angela Davis notes, "white men, by virtue of their economic position, had *unlimited access* to Black women's bodies." Davis, *Women, Race and Class* [1981] (New York: Vintage, 1983), 26, my emphasis.

41. Morrison, *Beloved* (New York: Knopf, 1987). *Beloved* won the 1988 Pulitzer Prize for fiction.

42. For more on black hair politics, see Ingrid Banks, *Hair Matters: Beauty, Power, and Black Women's Consciousness* (New York: New York University Press, 2000); Ayana D. Byrd and Lori L. Tharps, *Hair Story, Untangling the Roots of Black Hair in America* (New York: St. Martin's Press, 2002); or

Noliwe M. Rooks, *Hair Raising: Beauty, Culture, and African American Women* (New Brunswick, N.J.: Rutgers University Press, 1996).

43. bell hooks, "Selling Hot Pussy: Representations of Black Female Sexuality in the Cultural Marketplace," in *Black Looks: Race and Representation* (Boston: South End Press, 1992), 62.

44. Rob Davidson, "Racial Stock and 8-rocks: Communal Historiography in Toni Morrison's Paradise," *Twentieth Century Literature* 47.3 (2001): 362.

45. Davidson, 362.

46. As Hortense Spillers notes, "'Family,' as we practice and understand it 'in the West' [. . . is defined as] the vertical transfer of a bloodline, of a patronymic, of titles and entitlements, of real estate and the prerogatives of 'cold cash,' from fathers to sons and in the supposedly free exchange of affectional ties between a male and a female of his choice[.]" "Mama's Baby, Papa's Maybe: An American Grammar Book," in *African American Literary Theory: A Reader,* ed. Winston Napier (New York: New York University Press, 2002), 270.

47. Marita Golden, *Don't Play in the Sun: One Woman's Journey through the Color Complex* (New York: Doubleday, 2004), 15.

48. Spillers, 278.

49. To be fair, most critics of *Paradise* are less interested in the "white girl," per se, than they are interested in our inability as readers to identify her. Ana Maria Fraile-Marcos, for example, discusses the "blurring of racial boundaries that takes place in the Convent" in the context of the near-impossibility of "the reader's quest to identify the 'white girl'" (16); similarly, Magali Cornier Michael remarks that the "lack of certainty as to the identity of 'the white girl' marks skin color as in and of itself not of primary importance within the context of the Convent community" (653).

50. Kathryn Nicol, "Visible Differences: Viewing Racial Identity in Toni Morrison's *Paradise* and 'Recitatif,'" in *Literature and Racial Ambiguity,* ed. Teresa Hubel and Neil Brooks (New York: Rodopi, 2002), 226.

51. That city is never named, but the "Sisters Devoted to Indian and Colored People" (one of whom, Mary Magna, is Consolata's savior) are described as "six American nuns on their way back to the States after twelve years of being upstaged by older, sterner Portuguese Orders" (223). The likelihood that, in 1925, significant numbers of Portuguese nuns would be working anywhere in South America besides Brazil, Portugal's sole former American colony, seems small.

52. Samuel R. Delany, "Some Queer Notions About Race," in *Dangerous Liaisons: Blacks, Gays, and the Struggle for Equality*, ed. Eric Brandt (New York: The New Press, 1999), 267.

53. Although the text does not point directly to this, the fact that Consolata is situated outside of conventional U.S. class hierarchies may also make her impossible for the 8-rocks to read. Given that her presence in the Convent predates the founding of Ruby, her origins as an orphaned street child in Brazil are well obscured by time and distance by the time she encounters U.S. blacks. Thus she is neither a clear product of American poverty, as is Delia Best; nor is she clearly a member of the black elite, scripted into the protective fold of wealthy black patriarchy like the nineteen Negro ladies. As such, she troubles class categories in Ruby in a way that makes her "blackness," already ambiguous, nearly illegible.

54. Lubiano, "Standing in for the State," 159.

55. Lubiano, "Standing in for the State," 159.

56. I refer, here, to my friend and colleague, Stefanie K. Dunning; I am grateful to her for helping me, as I drafted this chapter, to think through this idea of cultural versus biological "purity" in the African American experience.

57. This is true even as so-called biological characteristics remain unacknowledged traces within the cultural concept of "race" in the American mind. Kwame Anthony Appiah writes, for instance, "current ways of talking about race are the residue, the detritus, so to speak, of earlier ways of thinking about race; so that it turns out to be easiest to understand contemporary talk about 'race' as the pale reflection of a more full-blooded race discourse that flourished in the last century." Appiah and Amy Gutman, eds., *Color Conscious: The Political Morality of Race* (Princeton: Princeton University Press, 1996), 38.

58. Patricia Williams, *Open House: Of Family, Friends, Food, Piano Lessons, and the Search for a Room of My Own* (New York: Farrar, Straus and Giroux, 2004), 196.

59. F. James Davis, *Who Is Black?*, 32.

60. Reid-Pharr, 80.

61. Stuart Hall, "Subjects in History: Making Diasporic Identities," in *The House That Race Built: Black Americans, U.S. Terrain*, ed. Wahneema Lubiano (New York: Pantheon, 1997), 299.

62. Schur, 290.

63. Delany, 268.

64. Williams, 196.

65. Reid-Pharr, 78.

5. Doing Violence to Desire

1. James Baldwin, "Alas, Poor Richard," in *Collected Essays*, ed. Toni Morrison (New York: Library of America, 1998), 251.

2. Baldwin, 251.

3. See, for example, Evelyn Brooks Higginbotham's comments on black women's "politics of silence" at the turn of the twentieth century in her essay "African American Women's History and the Metalanguage of Race," *Signs* 17.2 (1992): 251–74.

4. Baldwin, 251.

5. Bruce Kokopeli and George Lakey, "More Power than We Want: Masculine Sexuality and Violence," in *Race, Class, and Gender: An Anthology*, ed. Margaret L. Andersen and Patricia Hill Collins (Belmont, Calif.: Wadsworth, 1998), 470.

6. Leo Bersani, *A Future for Asytyanax* (New York: Columbia University Press, 1984), 302.

7. Elaine Scarry, *The Body in Pain* (New York: Oxford University Press, 1985), 59, my emphasis.

8. Bersani, 302.

9. Baldwin, "Freaks and the American Ideal of Manhood," in *Collected Essays*, 814–29.

10. Baldwin, "Freaks," 827.

11. Gayl Jones, *Eva's Man* [1976] (Boston: Beacon Press, 1987), 37. References to the 1987 edition will be cited parenthetically throughout the remainder of this chapter.

12. Zizek, Slavoj, "'I Hear You with My Eyes': or, The Invisible Master," in *Gaze and Voice As Love Objects*, ed. Renata Salecl and Slavoj Zizek (Durham and London: Duke University Press, 1996), 94.

13. Keith Harvey and Celia Shalom, eds., *Language and Desire: Encoding Sex, Romance and Intimacy* (New York: Routledge, 1997), 1.

14. Laura Tanner, *Intimate Violence: Reading Rape and Torture in Twentieth-Century Fiction* (Bloomington and Indianapolis: Indiana University Press, 1994), 4.

15. Madhu Dubey, *Black Women Novelists and the Nationalist Aesthetic* (Bloomington and Indianapolis: Indiana University Press, 1994), 102.

16. Zora Neale Hurston, *Their Eyes Were Watching God* [1937] (New York: Perennial, 1990), 140.

17. Kokopeli and Lakey, 471.

18. Mae Henderson, "The Stories of (O)Dessa: Stories of Complicity and Resistance," in *Female Subjects in Black and White: Race, Psychoanalysis and Feminism,* ed. Elizabeth Abel, Barbara Christian, Helene Moglen (Berkeley: University of California Press, 1997), 286.

19. Gayl Jones's first novel, *Corregidora* (Boston: Beacon Press, 1975), the story of a blues singer who grapples with the violent legacy of her slave ancestry, places significant emphasis on the idea of telling and retelling, and the relationship between oral narrative and historical trauma for people of African descent in the Americas.

20. Rhonda Williams, "Living at the Crossroads: Explorations in Race, Nationality, Sexuality, and Gender," in *The House That Race Built,* ed. Wahneema Lubiano (New York: Pantheon, 1997), 147.

21. Zizek, 94.

22. Dubey, 103, 104.

23. Francoise Lionnet, "Geographies of Pain: Captive Bodies and Violent Acts in the Fictions of Myriam Warner-Vieyra, Gayl Jones, and Bessie Head," *Callaloo* 16.1 (1993): 144.

24. Darlene Clark Hine, "Rape and the Inner Lives of Black Women in the Middle West: Preliminary Thoughts on the Culture of Dissemblance," in *Words of Fire,* ed. Beverly Guy-Sheftall (New York: The New Press, 1995), 382.

25. Alice Deignan writes, for example, that "It seems unsurprising that appetite for food is used to talk about sexual desire, given that hunger and desire are two of our most basic physical wants, and that satisfying each is a source of pleasure." Deignan, "Metaphors of Desire," in *Language and Desire: Encoding Sex, Romance and Intimacy,* ed. Keith Harvey and Celia Shalom (New York: Routledge, 1997), 30.

26. Alice Walker, "The Child Who Favored Daughter," in *In Love and in Trouble: Stories of Black Women* (San Diego: Harcourt Brace, 1973), 35–46.

27. Vanessa Freidman, "Over His Dead Body: Female Murderers, Female Rage, and Western Culture," in *States of Rage: Emotional Eruption, Violence, and Social Change,* ed. Renee R. Curry and Terry L. Allison (New York: New York University Press, 1996), 71.

28. Dubey, 103.

29. Slavoj Zizek, "Love Thy Neighbor? No Thanks!" in *The Psychoanalysis of Race*, ed. Christopher Lane (New York: Columbia University Press, 1998), 167.

30. Zizek, "Love Thy Neighbor?" 163, 164.

31. Baldwin, "Preservation of Innocence," in *Collected Essays*, 594.

32. Zizek, 166.

33. The full quotation is as follows: "Generally speaking I think one needs to look rather at how the great strategies of power encrust themselves and depend for their conditions of exercise on the level of the micro-relations of power." Michel Foucault, *Power/Knowledge*, ed. Colin Gordon (New York: Pantheon Books, 1980), 199.

Epilogue

1. Jason DeParle, "Raising Kevion," *New York Times Magazine*, Aug. 22, 2004: 27–53. I would like to thank my friend and colleague Monica Miller for bringing this article to my attention.

2. DeParle, 48.

3. DeParle, 48.

4. Harris self-published *Invisible Life* in 1991, and amassed such a following through his own efforts at promotion that the book was reissued by Anchor Books (Doubleday) in 1994. He has since published seven additional novels and a memoir. Harris's publishing success, along with that of popular black female author Terry McMillan (whose third novel, *Waiting to Exhale*, spent thirty-nine weeks on the *New York Times* bestseller list and was made into a feature film in 1995), has proven to mainstream publishers that there is a wide audience for mass-marketed black fiction. This audience, and the number of books produced for it, has continued to grow more than a decade after Harris's first book appeared on store shelves.

5. DeParle, 48.

6. Lauren Berlant and Michael Warner, "Sex in Public," in *Intimacy*, ed. Lauren Berlant (Chicago and London: University of Chicago Press, 2000), 313.

7. Berlant and Warner, 313.

8. Laura Kipnis, "Adultery," in *Intimacy*, ed. Lauren Berlant (Chicago and London: University of Chicago Press, 2000), 32.

9. Michael Warner, *The Trouble with Normal: Sex, Politics, and the Ethics of Queer Life* (New York: The Free Press, 1999), 27.

10. E. Lynn Harris, cited previously, achieved commercial publishing success largely through his melodramatic attention to the "down low" phenomenon in his fiction.

11. Keith Boykin addresses this issue in much greater detail in his recent book, *Beyond the Down Low: Sex, Lies, and Denial in Black America* (New York: Carroll & Graf, 2005).

12. Berlant and Warner, 312.

13. I should clarify that I do not make this distinction to distance myself from GLBT identity or orientation; such a move would be more than ironic given my personal identification as bisexual. In no way do I mean to suggest that "queerness as ideology" is acceptable, while gayness, as identity and practice, is not. Instead, my hope would be that an ideological embrace of queerness could make it that much easier for black GLBT subjects and their associated involvements to find greater awareness and acceptance in the larger black culture and community.

14. Cathy Cohen, "Punks, Bulldaggers, and Welfare Queens: The Radical Potential of Queer Politics?" *GLQ: A Journal of Lesbian and Gay Studies* 3.4 (1997): 458.

15. Devon W. Carbado, Dwight A. McBride, and Donald Weise, eds., *Black Like Us: A Century of Lesbian, Gay, and Bisexual African American Fiction* (New York: Cleis Press, 2002), xiv.

16. Marlon B. Ross, "Some Glances at the Black Fag: Race, Same-Sex Desire, and Cultural Belonging," *African American Literary Theory: A Reader*, ed. Winston Napier (New York and London: New York University Press, 2000), 504.

17. Maurice Stevens, *Troubling Beginnings: Trans(per)forming African American History and Identity* (New York and London: Routledge, 2003), 10.

18. Stevens, 10.

19. See Hamil R. Harris, "Some Blacks Find Nuggets of Truth in Cosby's Speech: Others Say D.C. Remarks about Poor Blacks Went Too Far," *Washington Post*, May 26, 2004: B05+.

20. Michael Eric Dyson, *Is Bill Cosby Right? Or Has the Black Middle Class Lost Its Mind?* (New York: Basic Civitas, 2005).

21. Online transcript of Cosby's remarks, May 17, 2004, Feb. 13, 2006, *American Rhetoric: The Power of Oratory in the United States*, http://www.americanrhetoric.com/speeches/billcosbypoundcakespeech.htm.

22. Ibid., paragraph 9.

23. Dyson, 4.

24. Here we might recall the list of scandal-hounded names offered in the introduction to this volume, including O. J. Simpson, R. Kelly, and Michael Jackson. Ironically, Bill Cosby also has faced public scandal, related

both to allegations in the late 1990s that he fathered a child outside of his marriage, and to more recent accusations of sexual harassment and assault. See Benjamin Weiser, "Cosby, an Unerring Father on TV, Speaks of Affair in Extortion Trial," *New York Times*, July 16, 1997: B1. See also Brodie Fenlon, "Cosby Denies Assault; Woman Claims She Was Drugged, Fondled in Star's Home," *Ottawa Sun*, January 21, 2005: 5.

25. As writers such as Evelynn Hammonds and Barbara Smith have noted, contemporary manifestations of "queer theory" in the academy, and of "queer politics" in the larger culture, have frequently marginalized people of color and the poor and working class, by failing to acknowledge the relative privilege of many of the white, middle-class subjects who self-identify as "queer." See Hammonds, "Black (W)holes and the Geometry of Black Female Sexuality," *African American Literary Theory: A Reader*, ed. Winston Napier (New York and London: New York University Press, 2000), 482–97, and Barbara Smith, "Queer Politics: Where's the Revolution?" *The Nation* 257.1 (1993): 12–16. See also Cohen.

26. Cohen, 440, author's emphasis.

27. Cohen, 442.

28. Cohen, 458.

29. Shay Youngblood, *Black Girl in Paris* (New York: Riverhead Books, 2000), 196. Subseqent references to this work are given parenthetically within the text.

Index

Candice M. Jenkins is associate professor of English at Hunter College, The City University of New York.